HIGHWAYS AND BYWAYS
IN
NORTHUMBRIA

Newcastle from the high level bridge.

HIGHWAYS AND BYWAYS
IN
NORTHUMBRIA

Peter Anderson Graham

Illustrations by Hugh Thomson

THE SPREDDEN PRESS
STOCKSFIELD
1988

First published by Macmillan, 1920
Reprinted 1921, 1928
Reprinted, 1988, with new introduction,
by
The Spredden Press,
Brocksbushes Farm,
Stocksfield,
Northumberland,
NE45 7WB

Introduction © The Spredden Press

Printed and bound by
SMITH SETTLE
Ilkley Road
Otley

INTRODUCTION

Peter Anderson Graham (1854-1925) came from an old Border family and was born at Crookham on the Northumbrian border, the nearest village to Flodden Field. One of a large family, he was destined for the church and sent to Durham University but he had been brought up on 'Burns, Byron and the Border ballads' and wanted to write. He became a journalist, working first in Edinburgh where one of his many friends was Robert Louis Stevenson.

Later he moved back to England and contributed articles to many well-known journals, among them *Country Life* and the *Morning Post* for which he became, in 1897, Special Commissioner for Agriculture. For the last twenty-three years of his life he was Editor of *Country Life*. He wrote two novels, one of them, *Red Scaur*, set in the north, 'by the pleasantest of the many streams which rise in the Cheviots', and some books on land use. He also edited a number of anthologies and collections of articles for *Country Life*. 'He was a master of style, admirably simple, concise and dignified', concluded *The Times'* obituary, regretting that so much of Peter Graham's work had been, of necessity, ephemeral.

Agriculture and the problems of those who work on the land and were forced, by poverty, to move to the towns or the mines, interested him deeply and his writing on this subject was based on an intimate knowledge of the people of the English countryside and his own wide sympathies. In a preface to one of his best books, *The Rural Exodus*: *The Problem of the Village and the Town* (1892) he wrote:

'I have wandered in most of the English shires, conversing freely alike with the landlord and the tenant, Anglican and Dissenter, the hind at his plough, the ratcatcher working ditches with ferret and terrier, the Agrarian lecturer, the village atheist, the poacher, the grocer and land agent, and it is my own blame if I have not obtained a tolerably correct notion of the ideas and aspirations of the English village'.

As Editor of *Country Life* Peter Graham spent most of his life in the south of England, but he retained a passionate loyalty to the land of his birth. 'He was most himself in his own country . . . His whole aspect changed when one saw him fishing for trout in his native streams or reading Border Ballads, or reciting his beloved Burns or "Marmion" ', wrote his son at his death. 'Being Northumbrian was almost nationhood to him.'

Northumbrians for him were different and, one suspects, superior beings. 'The genuine Northumbrian dislikes all unnecessary show and outward appearance because he is fond of doing things really well. The landlord expects a good rent, but does not shirk putting up solid buildings; the labourer gives a great day's work but expects an adequate wage for it. Every-where what is cheap and gimcrack is despised, be it food or furniture' (*Revival of English Agriculture*).

He had a longstanding friendship with Earl Grey of Fallodon, Foreign Secretary in the Great War, and author of those bestsellers, *The Charm of Birds* and *Fly Fishing*, and with Edward Hudson, owner of *Country Life* and of Lindisfarne Castle. He would often join Hudson's parties in the Castle, newly restored by Edwin Lutyens, or his picnics to Holy Island. He also knew the poet Swinburne 'whose talk ran very much on the ballads and superstitions of his county'.

Graham 'was a man of tall and striking presence' and in his young days was something of an athlete. He loved golf and all kinds of outdoor work, including harvesting. In later life he became an excellent chess player and his book on Blackburne, the great Manchester champion (*Mr Blackburne's Chess Games*) is still in print.

Macmillan could have made no better choice to edit the Northumbria volume in their successful series of guide books, Highways and Byways. The 1920s was a period of growing tourism and Graham was not uncritical of 'the aggressive tourist who has searched out all the prettiest and wildest nooks of England . . . and is constantly on the scent for old rights of way'. Yet his descriptions of a countryside that has changed less than most in Britain are exactly what the intelligent tourist requires. For Graham was deeply interested in the byways, the legends and stories, the small details of history as well as the main highways of fact for which he relied on his wide reading of local historians and antiquarians.

His guide is full of odd pieces of information: that you could get married *and* buy a glass of ginger beer at the Lamberton tollhouse; why the Yetholm gipsies were called muggers (because they sold mugs); and how the egg collectors risked their lives on the Pinnacles at the Farnes. The *Times Literary Supplement* reviewer concluded: 'Mr Graham is most in his element on the moor and by the burn; with the wild cattle of Chillingham, the gulls and guillemots of the Farnes and the wild fowl that haunt the Northumbrian lakes; in telling of angling on the Coquet, of salmon-spearing and otter-hunting . . . with other forgotten sports'. Yet he is good, too, on the cities: Berwick, 'the most romantic of the Northumbrian towns', and Newcastle whose 'paramount claim to attention is that in the whole world there is not a more stirring monument to human energy than is presented by the town and its river, the Tyne'.

Hugh Thomson (1860-1920), the distinguished book illustrator whose charming pencil drawings of buildings, landscape and people admirably complement this eminently readable guide, was an Irishman from Coleraine in 'Derry. He learned his trade as an illustrator from the chief designer at the Belfast printer where he started work at seventeen. In 1883 he came to London where he got work on the *English Illustrated Magazine*, edited by Comyns Carr, for which he worked for many years. He became a well-known and popular illustrator of works by Goldsmith, Miss Mitford, Mrs Gaskell, Jane Austen, Fanny

Burney, Thackeray and George Eliot and was described by Austin Dobson as 'the Charles Lamb of illustration'. But although he was best known for his comic drawings he was primarily a landscape artist. His biographers (M. H. Spielman and Walter Jerrold in *Hugh Thomas: His Art, Letters, Humour and Charm*, 1931) regretted that he did not give more time to pure landscape: 'None of his admirers needs to be told how well he used landscape not as mere background but as part of his figure pieces but it was not until he began work on the Highways and Byways series that he revealed his true gifts of that kind'. He illustrated several of this series and would travel round the countryside on a bicycle to collect his sketches. He died of *angina pectoris,* aggravated, it is said, by worry about Ireland.

G.M.D. 1988

PREFACE

THIS book deals chiefly with the modern County of Northumberland, all that is left of the ancient Kingdom of Northumbria, but as the historical interests of the one are intertwined with those of the other, it was decided to adopt the more comprehensive term. Northumbria casts a steady light on Northumberland.

The inhabitants of the most northern of our English counties have always been famous antiquarians and historians, and they know the books on which knowledge of the local past must be based. I think I have mentioned in the text all authors to whom I have been indebted, but for the use of those who still have before them the pleasure of exploring this most interesting and most romantic county a few of the more important authorities may be cited.

As a book of reference the monumental History still unfinished and now edited by Mr. Crawford Hodgson stands first. It is safe to say that no living writer knows Northumberland in more detail than Mr. Hodgson.

For the northern part of the county the *Proceedings of the Berwickshire Naturalists' Club* are invaluable. The club was formed in 1831 and from that time has lived up to the motto then adopted—

" MARE ET TELLUS, ET QUOD TEGIT OMNIA, CŒLUM."

It has maintained the laudable custom of visiting places of interest and discussing them on the spot.

The Newcastle Society of Antiquarians is an equally celebrated and energetic association, and its *Archaeologia Aeliana* is a mine of historical and antiquarian information.

Dr. Collingwood Bruce's *Handbook to the Roman Wall* has since his death been kept up to date and introduces the reader to the important authorities on this great monument of Imperial Rome.

Two books very imperfectly known have recently been translated by Sir Herbert Maxwell and are very illuminating in regard to the life and history of our Northumbrian ancestors. They are *The Chronicle of Lanercost,* 1272 *to* 1346, and *The Scalachronica of Sir Thomas Gray,* who died in 1369.

Raine's *Durham* is still an unquestioned authority on the ancient history of Norham, Islandshire, and St. Cuthbert.

All the important towns, Newcastle, Alnwick, Hexham, Berwick, have had their chroniclers, from each of whom something has been gleaned, but I would like to mention my special indebtedness to Mr. D. Dippie Dixon for his full and painstaking books *The Vale of Whittingham* and *Upper Coquetdale.*

For help and advice from the distinguished and the obscure I would like to express an equal gratitude, though I think the former will forgive me for saying that the greater pleasure is in hearing a story of the immediate past from the lips of a witness. Readers would think so too if I could reproduce the burr and the dialect!   P. A. G.

CONTENTS

xi

CONTENTS

CHAPTER XIX

CHAPTER XX

CHAPTER XXI

CHAPTER XXII

CHAPTER XXIII

CHAPTER XXIV

CHAPTER XXV

CHAPTER XXVI

CHAPTER XXVII

CHAPTER XXVIII

CHAPTER XXIX

CHAPTER XXX

CHAPTER XXXI

CHAPTER XXXII

CHAPTER XXXIII

CHAPTER XXXIV

CHAPTER XXXV

CHAPTER XXXVI

LIST OF ILLUSTRATIONS

HIGHWAYS AND BYWAYS

IN

NORTHUMBRIA

CHAPTER I

PHYSICAL FEATURES

Area—Population—Islands—Rivers—Lakes—Gate to Scotland—
Boundaries—Denes—a cradle of Christianity.

THE facts that the distance across Northumberland from a
point near Berwick-on-Tweed to Allenheads is seventy-one miles
and that the length of the coast from Lamberton to Tynemouth is
seventy miles show that it is, roughly speaking, square-shaped,
though the square is jagged and irregular. It has an area of
2,018 miles and divides naturally into East, West, and Middle.
The physical features conform in a general way to those of Great
Britain as a whole—hills in the west and an eastern slope to the
North Sea. The populations vary in accordance with the
physical conditions. Pleasant little bays, inlets and harbours
have encouraged the formation of fishing villages on the east
coast, and the fishermen form a distinct class, very clannish, and
inclined to marry only among their own folk. But they have
not proved immune from the vulgarising effect of certain modern
conditions. As the seaside habit grows among the industrial
communities, such fishermen as have not taken to trawling tend
to become sophisticated. The coble is turned into a pleasure-

Æ   B

boat, the owner hires himself and it out to row and sail, and he begins to look for tips. But occasionally one meets with men of the old type. Not infrequently they are on the parish, for the merry sailor is apt to forget that there ever will be a rainy day. But he does not lose heart, and remains to the last tough, weather-bronzed and cheery, telling with gusto the adventures and incidents of his past. From sailor he turned into a deep-sea fisherman. When he could not go out for cod he became a Tweed salmon fisher, and as the end of a mail-coach driver was often that of keeping a toll-bar, so the last resource of the aged sailor-man was often to work a ferry-boat. But the young and enterprising men have forsaken the line for the steam trawl, and the experience of the war has shown that they have lost nothing in seamanship or courage by the change. Meanwhile, the Northumbrian fishing villages have been transformed into seaside resorts. If you wish to know what they used to be like, cross the Border and go to Burnmouth or Eyemouth, where there is no accommodation for visitors, the half-tame gulls are playmates of the amphibious children, and the old-fashioned fishing village is unchanged.

Off the coast lie a number of islands which have special attractions of their own. They cast a spell over the naturalist, especially the devout lover of birds to whom an annual visit to the Farne Islands is a pilgrimage. In days when civilisation was young, they and Lindisfarne were famous as the abode of holy and very abstemious hermits and saints, who prepared for Heaven by starving themselves on earth. They loved the wild birds too, and the eider-duck were so fostered by the island saint that they are often called Cuddy's hens.

These are the chief islands, but Coquet Isle must not be left out, as, though small, it sustains the general characteristics of the rest.

Falling into the sea are the rivers of which Northumberland is proud. Most of them are dark and sombre as they approach the coast, as though reluctant to be merged in the infinite waters of the sea. That is a poetical way of putting it which the Tweed salmon poachers deny. They hold the law to be an ass because it deems that, as far as salmon catching is concerned, the mouth of the Tweed extends along the coast three miles north and three miles south. A legal subtlety highly inconvenient to those intent on netting salmon in the off season ! The Tweed, which only for a minute fraction of its course is an English river, proves our rule by being an exception. After leaving its various " dubs " (word abhorred by the late Andrew Lang !), it rushes madly under the arches of the old Border Bridge and at Spittal passes into the sea, gay and smiling to the last. One side is English, at Norham and Coldstream and Carham, but for the upper part of its course the Tweed remains " all Scotch." It has one purely English tributary in the Till, a slow and sinuous

Looking up the College Burn from Hethpool.

stream which creeps through a succession of low, green haughs from Bewick Mill to Etal. After leaving the boat-house and the old mill-cauld at the latter village, it splashes and dances over a rocky bed past wooded and hazel-clad banks to Tillmouth. It is more of a joy to the fly-fisher than might be imagined by those who know it only by repute.

On its way, Till receives many pleasant burns, such as that at Sandyfords, associated with the name of St. Paulinus. It is interesting, but only a streamlet " the breadth of a tailor's yard." At Ewart the Till receives the dashing and beautiful Glen

formed by the junction at Kirknewton of the rough and noisy
College and the staider Bowmont. In the upper part of its
course the Till is called the Breamish. As an old rhyme has it,

> Foot of Breamish and head of Till
> Meet together at Bewick Mill.

And if you follow its winding course you find it rises in Scotsman's
Knowe, not far from Cheviot Hill. In its upper course it passes
Ingram, Hedgeley, Chillingham and Chatton.

The Aln is a pleasant little seven-mile stream that rises near
Alnham and after passing Alnwick and Lesbury reaches the sea
at Alnmouth, famed for its golf course.

The Coquet is considered by enthusiasts, particularly fishing
enthusiasts, to be the finest of all the rivers of Northumberland,
and whether it be granted or not that proud pre-eminence, it
is at any rate in the first flight. It rises in the Outer Golden
Pot in the wild Thirlmoor Country, and after receiving near
Linsheels the waters of the Usway Burn from Cheviot, it passes
such a variety of country and so many things of beauty and
interest that a good day in Coquetdale is difficult to beat
anywhere. Before the war it used every year to attract crowds
of anglers to the ancient and rugged village of Rothbury and
will do so again now. As a chapter is given to Coquetdale, there
is no need to say more about the river here. It may interest
trouting anglers to know that the source of the Coquet is
near that of the Bowmont, which comes from Cocklaw Foot.
Cross the hill and you are in the region of Windygates, whence
are drawn the burns that unite to form the Coquet. It flows
directly to the sea while the Bowmont joins the College.

The gentle silvery Wansbeck issues from Sweethope Lough
and takes its name in all probability from the huge neighbouring
rocks at its source. They are called the Wannys—Great
Wanny, Little Wanny, Aird Law and Hepple Heugh. Mr.
Trevelyan suggests a different derivation in his volume called
" The Middle Marches," but Wannys Beck appears to be the
simpler and more natural. It sings its way past many famous
places, Wallington, Middleton Hall, Mitford, Morpeth, Bothal,
before it enters the sea at Cambois Bay.

At Belsay the Blyth is a pretty river and at Ponteland where
it is joined by the Pont. This character is maintained through
the Vale of Stannington and Plessey where are the " sounding

woods " of " Marmion." Its short course of twenty miles ends in the busy harbour of Blyth.

But the Tyne is the river of the county. It is to Newcastle what the Thames is to London. The word Tyneside calls up a world of collieries and their natural concomitants, engineering shops and factories, the hum of commerce, man the worker, and the much-sung triumphs of industry. But though the Tyne ends with the gravity and importance of a successful business man or a burgomaster, its slender youth is gilded with romance. If you start at Warden, where the North Tyne and the South Tyne commingle, and pursue these tributary streams to their source, you will, in the case of either, soon pass from the realm of industrial achievement. North Tyne oozes from the Deadwater in that wild Cheviot country whence issue Rule Water and Jed Water, rivers of Damascus (that is to say Scotland), but after being joined by the Kielder Burn, the Lewis Burn, and others, it darts away merrily down a valley that remains wild in the age of railways and was a terror to pass through before their invention. Even the names of the stations on the line running down the valley of North Tyne evoke memories—Kielder, Plashetts, Falstone, Tarset, Bellingham—each has its own story. It is difficult to say where the river is most beautiful. There is a fine stretch at Bellingham and a finer just above it, but this is the stream in youth with a waist like an eagle's talon, if one may be permitted an odd application of the fat knight's phrase. Flowing down Humshaugh and passing Chollerford to its junction with the South Tyne at Warden, through all its course it possesses a beauty different from, yet equal to, that of the Tweed at Melrose. It is no wonder that the Romans found a tutelary deity for this foreign river.

The South Tyne rises on Cross Fell, close to the source of the Wear, and flows down the famous Gap of Tyne to Newcastle— the Gap is the low ground which intervenes between the Pennine Chain and the Cheviots. South Tyne enters Northumberland shortly after leaving Alston and passes many historic places, Lambley Castle, the ruins of Bellister, Featherston Castle, Haltwhistle, Haydon and Warden. The Tyne receives the Devil's Water at Corbridge. Devil's Water is a turbulent and charming little river which does not owe its name to Satan, but to the long extinct family of Dyvelston. It is a good example of the type of river found in Northumberland. Long before it reaches the outskirts of Newcastle the Tyne doffs romance and plays the part of a quiet water highway running between a wilderness of buildings sealed with the mark of commerce and industry.

Northumberland, unlike its neighbours Cumberland and Westmoreland, is not very rich in lakes, which it calls loughs. Sportsmen, naturalists, and lovers of wild scenery delight in that picturesque group situated close to the Wall adjoining Housesteads. It comprises Greenlee Lough, Broomlee Lough and Crag Lough. There is another group, to one of which reference has already been made as the source of the Wansbeck ; the others are reservoirs belonging to the Newcastle and Gateshead Water Company. The largest reservoir is Catcleugh and it has the additional merit of being well stocked with trout. It lies at the foot of the Reidswire among wild surroundings full of Border associations. In the country are many delightful tarns and ponds that are called lakes, but are scarcely large enough to deserve the name. Some are interesting for their fishing, as that at Pawston ; some as breeding places of the black-headed gull, as Pallinsburn.

Northumberland has no very high mountains. Cheviot, the highest peak of the Cheviot Hills, has an altitude of only 2,676 feet. Coming near to that height are Cairn Hill, Hedgehope, Comb Fell, Windy Gate or Gyle, Cushat Law, The Schel, Dunmore Hill, Black Hag, Newton Tors and Hungry Law. A glance at any contour map of England will show how the Cheviots exercised an influence on history. Between them and the sea there is from ten to twenty miles of lowland. That is the gateway to and from Scotland. An army could march from Edinburgh to London along the east coast without encountering a hill 600 feet high till it came to the easily-surmounted North Yorkshire moor. The same route was followed naturally by the great North Road before and after the age of stage-coaches, and subsequently by the Great Northern and North Eastern Railway. Travelling this way, the passenger feels at points in danger of tumbling into the sea ; the waves lie at his very feet, but he catches no glimpse of hill scenery. In the centre of the county the steep hills interposed a formidable barrier. These considerations were taken into account in dividing the frontiers. Save for the little piece of land extending as far north as Lamberton, which is adjacent to the Berwick Boundaries, the March follows the Tweed as long as it constitutes a difficult obstacle. At Carham, about eighteen miles from Lamberton, the course of the river is left, and the frontier, after a short space in which the heights are inconsiderable, is carried through mountainous country. It is difficult to follow, for the country is very wild. Between the Venchen, which is visible through the hotel window at Yetholm in Roxburghshire, and Carter Fell many eminences over a thousand feet in altitude occur.

Northumbrian hills are not so high and rugged as, for example, those in the Highlands of Scotland. They have a tendency to be round, smooth and green. Bracken is as plentiful as heather. But they are cleft by deep valleys, glens and dales, down which the typical Northumbrian river, a purling stream in summer but a raging torrent in winter, chatters in the pleasantest manner imaginable. They live in my memory as they were when I used to go fishing at the dawn of a June morning, when cuckoos called on the slopes and the " whaup " or curlew swore at the intruder who came too close to his nesting-place in the slack or glidders, and the russet coat of the fox showed by a glimpse now and again under the green fern as he chased the rabbit. He who was after the trout raged too when the ragged Cheviot ewes sprang nimbly into the water and splashed across, to the terror of the fish. No wonder one grew up to like the hills, always looking so far away, mysterious and changing, now wrapped in fog, anon beheld in a bewildering twilight when the wind blew the mist from rock to rock in trailing veils.

The general character of the land can be best understood through its agriculture. For in the early years of last-century the Northumbrian farmer, like the rest of his tribe, had wheat fever badly. England was at war, and there were no controlled prices or ration books ! He grew seven and a half times as much wheat as he was doing before the German war broke out, and also far more oats. To-day Northumberland is the great sheep county. I need not give figures to prove the metamorphosis. Whosoever has fished the College or Bowmont must for ever remember the mournful " baa-ing " of countless sheep at night, when they were feeding their way to the high hills, and in the morning, when the shepherds with the aid of those wonderful clever little dogs of theirs drove them down to the fresh grass. of the valley. Another pleasant sound associated with the hills was the lustily-blown cow-horn calling the men to the foddering every night at eight o'clock. It used to sound more eerily from the farms in the dark nights of winter.

In a book of wanderings it is not necessary to say much about the geology of the county—its coal, shale, limestone, sandstone and other sedimentary rocks, its igneous rock of which Cheviot is built up, its basalt and Great Whin Sill. But at least one result of the disturbance of the earth's crust I would like to notice, because it has added to the charm of the county. This is the formation of numerous denes. A typical dene is a little gorge which looks like the furrow made by some titanic plough. The bones of one can be seen not more than half-an-hour's walk from the farm of Blink Bonny at the base of Flodden Hill. It was stripped of its wood and despoiled of its charm some years ago, but that enables the formation to be seen all the more clearly. At the top a ripple of water in late spring but a gush in winter tumbles down a rough rock ladder in a nook of which the nest of the ring-ouzel may be searched for, not in vain, close to the spray from the tumbling water. Numberless other nests may be found lower down in the holes and crevices of the banks, on the higher parts of which primroses used to appear in myriads. There used to be a constant cawing from the rookery above, where often the squirrel might be seen close to the dark birds.

Places like this occur very frequently in Northumberland, some on a smaller, some on a larger scale, but always with a peculiar and happy charm. They are worth looking for by such as love a cool retreat under green boughs, to sit on a log and listen to the voices of birds, the gurgling of water, and the swish of summer wind.

Northumberland to-day is a great energetic county. The mines, shipbuilding yards, factories and workshops are the admiration of the world, but as far as the spiritual transcends the material, its past was greater still. Two great days stand out in its history on account of the influence they exercise on succeeding events. One was that on which King Oswald raised the Cross as his battle standard and discomfited the heathen under Cadwallon at Heavenfeld. Till the fane erected by Wilfrid was destroyed by the Danes the monks of Hexham annually held a memorial service on the battlefield. Before Oswald the more splendid Eadwine with Paulinus for gospeller had Christianised on a great scale, but the movement lacked momentum and relapsed after his death.

The second great day was that on which Aidan crossed the sands at Lindisfarne from distant Iona and established there a monastery. We are apt to think of religious houses in the light of what they became in later days—houses of luxury and corruption. High ecclesiastics became grasping and ambitious, differing little from the unscrupulous soldier barons. Friars were too often ignorant and immoral, as Chaucer pictured them in the fourteenth century. But Aidan, simple, wise, and spiritual, belonged to the morning of the Christian faith. So did his immediate followers, in particular Cuthbert whose fame was to spread over the Christian world, become closely associated with Northumberland, and shed a glory over Lindisfarne.

Originally a Scottish " herd laddie," he emerges from a cloud of myth and legend, a simple, pious monk implicitly believing the truths of Christianity as they were accepted in his day. Not questioning, not speculative, believing the Way to be through prayer, fasting, and the mortification of the flesh, he appears to the modern eye too intent on his personal salvation, as one who had not altogether understood that whosoever would save his life shall lose it. He could never have guessed the truth underlying the apparent paradox that " Damn my own soul " is the first step towards grace. But his wise, sober common sense and the unaffected sincerity and homeliness of his conversation convinced those who heard him that his must be the right path. Under his guidance and that of his successors Lindisfarne became a fountain whence the civilising waters of Christianity, education, and art washed over the sea of the country? His was a doctrine of love which, like that of St. Francis, extended to beast and bird as well as humanity. Originating in Celtic sources, art as well as religion became moulded to the English character already in the making. Writing of the Lindisfarne Gospels the Rt. Rev. G. F. Browne, D.D., shows unanswerably that " the working out of the motive is Anglian not Celtic."

The Book of Kells, like ancient Celtic literature, is flawed with impurities of taste ; the art of the Lindisfarne Gospels is as English as a Shakespeare play or a Wordsworth Sonnet.

Until the arrival of the Danes, Lindisfarne remained the religious centre of Northumbria. It did not again assume that position. Durham, Hexham, Brinkburn, Tynemouth had the advantage of being on the mainland and passed it in the race.

After the Conquest the interest changes and the Border becomes the most famous place.

In Great Britain, for war and adventure, it supplied the stuff out of which were made the romantic ballads which to this day stir the heart like a trumpet.

Behind them in time legend dimly adumbrates great figures of the past like shapes that may be men or may be stones looking through the fog on a mountain side. Glendale has yielded the antiquary a rich store of prehistoric weapons and ornaments, but the oracles are dumb when asked who wore them. Yeavering Bell and the neighbouring hills carry traces that tell of a numerous highly organised tribe of inhabitants, but who is able to reconstruct their lives or tell their destiny ?

Figures of later date are equally elusive. Was King Arthur ever on the Roman Wall ? Was Bamburgh the Joyous Gard of Lancelot ?

The Dun Cow, Durham Cathedral.

CHAPTER II

Lamberton's great day—John de Raynton—Border marriages.

THERE are many ways of entering the modern county of Northumberland; through what was once Lamberton Toll, from Durham through Chester-le-Street to Gateshead, from Jedburgh to historic Otterburn; but I have a personal preference for the first mentioned.

Lamberton is about three miles north of Berwick-on-Tweed and in early days its tollgate used to separate England from Scotland. The gate is removed, but the house of its keeper remains. From St. Abb's Head it is a lovely walk to Lamberton by the wild rocky coast-line. Eyemouth and Burnmouth to be passed on the way will interest those who appreciate the primitive and picturesque. The associations connected with Lamberton form a contrast between the stately and the comically grotesque. Its greatest day in history was the 1st of August, 1503. The event was the arrival of the Princess Margaret, eldest daughter of King Henry VII, on her journey to Scotland as the wife of the Scottish king James IV. A vivid account of this stately pageant was written by John Younge, the Somerset Herald, who accompanied the party and acted as its historian. How he delighted to enumerate the great names and the sumptuous trappings of man and horse. To-day the splendour of the pilgrimage does not interest us so much as the consequences, only dimly foreseen by the wise and crafty Henry VII. Sympathy goes out to the child queen, a pawn in the game of politics, sent to marry a prince twice her age, who did not come to take her away. Instead, he sent as his representative " the Lord Archbishop of Glasco and the Count with a great retinue of knights, gentlemen and squires," and " there were five Trumpets or Claryons of the King that blewe at the coming of the said Queen, the which Melodye was good to here and to se." Her crossing of the Border was celebrated by High Mass at the great Kirk of Lamberton. Kneeling down to the ground, " they mayd the Receyving," and when the ceremony was over, " the said Lord of Northumberland mayd his devoir at the departyng of gambades and lepps as did likewise the Lord Scrop, the father and many others that returned again in making their congé." The Lord of Northumberland referred to here is the Percy nicknamed the Magnificent. At the time he was a gallant of twenty-four or five and Warden of the East Marches. He had entertained the Queen at Alnwick, to which he returned after the receiving.

Margaret went on to Fast Castle, where she was suitably entertained by its lord, while her retinue lodged at the Abbey of Coldingham. Fast Castle at one time was thought to be Wolf's Crag in " The Bride of Lammermoor," but Sir Walter Scott, while admitting the likeness, declared he had never seen the fortress. No doubt he knew many like it out of which he fashioned a suitable home for his impoverished hero. When the tragic story is read in its neighbourhood it is felt, as it cannot otherwise be, how faithfully he reproduced the character of the rugged coast-line and the melancholy or, to use a word of his coining, the sombrous sea. Margaret became mother of James V and grandmother of Mary Queen of Scots, whose son, James VI, united England and Scotland under one king. But much water was to pass under the bridge before that happened. The Earl of Surrey was one of Margaret's escorts to whom the King paid particular attention. Ten years only were to pass ere they met in a death grapple, but they did not dream of that in the summer days, when together they witnessed tournaments held in honour of the marriage, were spectators of the plays and moralities deemed appropriate to the occasion, listened to the minstrelsy and rejoiced in the young Queen's dancing. No one could in 1503 have foreseen the war of 1513 with its one renowned and melancholy battle when the Flowers o' the Forest were a' wed awa', and among them the King himself.

William Dunbar, the King's Rhymer, may have perished on the same occasion. He was never heard of again after the battle of Flodden. He was greatly attached to Queen Margaret and for her and her Court wrote some of his most frolic verse, as well as that lovely and imperial epithalamium " The Thrissill and the Rois." But the national welcome is more felicitously embodied in his lyric beginning

> Now fayre, fa yrest off every fayre,
> Princes most plesant and preclare,
> The lustyest one alyve that byne,
>   Welcum of Scotland to be Quene !

> Younge tendir plant of pulcritud,
> Descendyd of Imperyalle blude ;
> Freshe fragrant floure of fayrehede shene,
>   Welcum of Scotland to be Quene !

The Somerset Herald's description as preserved by Leland is worth reprinting to show what masters of pageant were our forefathers of the sixteenth century and is worth quoting here as far as it relates to Lamberton.

On the XXX and XXXI days of July 1502, the quene tarried at Barwyk, where she had grete chere of the said Capyiteyne of Barwyk (Sir Thomas Darcy) and hyr company in likewys.

That sam day was by the said Capyiteyne, to the pleasure of the said Quene, gyffen corses of chasse within the said town, with other sports of bayrs and of doggs togeder.

The first day of August the Quene departed from Barwyk for to go to Lamberton kerke in varrey fair company and well appoynted.

First of the said Archbyschops and Bischops, the Erles of Surrey and of Northumberland, the Lord Dacres, the Lord Scroop and his son, the Lord Gray, the Lord Latimer, the Lord Chamberlain, Maister Polle, and other Nobles and Knyghts. The young gentylmen were well appoynted at their devises, and ther was fou much of cloth of gold as of other ryche rayments. Their horsys frysks in harnays of the selfe : and of thos orfavery, sum others had campaynes gylt, the others campaynes of sylver. Gambades at plasur that it was a fayr thyng for to se.

The sayd Erle of Northumbrelaund was varey well mounted, hys horse rychly appoynted, his harnays of gold in brodeux, hymselfe in a jakette betten of gold, well wrought in goldsmith werke, and brodery and in a cloke of porple, borded of cloth of gold. His Hensmen appoynted as before mentioned. Incontinently before hym rode the Maister of his Horse, conveying the sam thre Hensmen arayed in jaketts all of orfavery and brodery, and ther harnays of their horsys in such wys of orfavery and brodery full of small bells that maid a grett noyse. After those cam a gentylman ledying in his haund a corser, covered to the grownde of a vary rich trapure betten of gold of orfavery and brodery in oraunge. And ichon of the sam a gren tre in the manere of a pyne, and maid the said Lord pannades and the weighted varey honestly.

After cam the said Qwene varey rychly arayde and enorned with gold and precyous stones, sytting in hyr lytere rychly appoynted. Her fotemen always ny to hyr well appoynted, and monted upon fayr pallefrys, and their harnays ryche in appareyll.

After cam her char rychely appoynted, fournysched of ladyes and gentylwomen well appoynted, and after that sum other gentylwomen on horsebak honorably appoynted.

The said Cappetayne of Barrwyk and my lady hys wyffe accompayned of many gentylmen and gentylwomen rychly arayde and clothed of a liveray went with the said Qwene to Edenburghe.

Before the said Qwene war by ordre Johannes and hys company (of players) and Henry Gloscebery and hys company, the trompetts, officers of armes and sergeants of mace, so that at the departing out of the said Barrwyk and at hyr Bedwarde at Lamberton Kirke it was a joy for to see and heare.

In such stat and array the said Qwene came out of Barwyk, ichon by ordre, the Lords and Nobles three and three togeder to the said Lamberton kirke, and the company behind well appoynted and in fair array, that it was estemed that thar war of the parte of the said Qwene xviii C or two M Horsys well Appoynted.

Before the said Scottysmen passed the Lords knights and gentylmen makynge Gambauds to the grett Gowre. And when the Qwene was come, the said byschop of Morrey, the said archbyschop (of Glasco) and the said Counte of Northumberlaunde avaunced toward hyr, and then knelling downe to the grounde mayde the Receyvinge. Ther was in presence the Archbyschop of York, the Bischop of Durham and the Erle of Surrey. After thys sche was brought to the Pavyllon ordonned for Recreacyon, and ny to that same sche was helped downe and kissed of the said Lords, and by them sche was brought to the Pavyllon wher no body entered except the Lords and Ladyes. And within the same was a Lady of the Countre, clothed with Scarlatte, with Gentylwomen appoynted after ther gyse who had brought sum new Fruyts.

Ny to that sam Pavyllon war other thre. The one for the Pannetry, the tother for the Boutry, the tother for the Kytchen; And ther ichon delibered hymselfe to make good chere and drynke. For ther was plante of Bred and Wyne so that ichon was contente.

After the Receyving doon, ichon put himself agayn in ordre, and the Qwene monted on Horsebak. The said Lord of Northumberland maid his Devor at the Departying of Gambauds and Lepps, as did lykewyse the Lord Scrop the Father and many others who retorned agayn, in taking their Congies. And of the Companie abydynge the Qwene was conveyed to hyr Lodgynge of Fast Castell, wher she was welcomed by the Lord of the said place and of the Lady sister of the said Bischop of Morrey, heir of Queen Elizabeth.

The Companie was lodged at the Abbay of Codyngham and in the Towne, where was ordonned Mett and Drynke for them, and also Liveray for their Horsys of Hay and Otts, ychon to his Quantyte.

The Nombre of the Scotts at the Mettynge of the said Qwene war by Estymacyon a thousaund Personnes, whereof ther might be v C Horsys of the thousand of grett price and well appoynted. And of the Companie passynge thorough with hyr to the Rylme of Scotland war in Nombre betwixt v and vi C well horsyd and appoynted.

The ij day of the said monneth the said Qwene departed from the said Fast Castell nobly appoynted and accompayned. And at the Departynge, they schott much ordonnance and had a very good chere and soe that every man was contente.[1]

From Fast Castle this princely train proceeded into Lothian by the Path of Pease, and staid during the night at the nunnery of Haddington. Next day they reached the Scottish Metropolis, where the royal nuptials were completed " amid the din of wassail, rout and revelry."

Exactly a hundred years after this, Margaret Tudor's great-grandson, son of Mary Queen of Scots and Darnley, heir of George the Steward of Scotland who founded the line of Stuart kings as James VI of Scotland and I of England, travelled the same road, reversing the steps of his progenitor, but he had no Somerset Herald to describe the pageant.

Lamberton has lost its old importance. In the thirteenth century it was part of the Barony of Mordington, and among the family papers of Mr. Campbell Renton and in the charter chest at Wedderburn Castle there are a number of charters relating to the lands of Lamberton. One of Mr. Campbell Renton's ancestors, John de Raynton, a rich burgess of Berwick-on-Tweed, who was taken prisoner by the Scots just before the battle of Halidon Hill (July 25, 1333), is given the lands and tenements of Over Lamberton of Agnes of Mordington. Another charter makes over to him the lands of Henry Cossar of Trebroun in the same town. From it we learn they were previously in the possession of Roger de Goswyc. Land in Kirk Lamberton was made over to him by William called Brune of the Borough Muir. Adam de Lamberton gave " my whole land of Lamberton in meadows and pastures to Gelfrio de Hessurle."

Little is left to remind one of Lamberton's history. A grave-

---

[1] Paper in the second volume of Leland's Collectanea, entitled, " The Fyancelles of Margaret, eldest daughter of King Henry VII, to James, King of Scotland ; together with her departure from England, journey into Scotland, her reception and marriage there, and the great feasts held on that account. Written by John Younge, Somerset Herald, who attended the Princess on her journey."

yard and some fragments of ruin are scarcely enough to distract attention from the moor and the sea.

Lamberton was notorious in the early half of the nineteenth century for the uproarious race meetings held on the moor and the Border marriages celebrated at the toll-bar. Both were vigorously condemned by the righteous, though there are unregenerates who still cherish memories of the former and philosophers who condone the latter. " A Toll wedding is

Coldstream Bridge.

better than none," said a comfortable-looking village woman to the writer; " they just used to gan thegither in my young days and if after they went sundry nobody cared." She was a village pagan who did not greatly believe in the niceness and fancy of the generation growing up beside her !

Lamberton and Coldstream Bridge were not gilded with the same air of romance as Gretna. At one period writers of novels were never tired of making the handsome young ensign run off to the Cumberland Border with the rich heiress, pursued, as often as not, by the irate father in his chariot. Very few

adventures of this kind are staged at Lamberton.   But in the
early half of the last century it was not uncommon for the
Northumbrian yokel, who still is very secretive about his love
affairs, to steal out at one end of the village while his nymph
took the opposite direction, the two meeting at an appointed
place, whence they trudged together to the toll.   At Coldstream
the priest was usually a blacksmith.   His shop and shoeing forge
continued to be used as a smithy up to a very recent date.   At
Lamberton Toll the ritual was performed by men of various
occupations.   In the *Proceedings* of the Berwickshire Naturalists'
Club for 1857 the advertisement of one of them is printed and
runs as follows :

BORDER MARRIAGES

ANDREW LYON

Begs respectfully to intimate that he can be found at
his   residence   Coxon's   Lane   adjoining   Walken
[? Walker] Gate any time his services may be required
by any person visiting the Hymeneal Shrine on the
Scottish Border

It was the simplest of ceremonies.   Legal marriage in
Scotland did not require more than a simple declaration on the
part of the man and woman.   Andrew Lyon's " Hymeneal
Altar " led to many irregularities, yet some regarded its
abolition as a mistake, because "couples might ha' done waur " !
Marriage was marriage, even when performed by a barber on
the open moorland.   An irregular kind of register was kept
and is still in existence, although its interest diminishes as the
actors die and are forgotten.

A jeweller who is now in a large way of business in another
part of the county told the present writer that he served his
time in Berwick-on-Tweed and is, indeed, a freeman.   He
recollected that on market days and holidays the firm for which
he worked would sell from twelve to eighteen wedding rings in
a morning for use at Lamberton Toll.   He also remembered the
famous notice stuck in the window of the toll-house : " Ginger
beer sold here and marriages performed " !

Berwick from the Pier.

CHAPTER III

HALIDON HILL

From Lamberton to Halidon Hill—The loveliest cliff-walk in
the county—The Battle.

FROM Lamberton the road goes its wide, spacious way towards
Berwick. The sea lies hidden beneath the high but flat fields
beyond the railway. At Marshall Meadows, a house in a clump
of trees, a path may be made to the sea by following a hedge,
or, better still, at the farm further on called Steps of Grace, a
little burn glides through a gentle valley dotted with gorse bushes.
A fence must be climbed, the railway crossed—all trespassing
but pleasant. In front the sea is spread and over a strip of land
are the cliff tops. Where a tiny stream has found its way a
path drops down to the shore, and on a green mound a deserted
salmon-fisher's shiel looks to the beach and the sea.
The burn falls over the steep bank behind, and down its course
meadowsweet and herb willow in high summer decorate the
slope. But when May flings its sweets, the primroses thick as
stars lighten the banks, and the violet too, for this bay is
sheltered from the north. In June the sea pinks clothe the sward

where it runs down to the rocks, and through a deep natural harbour the green water rushes to steal up the golden slip of sand. Far out are the brown sails of the fishing-boats or the streak of a steamer's smoke. Only the seagulls fly over to feed behind the plough on the uplands beyond. One always fancies that here the rock pigeon might murmur unmolested in crannies like the grey pipits which chatter on the patch of sand below. It is hardly possible to walk along the shore to Berwick, though this can be done when the tide is back ; but a coastguard's

The Greenses, Berwick.

path on the brink of the cliffs makes to Berwick a finer sea walk than can be had on any other part of the coast to Newcastle. Below are caves not very large, but still sufficient to suggest smugglers. When the tide comes in through narrow gullies and straits it has cut in the rocks, and dashes with clamour and fury into the caves, and hollow splashings and gurgles of rising and withdrawing water ascend to the listener on the green head of the cliff, there are some wonderful scenes. In one place the sea has hollowed a deep chasm in the land and on either side dark cliffs drop precipitously down into the turbulent water, and at high tide the inlet is full of the sound and fury of meeting waves. It is known as Maggie's Leap or some similar name, to

recall where a girl in some black hour jumped.   Then there
is the Needle's Eye, where the sea bursts through a slit in the
prominent cliff.   At the " Greenses " Harbour the cliffs stop.
" Greens," officials write, but " Greenses," say the people. Above
are wide pastures that stretch to the Bell Tower, and curving with
emerald green the crumbling sandstone heights drop towards
Berwick Pier.   At Greenses Harbour, besides artificial bathing
places when the tide is back, are beautful pools in the rocks
known to generations of schoolboys as the Poddlers and the
Narrow Way.   This is the way by the cliffs.   If the highway be
preferred it goes past a number of little farm-places.   A short
two miles, and rising to the right of the main road is seen the
long, upward road that leads past Conundrum, a farm curiously
named, to the wide romantic view that unfolds from the top of
Halidon Hill.   Here history was made.   Before that fated
battle Berwick was the greatest seaport of Scotland and its
commercial centre.   A well-known writer says : " Berwick-upon-
Tweed, the capital, took rank with Ghent, Rotterdam, and the
other great cities of the Low Countries, and was almost the rival
of London in mercantile enterprise."   The English indeed got
their revenge for Bannockburn, and, except for a brief period,
never again did the Scots hold that fair and thriving town under
their rule.   The Scots Gate was closed to their hungry fingers
and they hammered vainly on its iron-studded doors.   The
Scots, of course, could still annoy until the Union.   In 1558 the
French and Scottish soldiers at Eyemouth Fort fell on the
Berwick garrison, who were on Halidon Hill protecting the townsfolk, who were mowing—far to the north of the town lie the
freemens meadows even to this day.   The English were out
of their armour " to shoote, boule, coyte and exercise such lyke
games of pleasure," with the haymakers, no doubt, joining in
happily.   Under the hot sun from one till four they skirmished
with considerable loss on both sides.

After the battle of Halidon Hill, Berwick never again regained
the prestige of her ancient name.   Her fighting days passed
away with the stronger government of England seated within
her grey walls.

> The trumpet's silver sound was still
> The warder silent on the hill.

The formidable English bowmen soon to humble the pride of
France at Cressy carried away the honours from the Border town.

After the lion heart of Robert the Bruce had ceased to beat and had started on its last journey to the Holy Sepulchre with the gallant Douglas, the evil days fell on Berwick.

In February, 1333, the splendid army of Edward III invested the town, under Sir William Montagu. It was still holding out, though in desperate straits, when Edward marched from Newcastle. The Earl of Dunbar in the citadel, and Sir William Keith in the town, made a gallant resistance whilst the walls tottered before the furious English onslaught. The fate of Berwick was

Royal Border Bridge, Berwick.

sealed unless assistance arrived, so Keith promised to deliver it up by the 19th of July, and the sons of the principal townsmen were handed out through the blackened walls as hostages. An army did come from Scotland, but after crossing the Tweed and sending in men and food to the distressed town it marched on to the siege of Bamburgh, in which was Queen Philippa. The day arrived for the capitulation of Berwick, but the citizens refused, saying they had been relieved. The situation that arose was one of the most dramatic in Border history. Edward erected a gallows in full view of the Castle. It probably stood on ground near one of the arches of the modern railway bridge on the Tweedmouth side. Here he declared would be hung one of the hostages, a son of Alexander de Seton, a new warden of the town, if it did not capitulate. The heroic Setons refused to sacrifice the town. A tradition says that Lady Seton relented, but that is not borne out by Andrew Wyntoun, who lived close to the time, was related to the Setons, and wrote the well known " Chronicle of Scotland."

Wyntoun says that they had already lost two sons in the defence, but did not shrink from sacrificing a third.

> Then sayd the lady that she was young
> And her lord was young also
> Of power till have bairns mair
> And allow that they twa deid were there
> Yet of their bairns some living were.

From the Water Tower, part of whose strong walls the high tide still washes, to which descend the broken flight of steps now called the Breakneck Stairs, the Setons must have witnessed every detail of the heartrending scene. The knoll on which the gallows stood is still called Hang a Dyke Neuk. The impression that this poignant tragedy made actually lasted for over 500 years. Almost within living memory a skull was shown in Tweedmouth reputed to be young Seton's. This stern measure overcame the relatives of the other hostages. The English gave them fifteen days in which to surrender or give battle in the open and demanded three more hostages. Sir William Keith with a safe conduct galloped after the Scottish army invading Northumberland and overtook them at Walton Underwood. They found on reaching Berwick that the English army was arrayed on Halidon Hill about one and a half miles above the town. The Scots moved forward in four columns. Over the first floated the banner of John, Earl of Moray, and with him two notable veteran knights, John and Simon Fraser. Sir James Stewart rode at the head. The Regent Douglas commanded the third, supported by the Earl of Carrick. The reserve, the fourth, column was led by the Earl of Ross. It was July, when, even on that bleak coast, the richness of summer descends. From the height of Halidon the English hosts had on their right the silver winding Tweed, with the harbour at its mouth full of shipping, for Berwick was known then as the Alexandria of the North. On the southern side the rising moors stretched in the treeless solitude of that much-forayed land to the wide sides of noble Cheviot. On the left was the shimmering blue of the sea, calm in the brief Northern summer, and in front the huddled towers and roofs of Berwick that covered the suspense and suffering of the gallant townsfolk. On the flat Northumbrian coast sat the bold rock of Holy Island with its sacred edifice, and still further south the faint outline of Bamburgh. The Scots came forward to the foot of the hill and had to dismount. In front of them was marshy land, and above them the hill gleamed with the pennons and spears of English chivalry, and, most terrible of all, the kneeling bowmen. The Scots sent their horses to the rear whilst the English array watched them motionless. A huge Scot, called Turnbull, accompanied by a fierce mastiff, invited the English to produce a champion. A Norfolk knight, Robert Benhale, came forward. With one stroke he disabled the dog and then sliced off one arm of Turnbull and finally slashed off his head. It was an evil omen, and foreboding seized the Scots as they saw how closely knit stood the foe above them on the advantageous position, the sun glinting on their serried spears. The gallant Scots struggled through the marsh whilst into them poured sheaves of arrows. The ground was strewn with wounded and dying, and over them their comrades advanced and superbly drove with their long spears right into the thick formation of the English ranks. The unarmoured Irish slaves or mercenaries of the English army were thrust down and trampled on in the bloody clamour and the first ranks of the English were pushed back in disorder. Such was the onset of the Scots delivered with the renowned dash and valour which still to-day make the " kilties " the most dreaded opponents in a charge. Balliol and Darcy saw with dismay the wavering ranks they commanded. With the decision of desperation they rallied the firmness of the troops and hurried up the reserves and poured the unceasing, deadly shafts into the panting Scots who, hurling themselves up the steep, weighted with armour, bathed in blood and sweat, strove to gain a footing on the level crown of Halidon. Shouting, fighting, resisting with unsurpassable bravery, they were rolled down the hill. The flower of the knights were perishing, falling, trodden on, cruelly smashed as their companions were thrust over them towards the marshy base. In despair they refused to fly, striking down with wrath and vengeance their better placed foe. At last, in total disorder, they rushed to their horses. But the servitors in charge of them had fled. En-cumbered in mail, the Scots could make no headway. A fearful slaughter followed. Edward, coming up from Berwick walls, which he had been attacking, followed the fugitives for five miles with Darcy's Irish troops and English bowmen. The chronicler of Lanercost says: " The English pursued them on horseback, felling the wretches as they fled in all directions with iron-shod maces." The figures given of the slain are unreliable, as the English exaggerated and the Scots minimised their losses. As was characteristic of these Border battles the Scots lost a great many of their nobility, among whom were six Earls, Carrick, Ross, Athol, Lennox, Sutherland, and Menteith. The Regent Douglas also fell. It was a pitiful slaughter. Unhappy Berwick opened its gates to Edward. Near to the field of battle an altar was erected in a convent by the King, dedicated to St. Margaret, and £20 a year was granted to the nuns that they should for ever on the anniversary yield thanks to God.

A Sketch on the Northumberland Coast.

Berwick, from Spittal.

CHAPTER IV

BERWICK-ON-TWEED

BERWICK-ON-TWEED is the most romantic of the Northumbrian towns. Its history no less than its position entitles it to that distinction. It seems to have come into existence after the Battle of Carham and the cession of the Lothians to Scotland ; that would be early in the eleventh century. From that time until the Battle of Halidon Hill it was the scene of recurrent conflicts between the English and the Scots, remaining on the whole a part of Scotland. Indeed if it was not the greatest town of that country it was at any rate the leading borough. Its position is as striking as its history. Those who know it only from the map think that it is low, as it stands close to the sea at the mouth of the Tweed, but that part of the coast is high and rocky, and as a matter of fact Berwick-on-Tweed always gives the feeling of height. It is seen to greatest advantage by the traveller approaching from the Etal road. There is a rise about two or three miles from the town from which a fine view may be obtained of the bay, the curving pier, Spittal with its sands on the south side of the river, and the town itself, a mass of red pantile roofs clustering round the town hall, an eighteenth century building standing where the old Red Hall of the Flemings used to stand. But looked at from the north it is still more interesting. At the back of the spectator is that semi-moorland country which merges into the Lammermuirs, and far away to the south are the shadowy ranges of Cheviot, blue and dreamy in the distance. At the foot of Berwick, so to speak, and reached by a precipitous descent, is the Tweed, and when the tide is back flowing as silvery as it does at Melrose or Coldstream. Thomas Hodgkin, the historian, who lived at Bamburgh before he went to Barmoor, once drew attention to a kind of duplication of everything in Berwick. It is a walled town and it has two sets of walls, one Edwardian and the other Elizabethan. It has two bridges, a fine, tall, many-arched railway bridge which comes with a splendid sweep over from Tweedmouth to the place where the castle once stood. Indeed almost the whole of the ancient masonry was removed in order to build the station. The other is the famous Border Bridge, built at the instance of King James, who seems to have had some difficulty with the old structure on his march south to take possession of the English Crown. It is a quaint and beautiful bridge passing over the river about a quarter of a mile below the railway bridge. It is narrow, with curious little refuges at the arches, where if a passenger did not seek safety he would be in danger of being jammed whenever two carts met, so narrow is the roadway.

According to the Lanercost Chronicler Berwick was in the thirteenth century " so populous and of such trade that it might justly be called another Alexandria, whose riches was the sea, and the water its walls." But I think the best description of it in its ancient glory is to be found in the poem attributed to Dunbar, called " The Freiris of Berwik." Critics are agreed that whether this be Dunbar or not it cannot be later than the fourteenth century.

> As it befell, and hapnit into deid,
> Upon ane rever the quhilk is callit Tweid,
> At Tweidis mouth thair standis ane noble toun,
> Quhair mony lordis hes bene of grit renowne,
> And mony wourthy ladeis fair of face,
> And mony ane fresche lusty galland was:

Into this toun, the quhilk is callit Berwik
Apon the se ; thair standis nane it lyk.
For it is wallit weill about with stane,
And dowbill stankis cassin mony ane ;
And syn the castell is so strang and wicht,
With staitelie touris, and turatis he on hicht,
With kirnalis closit most craftelie of all,
The portculis most subtillie to fall,
That quhen thay list to draw tham vpon hicht,
That it may be into na mannis micht,
To win that hous by craft or subtiltie.
Thairto is it most fair alluterlie :
Onto my sicht, quhairevir I haue bein,
Most fair, most gudlie, and allther best besene :
The toun, the wall, the castel, and the land ;
The valayis grein vpon the tother hand ;
The grit croce kirk, and eik the Mason Dew.
The freiris of Jacobinis quhyt of hew,
The Carmelites, Augustins, Minors eik,
The four ordouris of freiris war nocht to seik ;
Thay war all in this wourthy toun duelling.

In spite of Berwick's antiquity there are, practically speaking,
no old houses in the town. The ancient dwellings have been
destroyed in the long succession of battles that have taken place.

The bridge—as we have said—dates from the reign of James I.
On his procession southward no doubt the dignitaries of Berwick
who welcomed him with pomp and enthusiasm took care that
he should thoroughly understand the deficiencies of the bridge
then standing. One cannot but wish, by-the-bye, that some
successor of the Somerset Herald had accompanied James and
written an equally picturesque account. The " Narration of
the Progresse and Entertainment of the King's most excellent
Majestie, with the Occurrents happening in the same Journey "
was obviously written by a courtier and a flatterer. It is very
certain " that the wisest fool in Christendom " said and did
many odd things in the course of this pilgrimage, especially
as his hopes and vanity were equally inflated by it, but if so
the recorder took care not to set them down. All that is interesting about his stay at Berwick is the description of the company
who attended or met him. Everywhere " the Lords Wardens "
of the border of England and Scotland received him, attended
by " the Lord Governour of Barwick " with " all the Counsell
of Warre," " the Constables with their Cornets of horse, and
divers of the Captaines, the Band of Gentlemen Pensioners,
with divers Gentlemen," and when he came near the gate " in

the clearnes of which faire time issued out of the Towne Mr. William Selbie, Gentleman Porter of Barwick, with divers Gentlemen of good repute." Before that the guns had roared out a welcome, and this the chronicler describes with great zest : " for from the mouths of dreadfull engins, not long before full fed by moderate artesmen, that knew how to stop and emptie the brasse and iron panches of those roring noises, came such a

A Byway, Berwick.

tempest, as deathfull, and sometimes more dreadfull than thunder, that all the ground thereabout trembled as in an earthquake, the houses and towers staggering, wrapping the whole Towne in a mantle of smoake, wherein the same was awhile hid from the sight of its Royall Owner." He ventures the opinion, or rather he says he " heard it credibly reported," that " a better peale of ordinance was never in any souldiers memorie (and there are some olde King Harrie's lads in Barwick, I can tell you) discharged in that place."

For centuries Berwick has had no suburbs or outlying districts. The tradition that safety lay within its walls has long survived— a strange anachronism handed down from the miseries of Border warfare ! Even yet the children play the game of " Scotch and English " in fierce realism. One consequence of the congestion of the town within its stone boundaries is the scarcity of gardens, the only gardens being attached to the houses within the vicinity of the Walls where grassy spaces still invite the washerwoman to dry her linen in the strong air from the sea.

The space in the town has been wonderfully utilised. All the
streets have " entries " that often contain the secluded pleasant
houses that the merchants of the past were content to dwell
within. The stranger passing these dark openings would expect
only a few back doors. Instead, he dives into a little street with
no outlet or view except perhaps the spire of the Town Hall
piercing the windy sky. There is possibly not another country
town in England within whose confines so little verdure or leafage
cheers the eyes of the inhabitants. The only colour comes from
the many red roofs which give Berwick such a delightful aspect
from the railway viaduct or from the Tweedmouth side, the
town ascending from the bank and clustering round the domin-
ating Town Hall. There are several entries worth penetrating.
In the Palace is Bishop's Entry, where the houses almost meet.
It leads to the old bowling green and the Governor's House
contained in an old quiet square. The Palace is entered by the
Sandgate on one side or at the entrance to the Ness Gate,
towards the pier, where the old Grammar School stands.

Church Street has many entries to be looked into. Above
one is the sign :

Fear to offende
Or marke the ende

In Eastern Lane is a fine seventeenth century house with a
handsome staircase, now divided up in smaller dwellings. But
in Bridge Street, into which Eastern Lane steeply descends, is
one of the most alluring byways in Berwick. It is the Sallyport, and connects the street with the quay and has a flight of
ancient and irregular steps to the Walls above. The Sallyport
is very narrow, with high gloomy walls and old houses that peer
into the sunless opposite walls. But here again venture through
one of the suspicious faced entries up which usually blows a
shrill, biting draught. The visitor may find a spacious cobbled
enclosure with a few humble but pleasant habitations, about
which the linen of mariners flaps as white as the wing of
the clamorous gull wheeling unexpectedly overhead. The
mariners are most likely workers about the quay, and the gull
is but a scavenger there for all his white-winged brotherhood
with the waves. Walking along the Walls in an evening past
the old fashioned houses of prosperous citizens, comes a strange
feeling of recognition of the romance of the past and the for-

gotten inhabitants of this crowded town passionate with race antipathy. Suddenly the houses break, and in the gap the setting

House in Eastern Lane, Berwick.

sun illumines the upper stories in the Sallyport, and below a sea-faring man lurches over the cobbles towards the dark entry to

the quay with the peculiar sway of the fishermen. It is only a
fleeting impression, but gathering twilight and solitary figure

The Sallyport, Berwick.

and the dark passage receiving it conjure up some of the unknown
tragedies enacted beneath these forbidding walls.

Not far from the entrance to the Sallyport in Bridge Street
there used to be a very old hostelry which had some fine carved
wood, a haunt once of the sailors who used to frequent Berwick
when there was a larger sea trade. The quay in summer is
busy with the herring boats—*Silver Queen*, *Two Brothers*, the
Marianne, etc., but the white fishing has declined owing to the
trawlers. Close against the quay, rising very gradually and

Spittal Ferry, Berwick side.

strongly, the old Bridge, the pride of Berwick, spans the Tweed,
and the masts of the fishing boats seem to overtop it.

The unsubdued past of Berwick speaks in its enduring gates.
The nail-studded oak, the massive keys, the archways' gloomy
strength, are no uncertain tribute to the marauding Scots and
Border hate.

On a summer day, to pass from the glittering Parade, flanked
by its handsome barracks, and the shadowless wall of the old
churchyard where no citizen is buried now, beneath the Cowgate
is to find a strange coolness, a lifeless quietness. The sun
ceases for a minute, the past claims its due, the spear of the

shadowy warder drops some antique salute, and the distant voice of the sergeant drilling his awkward Scottish Borderers, is but the echo of the Captain of the Guard three hundred years

The Cowgate, Berwick.

ago. We pass beneath the shadow, and before us lies the sun-bathed buttercup meadows of the Magdalene Fields (where stood the Hospital of St. Mary), and on the rim of the sky the quivering blue, the unforgettable blue of June on the North Sea. Another

D

sea gate, the Ness Gate, frames a picture as sudden, but with the
noble pier and lighthouse dividing river and sea.   The Ness
Street is a narrow grey thoroughfare where even in high summer
the air is keen.   It has some entries where lurk attractive cottages that receive the sun denied to the street.   At the end is
an entrance to the Walls, where one day in the year a sentry
stands forbidding entrance, thus preserving the rights of the
War Office.   Just in front is the dark archway, not so wide as
the Cowgate, sandy Spittal Point straight beyond, with the

Walls of Berwick, low tide, showing storm drum.

restless Bar narrowed by the long line of the pier, and the lighthouse, a strong tower often in winter white with the spray of the
terrible storms which sweep down the coast.   The pier is a great
promenade, and owing to the changeful character of the sea and
river mouth it never becomes monotonous.

The encircling Walls also provide a unique walk.   Cannon
still stand on Meg's Mount, and there used to be cannon placed
against the loopholes opposite the Carr Rock where the storm
drum hangs.   From the top of the Scots Gate we look down on
the busy High Street, and from the heights above, on the river and
its two bridges, Tweedmouth and Spittal, and the sea beyond.

But the whole area of the Walls is delightful, with sea and town.
The fortifications, grass-grown now, have been the playground
of generations of children.

It is a walk almost devoid of trees but always bracing with the
clean salt air.   Only in one hollow is a melancholy grove of trees
that rustle continually above the families who once walked the

Berwick from the Scots Gate.

pavements of the old town and now surround the parish church.
The trees grow so thickly beneath the shadow of the fortifications
that gloom invades the wanderer who meditates there.   The eye
cannot pierce the sighing leafage, but little imagination is needed
to see the grassy mounds and mossed headstones of citizens and
freemen of Berwick.   The church was built during the Pro-
tectorate, and on the same spot David Bruce was married to
Joan, sister of Edward II.   She, poor thing, was called Make

Peace, a bone flung amidst the embittered rivalry of the two nations. John Knox preached for two years in the church now standing, and later in the sixteenth century James Melville, who in exile wrote his famous diary.

Not far from this point in the Walls lie, on the outside of them, against the Magdalene Fields, the grounds called the "Stanks," used for skating in winter. As Berwickers use many perversions of speech, outsiders have supposed that the word was "tanks" with a superfluous "s." But it is probable that "stanks" is derived from the Gaelic *stang*, a ditch with stagnant water. We know water ditches surrounded the walls. Another word of perplexing etymology whose use has aroused the curiosity of visitors is "Dover," the water in which salmon is boiled and which is always served in Berwick with the fish. It is possibly from the old Celtic word which would be pronounced dóvŏr, from which is derived the modern Welsh word *dwr* (pronounced door), water. This derivation possibly links us to the remote times in which the luxury of sauces was introduced.

At the north end of the town, stretching towards the Magdalene Fields, parallel with the ruins and ditch of the Edwardian wall and the Bell Tower, lie the fishermen's quarters, known as Low and High Greenses. Here generations of a stalwart race of Burgons, Manuels, Buglasses, Pattersons, Jamiesons, etc., pursue the hereditary calling of toilers of the deep. They are not so numerous now, as since the advent of trawlers the line fishermen have not prospered notwithstanding a benevolent Government's assistance. The young men, it is to be feared, increasingly seek land occupations, though happily the navy found many recruits from their ranks, for the sea is in their blood.

The comfortable are apt to talk of the laziness of fishermen when they hang about the stile at the Fields watching for signs of the weather and discussing its endless vagaries. The townsman sees perhaps the sun shining, or a sweet grey gleaming sky arching the wide meadows to the edge of the circle that touches the distant moving water girdling the Fields. He thinks as he takes his easy constitutional or proceeds to his quiet office or shop that the fisherman is neglecting his duty of riding the waves and procuring his breakfast fish. He may not reflect that the baccy-chewing, spitting, jerseyed figure may have put out at 4 a.m. and had to return owing to heavy seas. Perhaps he may have got only a few fish in the clinging damp or biting

wind with the salt water eating into his blistered, "gathered"
hands as he pulled in the long dripping lines. As for pains of
rheumatism or toothache, the fisherman, were he minded, could
tell him many a tale. The days he spends " looking at the sea,"
are too often descanted upon by those whose feet have never
squelched in wintry brine, whose arms have never ached pulling
the heavy oar, or swollen with the sting of jelly fish in summer

Low Greenses, Berwick.

heat. Ask the fisherman's wife who, though usually happy and
healthy, sits for weary hours baiting the lines with the " lug "
she has dug up in the cold early morning on the wet sands behind
the pier. And along the cliffs she has gathered the fine grass
that she lays between the baited hooks. There are no women
now, except perhaps an occasional Eyemouth or Spittal wife,
who hawk round fish in creels on their backs, and they no longer
stand in short petticoats with copious pockets and chaffer at stalls
in the High Street, and praise shrilly and picturesquely the
quality of their husbands' haddies, ling, and cod. Such a one was

old Eppie, a Spittal wife who used to protest volubly with many an " eh, hinny, it's dirt cheap," as she smacked the scaly codling or haddie on the slippery board. But never for an instant did she expect or perhaps desire that her original price should not

At the end of the Greenses.

be well beaten down by the wary customer who usually prefaced her haggling interview with the belligerent inquiry " Hoo dear's it ? "

" Scratch a Russian and find a Tartar," and a fisherman of board schools is kith and kin to a remote ancestry who read the stars and feared the supernatural in every form, and found it in details of life so trivial that it is impossible to work out the origin of their superstitions. Yet a diligent student might perhaps find out here and there some reason behind their blind dread. A typical example is that of a fisherman who traced a string of misfortunes to meeting a woman going boatward in the morning. As a first mishap he will tell you he slipped going down the cobbled way and his lines got tangled. After infinite trouble this would be rectified, but getting into the boat he would twist his leg, then an oar would drop overboard, the wind would rise and the sail refuse to be adjusted. Then at sea he cast his line, but it got fastened to another man's or caught by a trawler or among the rocks, and after losing a good part of it the remainder was pulled up to exhibit as his catch a few starfish. He may cast it again, but the result is only what he expected—*nil*. Disheartened, he thinks he will go and pull up his crab pot which was set a few days ago. He finds the mark of its whereabouts gone and cannot trace it anywhere. Finally, after having cut his fingers somehow and being knocked over by the mast and sworn at by his mates, he gets to harbour through a heavy sea, having just escaped with his life. One listens to all this circumstantial tale, which cannot be told in less than an hour, with many references to the signs in the sky, and the boats that were passed, and the wisdom with which his mates foretold disaster, and wonders at the childlike credulity from a man who is full of natural wit and shrewdness.

CHAPTER V

From Berwick to Norham—Horncliffe Glen—The Castle—Origin of ' Robin Adair ''—Mons Meg at Norham—William Marmion's adventure.

NORHAM is easily reached by train from Berwick, but the walker or cyclist will get a finer impression of the country on either side of the Tweed as it widens out towards Spittal. It is not easy to follow the river, as there is no continuous path. About two miles above Berwick on the north side the Whitadder, a lovely Berwickshire stream, falls into the Tweed and can only be crossed by following its banks to Canties Bridge, which is still within Berwick bounds. But the Bounds road is passed before reaching Paxton. The village of Paxton lies to the right and the road goes past the policies of Paxton House. If instead of keeping to the road the pedestrian about one mile from Canties Bridge takes any of the field gates that lead to the river, he will walk to the Chain Bridge where the Tweed, silver and gracious, flows past Paxton Woods. A path skirts the edge of the river along the grounds of Paxton House. On the opposite side are green haughs, and, beyond, the rising farm lands. Here Charles I had a large camp on his way to Scotland to meet the Covenanters. The pleasantest way to reach the Chain Bridge from Berwick is by boat, which can be hired at Berwick. The idea is to go up with the tide and after picnicking, return with its ebb. Above the bridge, high on a cliff can be seen the roofs of the pretty village of Horncliffe—still by the rustic called Horckley as it used to be written—and about a quarter of a mile beyond it, where the Mill waters run into the Tweed, one of the loveliest glens in this part of the world.

Horncliffe Glen is noted on the Borders. It is a deep ravine, woods on one side where the primroses in spring are wonderful, bracken and whin on the other. A path runs up the burnside, and as there is no particular object in visiting Horncliffe, unless to see the low thatched cottage that is said to have sheltered Cromwell when the army crossed the Tweed, the visitor can either follow the stream that way or take the path on the precipitous bank above and thus reach Horncliffe Mill.   There

Norham.

is no more exquisite scene in North Northumberland. The moss-grown mill, with a quaint vane and an outside stone stair, stands under an overhanging sandstone cliff, the water babbling at its base, ferns peeping from every crevice. The complete seclusion, the protection of the high banks which allow ferns and many a flower not usually found in the neighbourhood to adorn the rocky sides of the stream here, suggest Devonshire's mild and humid air. By clambering across the stream behind the mill a path will be found right through the woods for possibly two miles, when it emerges on the Norham

Road. No visitor to Berwick would, seeing the scarcity of woodland in its neighbourhood, guess the existence of such a lovely, wild, remote glen in which the March sun always feels like May, so perfectly has nature sheltered it. Keeping to the right on emerging on the Norham Road, which is reached either by a stile or a fence, the traveller finds himself on a pleasant highway which leads from farm to farm till suddenly, after passing the park wall of Morris Hall on the left, he sees the bare grey ruined keep of the famous Castle over ninety feet high and the strong remains of the outlying curtain walls. Before giving a slight sketch of Norham's historic past it will be as well to describe the route which the cyclist who did not strike off the main road beyond Canties Bridge to the Tweed would take. The road lined with trees passes a few steps from Paxton village. The song of " Robin Adair," with its haunting regret, sprang from a rude ballad written in Paxton early in the eighteenth century, of which one verse runs :

> Paxton's a fine snug place, Robin Adair,
> It's a wondrous couthie place, Robin Adair ;
>   Let Whitadder rin a spate
>   Or the wind blow at ony rate,
> Yet I'll meet thee on the gait, Robin Adair.

The concert room for generations has made us familiar with the refined pathos of the later version :

> What's this dull town to me ? Robin's not near.
> What was't I wished to see, what wished to hear ?
> Where's all the joy and mirth
> Made this town heaven on earth ?
> O they're all fled with thee, Robin Adair.

Some of us prefer the homelier but not less tender words of the original.

Whatever words are sung to it, the ancient air " so simple in construction, so full of power and pathos," is a gem of purest beauty.

The local saying that Paxton was famous for "Drunken old wives and salmon sae fine," evidently originated in the mind of some misbegotten knave who lived on the other side of the Tweed. Paxton belonged to the Paxtons of that Ilk who were among the unfortunate Borderers who in early times held land in both kingdoms and experienced the usual difficulty of serving two masters. The Paxtons were forfeited both by English and Scottish Kings. Paxton was burnt by the Duke of Gloucester in 1482 and by the Duke of Norfolk, who laid the neighbourhood waste in 1540. At the Union the Paxtons only had a few acres left. Sir Joseph Paxton, who built the Crystal Palace, came of that stock. Paxton House lies to the left, the policies bordering the road. It was built by the Adams in 1777 for Ninian Home, who bought the estate.

A very pleasant road continues to Horndean, a tiny village, and thence, studying the finger-posts, to another hamlet famous for its small church, Ladykirk, once called Upsettlington. Before its name was changed one sunny day in August, 1497, James IV sat playing cards in the shade with the Spanish Ambassador. The six horses who were drawing Mons Meg to subdue " Norem " were doubtless tired and, like their masters, glad to rest in the cool air above Tweed's serene flood. It was through James that the modern name of Ladykirk arose. The story is that James IV, returning from a raid into England in those days when Flodden was still unfought, found just above Norham that the river had risen at the ford. He made a vow that, if he and his men got safely over, on the high bank on the north side he would build a Kirk to Our Lady which fire would not burn nor water destroy. Thus rose the grey stone chapel roofed and seated with stone on the pre-cipice overlooking Norham. It is modernised now with wooden seats, but by its walls we seem still to hear beyond the murmuring Tweed the shouts of horsemen and the rattle of harness and sword as the weary steeds and heated driven men scramble up the steep sides of Tweed's north bank. It was home to them, even as to this day it is north country to the English wayfarer who, coming from the pleasant burr of the Norham villager, meets on the Ladykirk Road the broad accent of the Scottish hind. The little graveyard of Ladykirk has, or had, sixteenth century stones with cross-bones and skulls still spelling out their hiero-glyphic comment on the final destiny of kings and church-builders and knights and rustic man and maid. The church is built of polished freestone in the form of a Latin cross and is Gothic with the exception of the steeple, added two hundred and forty years after the original building. The roof is very notice-able, being covered with wrought ashlars jointed and overlapped so that the rain is carried off as if the roof were in one piece.

The walls have bullet marks. Ladykirk was one of the last pre-Reformation churches erected in Scotland.

To approach Norham (North Town, on account of its position) from the Scottish side is far more arresting to the imagination than reaching it from the Berwick Road or from the railway road, the only other two entrances. From Ladykirk bank the high road between woods descends to

Ladykirk Church.

Norham bridge. In autumn it is singularly beautiful to look on the coloured trees down the slope below which rolls the Tweed with leaves dancing on the flood of brown waters. Beyond, the sunshine lingers in the long neutral tinted village that seems to lead right up to the woods around the grey castle. The ancient church of Norham is hidden away to the right not far from the banks of the river. Here on the English side Tweed runs by pleasant haughs where the fishers cast their nets for salmon. Village gossips still recall that about a hundred years ago at a ford below Ladykirk the Norham doctor of the day, hurrying to a case, was caught by the flood and he and his horse whirled away.

After crossing the bridge the village lies to the left. To the right the road goes to a picturesque cottage known as the Boathouse, and a little further up is Norham Glen, a beautiful place, but not to be compared with Horncliffe. The Tweed is here at its loveliest.

Norham's centre is the Cross which stands on its ancient base. The village had a charter given by Bishop Pudsey in the twelfth century. Its weekly market, says an Elizabethan Survey, was " keept on the Sundaye which by reason it is undecent is therefore the less used or esteemed." There are still a few thatched cottages, but no old houses. It is a favourite residential place, as it lies warm in the valley away from the east winds that torment the coast. It always appears the most restful of villages, for it is one mile from the station, and its large, quiet, sunny spaces between the opposite sides of the street give it dignity and aloofness. Even in this remote world every village has its own character. The neighbours do not shout across the street as they do at democratic Eyemouth. Houses are not merely the cottages of hinds as at Ladykirk, or crowded within the circumference of a great wall as at Berwick, or let in lodgings as at Spittal. At Coldstream there is a bustle of trade and shops as if it were a Wolverhampton in miniature. At Norham the shops are few and retiring. They are lost sight of between the varying sizes of cottage and villa. They but wait on necessity and ignore the superfluous. Even religious buildings do not clamour for attention, and manse and vicarage are hid from the casual visitor. The old church has to be sought, and the church-yard where the sheep nibble on the old green graves, green for so many forgetful years. A clump of dark yews covers a family vault, and the paths wander about above the dust gathered there since the Saxons worshipped within sound of the running Tweed. It is only ten minutes' walk to the Castle from here, and yet how far away from its repose the shouts of those who defended and assailed that solitary and majestic relic of power above the woods of Tweed ! When the village was called Ubbanford (Ubba or Offa would be the name of some important person), there was a Saxon church built by Bishop Ecgred about 830 in which was buried saintly King Ceolwulf, his shrine being transferred from Lindisfarne by the Bishop who dedicated the church to St. Ceolwulf, St. Cuthbert and St. Peter. Bede dedicated his History to " Ceolwulf the Most Glorious." The present building was contemporary with the Castle, and is supposed to have been built by Flambard. Edward I. met in the church the Scottish nobles at the famous arbitration when the claims of John Balliol were discussed. In the reign of the Conqueror Earl Gospatric was buried in the church porch. Built up into a pillar in the churchyard are a number of stones dug out from the foundations of the Saxon church, and in the opinion of Dr. Raine they are of the same date as the cross at Bewcastle. They are ornamented in beautiful ninth century style. One of them has an inscription *P. Anima Ælfa*, meaning, probably, Pray for the soul of Ælfa. From the churchyard a short, narrow path runs between hedges to the river, and turning to the right a beautiful view of the Castle is in sight. Valiant, it looked forth in its youth, fresh and fearful from the masons' final touches, with watchful eye on the menacing north. To-day its brave age has seen from north bank and south bank men who have marched past its walls to die for a higher cause than Border feuds. Would the Northumberland Fusiliers have fought as well in France and Flanders if their ancestors had not listened often for days to the tramp of hosts and opposing cries, or the clatter of late forayers returning at night ?

The famous episode of Sir William Marmion's visit to Norham is fully related by Thomas Grey in " The Scalacronica." The Thomas Grey mentioned in the story was his father. It will be remembered that the author when himself Captain of Norham was captured and taken to Edinburgh Castle, where he wrote his book. The following is his spirited history of Marmion's adventure :

" At which time at a great feast of lords and ladies in the county of Lincoln a young page brought a war helmet, with a gilt crest on the same, to William Marmion, Knight, with a letter from his lady-love commanding him to go to the most dangerous place in Great Britain and there cause this helmet to be famous. Thereupon it was decided by the knights present that he should go to Norham as the most dangerous and adventurous place in the country. The said William betook himself to Norham, where, within four days of his arrival, Sir Alexander de Mowbray, brother of Sir Philip de Mowbray, at that time Governor of Berwick, came before the Castle of Norham with the most spirited chivalry of the Marches of Scotland and drew up before the Castle at the hour of noon with more than eight score men-at-arms. The alarm was given in the Castle as they were sitting down to dinner. Thomas de Grey, the constable, went with his garrison to his barriers, saw the enemy near drawn up in order of battle, looked behind him, and beheld the said knight, William Marmion, approaching on foot, all glittering with gold and silver, marvellous finely attired, with the helmet on his head. The said Thomas, having been well informed of the reason for his coming to Norham, cried aloud to him : ' Sir Knight, you have come as knight errant to make that helmet famous, and it is more meet that deeds of chivalry be done on horseback than afoot, when that can be managed conveniently. Mount your horse : there are your enemies ; set spurs and charge into their midst. May I deny my God if I do not rescue your person, alive or dead, or perish in the attempt ! '

" The knight mounted a beautiful charger, spurred forward, and charged into the midst of the enemy, who struck him down, wounded him in the face, and dragged him out of the saddle to the ground.

" At this moment, up came the said Thomas with all his garrison, with levelled lances, which they drove into the bowels of the horses so that they threw their riders. They repulsed the mounted enemy, raised the fallen knight, remounting him upon his own horse, put the enemy to flight, of whom some were left dead in the first encounter, and captured fifty valuable horses. The women of the Castle then brought out horses to their men, who mounted and gave chase, slaying those whom they could overtake. Thomas de Grey caused to be killed in the Yair Ford a Fleming named Cryn, a sea captain, a pirate, who was a great partisan of Robert de Brus. The others who escaped were pursued to the nunnery of Berwick."

Norham Castle, built in 1122 by Flambard, Prince Bishop of Durham, that upstart, pushing, mediæval ecclesiastic, full of " craft and wile," was the most important fortress on the Borders and the scene of not only great exploits but great meetings between the rival countries, and many times it changed hands. King John met William the Lion here to make one of the many treaties intended to secure peace on the Borders. The latter's son, Alexander II, stayed here ; Edward I met the Scots camped at Upsettlington, on Holywell Haugh, a meadow facing the Castle on the opposite side, and discussed their differences, and the result was his selection of the ill-fated John Balliol as King of Scotland, who swore fealty to Edward in the Castle. After that the story of sieges and surprises goes on without ceasing. One unfortunate sovereign who tried to secure it was Henry VI, and Queen Margaret after the battle of Hexham. James IV brought the famous cannon Mons Meg (so called because made at the Mons renowned now as the point from which the " Contemptibles " made their immortal retreat, and as the spot where the Great War ended with the defeat of Germany) from Edinburgh for the attack, and there are still preserved near the Castle some of the missiles discharged from it. When James made his last sally from Scotland on his way to Flodden, Norham held out for five days. The Scots' last attempt to secure it was in 1530, and after that, the power of Norham gradually declining with the union of the kingdoms, it fell into decay. In Camden's time the Castle had " an outer wall of great compass with many little towers in the angle next the river, and within, another circular tower much stronger, in the centre whereof rises a loftier tower." The complete decay of the Castle now is due to the undermining of the river.

It stands on an almost perpendicular bank rising above the Tweed, and is protected like so many Northumbrian strongholds on one side by a precipitous climb from a ravine where a thread of water runs into Tweed. The stranger entering through the curtain wall that skirts the road by an ancient archway sees outlined against a half circle of trees the bare walls of the keep seated on a considerable mound. The grass runs up to it over masonry and ditch, banks and hollows all green now above the strength and splendour which Scott's romantic eye saw so plainly. Perhaps he only saw it once in his unforgetting fashion when autumn had painted the encircling trees and the red October sunset was staining the broad bosom of his beloved Tweed. As a recent writer [1] says of his description, " the close succession of minute touches neither oppresses us nor distracts us in our enjoyment of the complete effect."

[1] " Scottish Literature," by G. Gregory Smith. Macmillan.

Day set on Norham's castled steep
And Tweed's fair river, broad and deep
  And Cheviot's mountains lone ;
The battled towers, the donjon Keep,
The loop-hole grates where captives weep,
The flanking walls that round it sweep
  In yellow lustre shone.
The warriors on the turrets high,
Moving athwart the evening sky,
  Seem'd forms of giant height ;
Their armour as it caught the rays,
Flash'd back against the western blaze
  In lines of dazzling light.

St. George's banner, broad and gay
Now faded, as the fading ray
  Less bright, and less, was flung ;
The evening gale had scarce the power
To wave it on the donjon tower,
  So heavily it hung.

A Cheviot Stream.

E

CHAPTER VI

THE BATTLEFIELD OF FLODDEN

THE FORD

" So that the Night Watch of Ryddysdaill shall join the Night Watch of Tyndaill at the Stoneyford."

Leges Marchiarum.

First Watchman.

O watcher at the ford, your streams run low,
Did any rider cross ?   Did any go
Your way beneath the moon ?

Second Watchman.

The moon is young ; I saw the crescent stoop
Till imaged in the pool her silver loop
No more.   She set too soon.

First Watchman.

O watcher, heard you at the strait no sound
Of feet that stumbled on the stony ground,
Where one might take the hill ?

Second Watchman.

I heard the water wash among the weeds,
A hunting otter rustled in the reeds,
Naught else.   The night was still.

First Watchman.

The night was still, I rode beside the stream—
Heard you no cry ?   I saw a lanthorn gleam,
For what searched you the wood ?

Second Watchman.

There screamed some vermin tangled in a snare,
It was a thieving fox that I found there,
And flung him to the flood.

FIRST WATCHMAN.

O watcher, where you marked the driftwood ride
The flood—saw you naught else go down the tide ?
At dawn the spate rose high.

SECOND WATCHMAN.

Above this ford you know the haughs are green,
And many cattle graze. I may have seen
A foundered steer go by.

MARNA PEASE.

FLODDEN FIELD was the greatest battle fought in Northumberland. But it is one of the " old unhappy far-off things " over
the details of which there is endless discussion. There was no
Froissart in 1513 to describe the battle and the deeds of heroes,
and desperate men fighting for life know only what happens to
themselves. Still the main facts are well established, and to
piece together a coherent picture of the battle adds to the
fascination of a fine Border landscape. Glendale is an angler's
Paradise, and the disciple of Father Izaak, if he puts a few books
about Flodden into his bag, will even if alone enjoy his Pastime
with Good Company. First place should be given to Marmion,
the best battle piece out of Homer. Sir Walter with sure instinct
seized upon the salient facts, and his account is as true as an
imaginative picture need be. A curious effect of his poem was
to cast a new glamour over the name Sybil, and that by means
of an inexactitude. A very lovely inexactitude ! When Clare,
a ministering angel to the dying Marmion, in answer to his
agonised cry for water, took his casque and

stoop'd her by the runnel's side,
But in abhorrence backward drew ;
For, oozing from the mountain's side,
Where raged the war, a dark red-tide
Was curdling in the streamlet blue,

her eyes caught sight of a little fountain cell, " where water,
clear as diamond-spark, in a stone basin fell." As long as I
can remember it was a delight to croon over the legend printed
in old English letters in the editions of Marmion :

Drink . weary . pilgrim . drink . and . pray .
For . the . kind . soul . of . Sybil . Grey .
Who . built . this . cross . and . well .

E 2

For long this well was identified with a little spring on Flodden
Hill, and Louisa, Marchioness of Waterford, about the time when
she planted the strip of conifers stretching from the hill down
to the Wooler road, erected a little fountain for visitors, who
could drive in a straight line from Ford Castle to Flodden.
At the well they might drink cold water and meditate the scene.
But she was a very Protestant lady who did not believe in prayers

Ford Castle, Northumberland.

for the dead, and therefore substituted an invitation to rest for
the second line—

> Drink, weary pilgrim ; drink and stay
> Rest by the well of Sybil Grey.

The well, now called Marmion's Well, that Scott evidently
had in his mind, is close to Branxton, the real battlefield.

In Sir Walter Scott's time the county was bare, as may be
judged from his phrase, Flodden " bent," meaning it was covered

with bents or rough grass, as in the ballad phrase " the bent and the heather." As late as 1839 the Rev. Thomas Knight, Vicar of Ford, described the hill as " now covered by peaceful flocks and golden cornfields." That was its appearance between the novelist's day and the woody landscape it forms now. The change is of historic importance, as it shows that those who were with James could in good weather better watch the movements of the enemy since these movements were not shrouded by trees.

Sir Walter Scott was well entitled to take liberties with history, and no one can regret his doing so who follows the old road to the hill. " Dark Flodden " is an outspur of the Cheviots which stand behind it in massive formation. Its epithet " dark " renders the effect produced by the oaks crowning the summit. The best way is through a gate just after crossing the burn in which Paulinus is said by tradition to have performed some of his numerous baptisings. The way is now up a lane called " the Sandy Lonnin," which leads past a lovely dene. Canon Greenwell records that upon a swelling piece of ground near this dene several hollows, each covered by a flat stone and filled with burnt bones, were found. In one of these hollows lined with small stones was a necklace of jet beads strung round the neck of an urn. Unfortunately, he adds, neither the urn nor beads have been preserved. No tumulus seems to have covered these graves, but it is surmised that the rounded hill itself formed a natural tumulus. One cannot help regretting that this is all to tell of what seems to have been a pathetic memorial raised by one of the myriad of native British who in prehistoric times peopled these vales. A little further on is a farm with the pleasant name of Blink Bonny. Not far off is another called Encampment, which may have been a most suitable camp for the army of King James. At Blink Bonny the turnpike is crossed by a road which goes by Mindrum and Pawston to Yetholm in Roxburghshire, and the way continues by a field lane which, with plantation on one side and open ground on the other, leads up to Flodden by the quarry.

Lady Waterford's drive round the summit of the hill was thick with short grass and mosses last time I saw it, but the well and the cup and the water still remain. No pleasanter place to saunter in a summer afternoon.

> Oft halts the stranger there,
> For thence may best his curious eye
> The memorable field descry ;
>   And shepherd boys repair
> To seek the water-flag and rush,
> And rest them by the hazel bush,
>   And plait their garlands fair.

The scene of the battle was Branxton Hill, not Flodden Hill. Indeed, by many old writers it is called the Battle of Branxton. By a coincidence, it was the Rev. Robert Jones, Vicar of Branxton, who in the early part of the nineteenth century, making a study of the battle the hobby of his life, worked out something like its real history. This account is as well written as it is well informed, and is published in pamphlet form for the convenience of those who like to study the landscape with the written history before them. It is excellent reading. With it the studious angler should put in his bag the clear and concise account of the late Captain Norman—whose obsequies, alas! are taking place as this is being written—and the careful study by Dr. Thomas Hodgkin.

Imagination finds it difficult to reconstruct the landscape as it must have appeared at four o'clock on the misty, drizzling September afternoon when the battle began. The main features, however, are unchangeable. Behind Flodden are the Cheviots, scrub-clad on their lower slopes, grass and bracken and heather further up. A little nearer and you would hear the bleating of their countless sheep. Far away to the north rise the Eildons "cleft in three," romantic in the distance. Coldstream, where James crossed into England, is not visible from the hill. "Auld Wark upon the Tweed," which he assailed and took, has disappeared. Etal Castle is but a home for owls and jackdaws. Ford Castle stands restored among its trees. "The sullen Till" serpentines through its green haughs.

Surrey's army had been assembled at Pontefract, whence the soldiers were shipped to Tynemouth. There they were reinforced by 5,000 soldiers sent by Henry VIII from France. Surrey advanced northward by Alnwick, making his camp at Bolton, a village about six miles from that town. In the chivalrous manner of the time, he had offered to meet James in pitched battle at the village of Bolton or on Milfield Plain. But James declining to leave his fastness, Surrey crossed the Till at Weetwood, about two miles from Wooler, and the night

before the battle camped behind Barmoor Wood. Looking
down at it to-day one sees a fertile, highly-cultivated district.
This part of Glendale stands high agriculturally. It is laid
out in fields hedged with quick in the usual Northumbrian
style. Stone-built farmhouses are dotted over it, the red
gleam of their pantiled roofs showing pleasantly through the
green leafage of sheltering trees. But in the raiding times the
scene was different. Until well on in the eighteenth century
the land was practically unenclosed and undrained. Broom
was a predominant plant. It covered Milfield Plain, and a
broad belt stretched from Flodden almost to Wooler. That
was the state of things until the time of Matthew Cully of
Coupland Castle, a famous agriculturist, who both by precept
and example taught the advantage of growing turnips. Only
a few patches of broom remain here and there to suggest a state
of things to which writers on farming only make brief allusion.
You must see Belford Moor in late spring when the " unprofitably
gay " broom and gorse are in their glory to realise what the county
must have been in the old time.

From the eminence of Flodden Hill the movements of the
army may be puzzled out if the day be clear. Critics of Surrey's
generalship, however, do not take sufficiently into account the
fact that the afternoon was drizzly and misty, of low visibility,
in the language of the most recent warfare, following a period
of rain that had filled the Till to overflowing. James must have
experienced great difficulty in obtaining knowledge of his enemy's
movements and Surrey enjoyed the military advantage of
approaching under cover of the haze. His plan was to send
Howard with the artillery across the single-spanned bridge at
Twizel, which is still standing, and so interpose between the
Scottish army and the Tweed. No doubt that movement
was the first of which James got wind, and he correctly divined
its intention. Scott represents him as setting fire to his camp
and rushing downhill, but it is four miles from Flodden to
Twizel. What James actually did under cover of the smoke
caused by burning the camp refuse was to change his position
from Flodden Hill to Branxton Hill, a mile northward. Mean-
time Surrey himself was leading the rearguard across the Till
at two fords which are still known by the names they then bore.
One was Sandyford, also called the Cradles, where the Back
Burn—the burn of Paulinus—enters the Till. It no doubt

was the brook " a tailor's yard wide " of the old chronicler.
The other was the Willow Ford, a little down the stream nearer
Etal. In that neighbourhood the Till is still lined with willows,
as it probably was in the sixteenth century. The obstacle
that the rearguard had to get over was a great bog or morass,
most of which has now been drained. Parts of it remain,
however, between Mardon Hill and the Blue Bell Inn on the
Pallinsburn estate. Until very recently the remains of the

Branxton

bridge existed, by which it was crossed at its worst part. When
James, who was not without leadership, saw what was happening,
he prepared to charge down the hill, and this was the beginning
of the battle. The extent of the forces engaged is not easily
determined now. The army originally brought together by
the Scottish king was said to have numbered about 100,000,
but in those days an army did not grow on the march, and 100,000
certainly does not mean anything like that number of effectives.
Captain Norman estimated that the Scots might have had
35,000 soldiers but those, be it remembered, were " the flower

of the army." Then the followers of Huntly and Home shortly after the beginning of the fray withdrew from it, perhaps for plunder, or it may be for reasons connected with precedence, so often a bone of contention with the proud Scot. The relative positions of the armies have been made clear by the cannon balls from time to time turned up by the plough. Those used by the Scots were leaden, while those of the English were of iron. But the feature of the day was the fearful hand-to-hand fighting, and no description of it has ever been or is ever likely to be written equal to that of Sir Walter :

> But as they left the dark'ning heath,
> More desperate grew the strife of death.
> The English shafts in volleys hail'd,
> In headlong charge their horse assail'd ;
> Front, flank, and rear, the squadrons sweep
> To break the Scottish circle deep,
>   That fought around their King.
> But yet, though thick the shafts as snow,
> Though charging knights like whirlwinds go,
> Though bill-men ply the ghastly blow,
>   Unbroken was the ring ;
> The stubborn spear-men still made good
> Their dark impenetrable wood,
> Each stepping where his comrade stood,
>   The instant that he fell.
> No thought was there of dastard flight ;
> Link'd in the serried phalanx tight,
> Groom fought like noble, squire like knight,
>   As fearlessly and well ;
> Till utter darkness closed her wing
> O'er their thin host and wounded King.
> Then skilful Surrey's sage commands
> Led back from strife his shatter'd bands ;
> And from the charge they drew,
> As mountain-waves, from wasted lands,
>   Sweep back to ocean blue.
> Then did their loss his foemen know ;
> Their King, their Lords, their mightiest low,
> They melted from the field as snow,
> When streams are swoln and south winds blow,
>   Dissolves in silent dew.
> Tweed's echoes heard the ceaseless plash,
>   While many a broken band,
> Disorder'd, through her currents dash,
>   To gain the Scottish land ;
> To town and tower, to down and dale,
> To tell red Flodden's dismal tale,
> And raise the universal wail.

Tradition, legend, tune, and song,
Shall many an age that wail prolong :
Still from the sire the son shall hear
Of the stern strife, and carnage drear,
   Of Flodden's fatal field,
Where shiver'd was fair Scotland's spear,
   And broken was her shield !

Little remains to be added. The spot at which King James fell is now marked by a great granite monolith with the date of the battle on it, and an inscription as terse and appropriate as could possibly be imagined : " To the Brave of Both Nations."

The old legend that fixed upon the great stone on a level field near Crookham West Field has no basis in fact. The stone is a very ancient one and had stood there for centuries before the battle was fought. The field was part of Crookham Moor, the gathering place of the local clans when a Scottish foray was to be resisted or an English foray made into Scotland.

Of the poetry to which the battle has given rise the finest beyond question is " The Flowers of the Forest." Sir Walter's prophecy has been fulfilled to the letter, but no other tradition, legend, or song describes "the end of the hunting " with a homelier or more sincere pathos than the ballad of Jane Elliot.

I've heard them lilting, at our ewe-milking
  Lasses a' lilting before dawn of day :
But now they are moaning, on ilka green loaning,
  The Flowers of the forest are a' wede away.

   .   .   .   .   .   .

Dool and wae for the order sent our lads to the Border,
  The English for aince by guile wan the day :
The Flowers of the Forest that fought aye the foremost,
  The prime of our land are cauld in the clay.

We'll hear nae mair lilting at the ewe-milking,
  Women and bairns are heartless and wae,
Sighing and moaning on ilka green loaning,
  The Flowers of the Forest are a' wede away.

Of the relics the most poetical are the famous banner carried by the Soutars of Selkirk, now preserved in the town, and the other scarcely less famous borne by the Seven Spears of Wedderburn and now preserved, torn and frayed, in the Castle of Wedderburn.

The following description of the memorial is by Commander Norman, who was mainly instrumental in collecting funds for it. It " stands on a piece of ground generously presented by John Carnaby Collingwood, Esq. (one of the Club members), as consisting of a Celtic Monolith Cross of Grey Aberdeen granite, 12 feet 6 inches high, and 3 feet 9 inches across the arms, raised on a rustic base or cairn, 6 feet high, of rough-hewn granite blocks upon a solid concrete foundation, the whole being enclosed with a fence of massive granite posts connected by galvanised iron bars. The inscription—besides which there is no lettering of any sort—is

FLODDEN 1513
TO THE BRAVE OF BOTH NATIONS.
ERECTED 1910.

in incised letters on a slab on the north side of the cairn. Access to the Memorial is through a wicket-gate in the hedge at the nearest point of the road, 99 yards distant, and by no other way."

The Ford at Coldstream.

. . . Many a broken band
Disordered through her currents dash
To gain the Scottish land.

CHAPTER VII

ALONG TILL SIDE

A primæval lake—Till rhyme and legend—Pack horse mills—Etal
village and ruins—A submerged bridge—Pallinsburn and its
gull pond—Crookham and Dorothy Forster—Ford in Lady
Waterford's day—A hunting anecdote—To Milfield and
Wooler.

FOLLOWING the course of a river is a pleasant but long business,
and Till is a meandering stream. Often as a boy I listened to
a rustic but highly intelligent native arguing that the flat green
haughs above Etal and Milfield Plain must at one time have
been submerged by a gigantic lake. Mr. G. G. Butler, in an
address delivered in 1904, set forth a similar idea and supported
it with geological data. One of his points was that beds of clay,
not mixed with stone and boulders as it is when of glacial origin,
but deep and continuous, are formed by the deposit of the finest
river sand in still lake water. This condition is fulfilled at the
tile-sheds of Flodden and Ewart. Borings by Sir Horace St.
Paul produced even stronger evidence. On low haugh land
near Humbledon Buildings, where clay is at the surface, he bored
seventy feet without getting through it. At another place he
bored first through twenty-five feet of dry sand and gravel,
then through soft and wet sand and gravel, after which he came
to a bed of clay, which he bored to a depth of a hundred feet,
when the rods broke. It is at least imaginable that the Till at
that epoch found an outlet through the now dry gorge of Haiden
Dene and flowed directly into the North Sea.

When Sir Walter Scott characterised the river as the " deep
and sullen Till " he had probably been looking at it from Flodden
Hill. Primitive man gazing on the same prospect would, according to the hypothesis, have seen a great sheet of still water on

which floated the coracle canoe or whatever was used for water transport by " the man in the barrow."

There is still a suggestion of the lake about the Till above Etal. A stranger would have to fling in a stick to find the way it travels, and in stormy weather it produces quite formidable wavelets. It has always been dangerous mainly because its deepest holes are nearest the edge. A bathing schoolboy may wade for long distances in mid-stream while a six-foot man could not keep his head above water if he tried to stand upright near either bank. This and the tremendous floods which occur when its feeders are swollen with rain may account for its surly rhyme, which, however, according to an old tradition, bears a reference to the Scottish flight after Flodden :

> Tweed said to Till
> What gars ye rin sae still ?
> Till said to Tweed
> Though ye rin wi' speed
> And I rin slaw
> Yet where ye droon yin man I droon twa.

But it is no longer surly or sullen when once it has tumbled over the cauld at Etal. Just below that are stepping stones over which the impecunious schoolboy may cross when he has not the copper which Charon exacts at the ferry. This change in character is reflected in the fishing. In the still reaches by the haughs lie the monsters. You may, on an autumn day, watch the salmon leaping the mill dam on their way up-stream. The bull trout and whitling, the pike and the perch, have innumerable strongholds in the pond weed which flourishes. Shoals of red-finned perch, in the deeper pool, tempt the child with his first home-made rod. But when Till, like a quick-change artist, doffs the sober livery in which he has been clad and streams away towards Twizel, rippling and singing over rock and stone, he becomes a joy to the trout fisher, who, however, finds one drop of bitterness in his cup. He likes not the grayling introduced some years ago.

The vegetation on the bank, too, is different. By, or rather in, the still waters grow borders of sedges—usually called " segs " for short—with rushes here and there. In old days when bee-hives were made of straw laced with willows and basket-making, particularly swills—an extra long basket used on the farm for potatoes and turnips—willows were planted on the banks. That the name Willow Ford is as old as the battle of Flodden suggests that the industry is as old too. But the willows are neglected now. If a typical one were photographed it would significantly illustrate the line in " Hamlet," " a willow grew athwart the stream." Untended, they are more picturesque than ever.

But where Till is prettiest the sky is shut out with the foliage of trees. They are of sorts which vary from the hazel to the oak.

Twizel Bridge.

Recent plantings have been mostly of Conifera. Soft woods are the fashion just now both for use and beauty, but they give a certain park-like and artificial appearance which spoils the simple primitive charm of the timber trees beloved of our forefathers.

It makes very little difference whether you walk up or down the bank of a river ; but up used to be convenient when bent on a walking tour, because there is a railway station at Twizel and it makes a good starting point.

The famous bridge is the best place at which to leave the high road. One is glad to omit the short section of the river between it and Tillmouth where " the chapel fair " referred to in ' Marmion " has been hopelessly " restored." Once a castle of note stood at Twizel, but it was destroyed during the war which followed the espousal by James IV of the cause of Perkin Warbeck. A ruin visible from the railway carriage represents an effort at building made in the eighteenth century by the

Twizel House.

Sir Francis Blake of that period. It was never completed, or indeed used, except as a quarry for stones when the present residence of the Blake family was built.

The grey Tudor bridge can never be seen too often. " Greate and strong and of one bow," as Leland described it, it is a good example from a good period. But were it a cast iron County Council bridge of to-day it would be interesting because of its past (I hope the bull will not obscure the meaning). Over it on the fateful day of Flodden passed Surrey's vanguard and artillery.

The walk up-stream discloses little of antiquarian interest. It is impossible to go anywhere in Northumberland without coming across remains of fortified buildings. From the twelfth to the seventeenth century Border people had always to keep watch and ward against the foe. The owner of a few cows and a nag or two had to have a place to drive them when a foray

Looking up Till from Twizel Bridge.

was on. One can realise the life they led from what happened in London when an air-raid was always a possibility.

The pleasure of this walk is mainly derived from nature. Under the leafy shade it is cool on the hottest summer day; cool too are the very colours of running water, here showing a million reflections in its brown depths, there gleaming fresh and white as it foams over a boulder whereon alights that energetic companion of your walk, the water ousel, ever like the village idiot nodding his head. The heron and the kingfisher love the shallow streams, and often the brown owl mistakes the gloom of the forest for the passing of day.

Old mills, mostly ruined, occur frequently between Twizel and Etal. They are generally approached by bridle paths only, and so recall the time when yeomen took their corn to be ground on the back of a packhorse and brought home the meal less the millers " moulter " or multure. The miller continued to be the " stout carle " depicted by Chaucer up to the time of Thomas

Etal Village and Castle.

Bewick. Later it became more usual for the meal to be delivered by the poker—the word was probably connected with ' pokes,' as bags or sacks were called. Much cheating went on over that indefinite levy on the ground corn, the multure, pretty much as Chaucer described in the Reeve's Tale.

Etal Village, embowered in trees, with thatched houses and gay little gardens in front of them, is one of the prettiest villages in the county.

Etal Castle was " in very great decay " when the Border Survey of 1542 was made. It never recovered from the hammering it got before Flodden and is now ruinous. Bowes described

F

it as " being of the Erle of Rutland's inheritance," and it was a Manners who built it in the twelfth century. His arms may yet be seen above the entrance gate. There remains also " the wall of stone and lime " built by Sir Robert de Manners in 1342; when what seems to have been originally a mansion-house was crenellated and fortified.

In the time of Queen Bess it was held by the Collingwoods under a lease of three lives. Afterwards it passed into the hands of George Home, Earl of Dunbar. a Scottish favourite of " the wisest fool in Christendom." Dunbar sold it to the Carrs, from whom Lady Fitzclarence was descended. She was married in May, 1821, to Lord Fitzclarence, son of William IV and Mrs. Jordan. Hence the portraits of that famous actress and the souvenirs of William that used to adorn the interior of Etal House before it was sold on the death of Lady Fitzclarence.

The river, held in check by the mill-dam, is here like a pond. It is crossed by a ferry which starts at the bottom of a declivity on the summit of which the castle is placed. Up stream on the right bank a footpath goes. Follow it and before crossing to the green haugh look into the stream, and if the water be clear you may see the ruins of a bridge. Where they reach the other side there is an avenue of trees showing where the main road used to go. What would one not give to be carried back on a Time Wishing Carpet to Mid-September, 1513! for over that bridge and along the road, grass for four hundred years, were drawn the Scottish guns captured at Flodden and the English artillery. One looks, till the oaths of the teamsters, the orders of officers, and the jabbering of victory-flushed men seem to rise above the clamour of the jackdaws on Etal Castle.

This was the " brigge at Etayle " the decay of which is lamented by Bowes. It " afforded ready passage when the river.Tyll is waxen greate and past the rydinge upon horseback." So he calls out to have it " re-edyfied," and during the last four centuries this has been suggested again and again. The very last time I was at Etal an old inhabitant dwelt upon the advantages, and showed how without a bridge at Etal the way is very roundabout to places on the main road between Cornhill and Wooler. But no one has yet re-builded the bridge.

The ferry used to be kept by an old man who had in his cottage two fine pictures of a Peregrine Falcon and a Hen Harrier, both from Henhole near Cheviot. Every time he showed them he told the same story of the painter who, burning with enthusiasm, took these and other pictures to an Edinburgh publisher. What surprised the unworldly artist was that the Scot, though acknowledging the merit of the drawings, asked, "But would it pey?" He was struck dumb for a moment by a question which was the last he would have thought about; then, with a "It'll

Ferry over Till at Etal.

take a langer shot than me to tell that," he folded up his possessions and took his departure. How times and manners change! The artist of to-day would put that query first.

There is no trace of a road now except a footpath across the green haugh with a rush-covered bog in the middle of it, while to the right of it is a declivity still called the Balks, an interesting survival of the open-field system of cultivation. The names of many hamlets are reminiscent of the same system. Such are

F 2

Crookham East Field, Crookham West Field, Ford West Field, and so on. The common field was divided into what are variously called ridges or riggs, selions or stitches. A three-course rotation prevailed. Autumn-sown wheat or rye one year, spring-sown corn the next, or, as an alternative, peas or beans. Every third year the land was fallowed.

Above the Balks is a hamlet named Keek Out, where watch was kept for the marauding Scot. Not far off is Pallinsburn House, with a fox-cover at the back and in front a wooded park sloping gently down to the edge of the gull-pond, a famous breeding resort of *Larus ridibundus*. The gulls used to be called Askew's Hens, from the name of the family, one of whom built the house. Watson Askew forbade his guests to shoot there—a severe trial for a sportsman, since wild duck come to it in considerable numbers, as well as water-hens, coots, grebes and their kind. Often Colonel Askew, a fine old sportsman who used to be a frequent visitor, was heard to mutter as the duck came flying over in the dusk : " Damn you, I'll shoot you ! Damn you, I'll shoot you ! " But he never did. Tradition says the gulls came from Morebattle about 1750, when the Kale, then a tributary of the Bowmont, broke its banks and flowed to Teviot, the water of the lake escaping too. But Marden Bog must have attracted *ridibundus* in the dark ages, and the pond was a part of it.

It is beautiful in spring to see the pond, which is set with wild flowering shrubs and trees, such as gorse and broom, the white-thorn and the laburnum. The noisy birds make a Babel of the place, and as they fly to and fro their white wings flashing among the tree shadows of the adjacent old plantation and the clamour of their voices bring a touch of the sea inland. They usually come when March is blustering out the last two or three of its days, and go away when the harsh note of the corncrake rises from the fields of waving corn and clover.

Seven miles from Berwick, on the way to Etal, is the hamlet of Duddo—from *Dod*, a round-topped hill, and *hoe*, a height. On a rocky eminence which rises unexpectedly from the surrounding cornfields are the walls of an ancient pele of the Lords of Tillmouth, which was destroyed by the Scots a few days before Flodden. It was further ruined by the working of the neighbouring coal seams. There are only a few cottages by the roadside, called the village. On Grindon Rig, in the direction of Norham, are the Duddo Stones, striking monoliths, from five to ten feet high. They may have formed part of a Druidical circle.

Crookham, standing high on jutting ground, is a finely situated village looking across Till to the Etal Haughs, and with Flodden and the blue Cheviot range in the opposite direction. But it has no resident squire to beautify it, no church except a plain, square slated Presbyterian meeting-house, and for long its

Duddo Tower.

population has been dwindling. In old times it was a nest of farmers and yeomen, and no other village near could turn out so many tough fighters, each on his own nag. During the early years of Lady Waterford it had a miscellaneous population of horsecopers, crofters, and other smallholders, bondagers, and those who kept lodgings for the packmen, pedlars, clock-menders, and the other "gaun-folk." Many of them lived in houses thatched down to the ground, and each cottage had a midden at the door. Mrs. Armstrong (Besant's heroine, Dorothy Forster) ended her days here as the wife of a faithful old farmer.

There is a ruinous stone building which tradition asserts to have been a tavern at the Battle of Flodden.

Leaving it and going along the river bank one passes Ford Forge, which was one of the last places in Great Britain where spades and shovels were forged by the agency of water-power.

Ford Castle stands in a well-timbered park on ground which rises from the north bank of Till at a distance of about a mile

Ford Church.

from the river. It was a strong Border tower till partially destroyed by James IV before Flodden. The legendary tale that the royal squire of dames lost the battle through dallying with Lady Heron is not in accord with fact. Ford Castle is well placed for watching what takes place in Glendale, a fact illustrated by a pleasant anecdote. For more than half a century the vicar of Ford was the Rev. Thomas Knight. Old inhabitants still remember him in an old age " frosty but kindly "—the frost is purely an allusion to his snowy hair ; a warmer-hearted man never lived. Mr. Knight in his young days was a bit of a sporting parson, but, becoming involved in the Oxford Movement, he thought it best to give up every form of sport except fishing, to which he remained addicted to the end of his life. But he ceased to shoot or hunt. Nevertheless e'en in our ashes glow their wonted fires ; though he would not ride to hounds any more, he mounted the old rectory tower part of the castle, from which he could follow almost every run, thus at the same time enjoying the hunt and salving his conscience.

This was in the day when the old Earl of Wemyss was M.F.H. Of him many a good story is told. Once at least the laugh was against him. He hated the music of wandering minstrels with a mania almost. One day the meet was at Ford Bridge. As the field began to gather, a man appeared on the scene with a barrel organ. It happened that Captain Gooch, brother to the Rev. Harcourt Gooch, then curate to Mr. Knight, was present. He did not lessen the M.F.H.'s annoyance by his question : " I say, Wemyss, do you *always* have music at your meet ? "

Ford Castle was built in 1282 by Odinel de Forde. His daughter married Sir William Heron, who thus became owner of Ford. Since his day it has been in the possession of Carrs, Blakes, Delavals and Beresfords. From one of the last-mentioned it was purchased by Lord Joicey.

As a military stronghold, Ford ceased to have importance after the battle of Flodden. Sir Robert Bowes, in the "Book of the State of the Marches," says it was burnt by James IV a little before he was slain. The antiquarian interest was fatally injured by Sir John Hussy Delaval, who, in 1761-4, rebuilt much of it in the sham Gothic of the period. Lady Waterford, a hundred years later, tried to undo the mischief, but the feat was impossible. The church is of the thirteenth century, but restoration and improvement have obliterated many of the most interesting features.

Ford's pleasantest time occurred when Louisa Lady Waterford was in her early widowhood. Thomas Knight was rector and Lady Fitzclarence was at Etal. Lady Waterford was a Stuart, the third daughter of Baron Stuart de Rothesay. At Lord Eglinton's famous tournament, a revival due to the influence of Sir Walter Scott, she had been chosen Queen of Beauty, and retained her charms to the end—a countenance that one would not call majestic only because of the vivacity with which it was so frequently relaxed, mobile lips, large grey eyes set wide apart and shining with native kindness and candour, won friendship at a glance. The only fair criticism I ever heard passed upon her was that of a lady belonging to a neighbouring family who

Ford Castle from the Road.

called her " an organisation for relief of the undeserving poor." The hit did not imply that the poor were undeserving, but that Lady Waterford, in her *rôle* of Lady Bountiful, was at the mercy of every knave who could fabricate a pitiful story—a weakness no doubt, but a lovable weakness.

Lady Waterford was one of the many Northumbrian friends of Rossetti and the Pre-Raphaelite Brotherhood, and no inconsiderable artist herself.   The school at Ford is decorated with a series of frescoes illustrative of Bible scenes and characters, such as Adam and Eve, Cain and Abel, Jacob and Esau, Moses among the bulrushes, etc.   Local interest used to be stimulated by the fact that Lady Waterford used a number of the villagers

Wooler.

as models for her figures, but as these characters die or leave the district the identification tends to become lost.

Mr. Knight, the rector, lived several years after the celebration of his jubilee, and his personality is still affectionately remembered, not least by the large proportion of English Presbyterians in the neighbourhood.

The village of Ford has been highly extolled for its beauty. As a matter of fact Lady Waterford trimmed it up so that it lost some of the most typical characteristics of a Northumbrian village.

Let it not go unchronicled that the Castle used to have its

ghost. It was firmly believed in the countryside that the ancient and stately shade of Lady Delaval used to parade certain of the rooms and had been seen by countless visitors.

Milfield is a village on the high road about a mile from the river. In that ill-conceived incursion of the Scots called " the Ill Road," just before Flodden, Sir William Bulmer was able to conceal his horse, archers and bowmen in the tall broom between Wooler and Milfield, so that he surprised Lord Hume and his 3,000 horsemen, killing 400 and making 200 prisoners.

There is a pleasant little house of the Greys at Milfield Hill.

Ewart House, where Sir Horace St. Paul, a famous worthy of

Approaching Wooler from Ilderton.

the nineteenth century, lived, is a little higher up still. Internally it is interesting, with its pictures, tapestries, and old nicknacks.

Near it is the interesting hill called Yeavering Bell. It is worth climbing if only for the fine view from the summit, which gives you at a glance the typical features of a fertile Northumbrian landscape in Glendale. Streams meandering through neatly hedged and well tilled fields, rows of hinds' cottages, farmhouses with a warm glow of red pantiles, and far away the Eildon Hills in one direction, Holy Island in another.

Farther on is Wooler, beloved of anglers, who from this centre can fish the Till and easily reach the Glen, the College, and the Bowmont if their taste lies in the direction of burn fishing and Cheviot air. Wooler used to have the distinction of being a market town with no railway station near it, but this was changed with the opening of the Alnwick and Kelso line. To-day it has added golf to its other attractions, and indeed must

be a place of healing to the busy who come in to rest and rein-
vigorate nerves worn out by the strenuous life of the local
metropolis.

Henry I granted the barony of Wooler to Robert des
Muschamps, and the name in a variety of spelling crops up
continually in the deeds relating to its wide territory. Muschance,
Muscynes, and Musceyne are Northumbrian renderings of it.

Wooler has a wishing-well which is sometimes described as a
monument of dead superstition, but the last time I was there
the number of crooked pins dropped into the well and lying
under its clear water indicated that the old beliefs had not yet
died out.

*We hae nae shoemakker here and we hae to go to Belford for the doctor.
There's a lot we hae nae, but we can always get a bit o' meat.*

CHAPTER VIII

" To add to my satisfaction, we are amidst places renowned by the feats of former days ; each hill is crowned with a tower, or camp, or cairn, and in no situation can you be near more fields of battle : Flodden, Otterburn, Chevy Chase, Ford Castle, Chillingham Castle, Coupland Castle, and many another scene of blood, are within the compass of a forenoon's ride."—Walter Scott in a letter to William Clerk dated 26th August, 1791.

THAT part of the English Border in which stands Chillingham Castle is the most romantic spot in the British Islands. Nature on the county has lavished her treasures, such as fertile fields, running streams, diversities of hill and plain, a coast well deserving Swinburne's line : " The lordly strand of Northumberland." Romance dwells by its rivers and in its valleys and peers out from its fortress ruins, which fancy easily fills with the stern faces that must often have watched from the loopholes. Even its waste places, its moors and commons, hags and mountains, are delightful to the eye. But the past of this fair demesne was more favourable to the development of romantic ballads than fine building. In those days of " ffra and foray," which began nobody knows exactly when and lasted till the beginning of the eighteenth century, the Borderer had ever to look out for the reiving Scot who issued forth to burn and steal. Besides, he was kept in a state of poverty as a net result of these attacks and reprisals. Thus, if we except the great places built so strongly as to defy the marauders, there are few, if any, fine old houses in the neighbourhood. Castles and towers there were in abundance, as Sir Walter Scott was quick to notice when, as a young man, he sojourned in the Cheviots to breathe the mountain air and drink goats' milk.   The district was very much to his mind, because it teemed with places famous in legend and song.

As the Great North Road runs from Alnwick to the Scottish Border, a range of moor with craggy summits lies between it and the valley of the Till.   From the top of the highest peak the view stretches from the Farne Islands and the sea far over the domed heads of the Cheviot Hills on the west.   The summit of Roscastle looks down upon Chillingham across a wide stretch covered alternately with heather, woodland, high ferns, and

Chillingham Castle.

grass.   The castle stands on the bank of the Chillingham burn, a grey quadrangle, with towers of heavy masonry at the four corners.   On the east is the burn, on the north the entrance gate, on the west an Italian garden covers the site of the jousting ground, on the south a lawn is banked up above the former level of the ground floor.   There was once a moat here, and the culvert which remains suggests that it circled the castle on all sides.

What the life at Chillingham was in the old days is best shown by Cadwallader Bates, historian, antiquary, good Northumbrian, who fished up an old document, the *Proof of Age* of Margaret, daughter of Sir Henry de Heton, a curious record of an ordinary

day's doings at Chillingham in the last days of the fourteenth
century, which stirs the historic imagination.   Margaret was
born on January 14th, 1395, and on the day of her christening,
which took place in Chillingham Church, Nicholas Heron was
married, and John Sergeant at the same time wedded Alice de
Wyndegaltes.   At the castle, Sir Henry de Heton, the baby's
father, bought a white horse from William Cramlington, and
sent Wyland Mauduit to Newcastle to buy wine.   John Belsise
rode to Alnwick with a letter to the Duke of Northumberland,
William Cotys killed a doe in the field of Chillingham.   John
Horsley was captured and carried off by the Scots, and John
Wytton caught a Scot, Thomas Turnbull, and clapped him into
Chillingham gaol.   On the same day Robert Horne was
captured by Sir Thomas Grey of Heton and thrust into Norham
Castle.   The day was no extraordinary one.   Its events have
been recorded and handed down by chance.   Yet how vividly
it calls up the life of a Northumbrian gentleman of those days.
He slays venison and buys wine, adds to the horses which he
kept ready for riding, has a follower captured and himself
captures a prowling enemy, and is apparently engaged in a
family feud.   These were the commonplace occurrences of daily
life ; what would it be like in really stirring times ?   Besides
formal invasions, such as the expedition to Flodden, when the
army was encamped for a long space of time in the neighbourhood,
the Scots kept the English Borderers perpetually on the alert
by their raids.   Watchers waited at the fords through the autumn
nights and beacon fires were ready piled on the hills to warn
men that the Scots were " riding."   The habit of violence was
ingrained in the Borderers.   Blood feuds and private wars
were carried on from one generation to another, and religious
quarrels added to their bitterness.   In the history of these
embroilments the masters of Chillingham sometimes figure.
Several of them held official posts ; one was Warden of the
West March, another Deputy-Warden, a third a frequent
correspondent of Robert Cecil and recommended by a Warden
as " the perfectest I knowe " to be on the March Commission.
They had no blood feuds with the Scots.   Their name, at
least, does not figure in a long list of Border feuds in 1595.
But they had their troubles at home with the neighbouring
families of Selby and Widdrington.   Sir Ralph Grey the fifth
was at feud with Henry Widdrington.   He and his brother

were involved in an affair with the Selby family, which epito-
mises a whole chapter of Border life.   An old grudge was stirred
to a blaze by a tenant of Ralph Grey bringing an accusation

The Cloisters, Chillingham Castle.

against a Selby.   Challenges passed, and Edward Grey agreed
to meet William Selby in Berwick churchyard.   They met and
adjourned their conference to the " backside " of the church,
while the partisans hung in two small groups at the east and

west ends. Grey's friends came up " offering no stroke to offend." But somehow old William Selby had presently fallen down upon his back, the minister was out of the church, and women were screaming. Reinforcements came upon the scene, called by Selby " certaine of my friends in the towne," but, according to Grey, " six or seven of the most notorious common fighters in Berwick." Edward Grey was wounded and his man, Bryan Horsley, was run through with a rapier. Then, in a cloud of recriminations and letters to the Secretary of State in London, the story passes out of sight. Another picture is of a Sunday morning in March, when Queen Mary was reigning. The master of Chillingham is riding with a cavalcade over to Ford Castle. He is a Justice of the Peace and Deputy-Warden ; with him are the mayor and treasurer of Berwick. Suddenly an ambuscade sets on them. The treasurer dies with fifteen wounds in him, and the mayor " after his stroke never spake a word." More followers came up on Sunday afternoon and the fight went on. The quarrel was over the possession of Ford Castle, which lay in dispute between the Herons and the Carrs. To fill up the picture we must add Chillingham, with watchmen on the towers and women looking down from the deep windows and waiting for news.

" In these parts," said a sheriff, " almost no person rideth unarmed, but as surely upon his guard as if he rode against the enemy of Scotland." In England it was an age of splendour, in which luxury and civilised arts flourished, and Northumberland felt the new influence. The fifth Earl of Northumberland earned his title " the Magnificent " and was among the heroes of the Field of the Cloth of Gold. A mistress of Chillingham Castle in 1581 left her son silver bowls and spoons and a silver and gilt salt-cellar, and to a daughter gold bracelets, " my best velvet gowne, and a kirtle of velvet embroidered." Coal began to be burned in gentlemen's fireplaces and glass was used in their windows. In the south, the days of the castle were over ; defensive precautions were no longer studied, and the mansion and manor house were built for domestic convenience. But within sight of the Scottish Border a home was still a strong-hold first. Strong walls, arms and horses formed the bases of civilised life, and the bowls and spoons and velvet but a veneer. So the Tudor builders who put Chillingham in " measurable good reparacions " added corridors and built larger state rooms, but left the castle a place of defence. Since that period alteration has taken the form of adapting rather than of rebuilding ; the result is that the old remains behind the new, and Chillingham is a house of secrets, some of which are only now yielding to patient research. Old stairways have been found, mounting the deep walls of the southern towers. The original floor of the solar has been traced behind the old hall on the east. The pigeon-post has been discovered in the north-eastern tower, and a large space between walls has been opened on this side. Elsewhere a fireplace and windows long obscured behind plaster have been retrieved. The coatings of intervening years are being stripped off and the life-history of the castle is being revealed in fuller detail.

THE WILD CATTLE

The famous wild cattle at Chillingham have been so often painted and described that little remains to be said about them. Yet they are of perennial interest, and the park itself is a noble one and well worthy of a visit. It extends over a thousand acres, of which a considerable part is woodland, and the whole is beautifully undulated. Sir Edward Landseer's pictures and the well-known description by George Culley have made the appearance of the animals familiar. It would appear, however, that they have changed in some important points during the centuries. From a passage in the Account Book of William Taylor, steward of Chillingham, dated 1692, which is given in " The Border Holds of Northumberland," by Cadwallader Bates, there seems to have been a mixture in the herd. The passage is as follows : " Beasts in ye Parke, my Lord's—16 white wilde beasts, 2 black steeres and a quy, 12 white read and black eard, 5 blacke oxen and browne one, 2 oxen from Wark June last." The point to be particularly noticed is that there were white, red and black eared among them. On this point Mr. Lydekker says that " whereas the ears of the Chillingham cattle are now red, in former days they were generally black." He makes a reference to Thomas Bewick, who, in his " General History of Quadrupeds," of which the first edition was published in 1790, stated that in his time a few of these cattle had black ears, while in 1692, says Mr. Lydekker, black ears were in the ascendancy. George Culley, writing in 1786, describes the wild habits of the cattle in a manner that would apply at the present

G

The monarch of the herd.

moment. Thus when the cows calve they hide their young just as such a wild animal as the hare does, and if the little beasts are taken by surprise they cower down on the ground to conceal themselves in the same way as rabbits do, or like hares in a forme. Another writer, Mr. Hindmarsh, writing in 1839, dwells on the same wild characteristics. He says : " They hide their young, feed in the night, basking or sleeping during the day : they are fierce when pressed, but, generally speaking, very timorous, moving off on the approach of anyone, even at a great distance." The late Lord Tankerville enlarged the same point. After dwelling on these traits to which we have alluded, he said : " They are fierce when pressed, but, generally speaking,

Cows and a calf.

very timorous, moving off on the appearance of anyone even at a great distance ; yet this varies very much in different seasons of the year, and according to the manner in which they are approached. In summer I have been for several weeks at a time without getting a sight of them—they, on the slightest appearance of anyone, retiring into a wood which serves them as a sanctuary. On the other hand, in winter, when coming down for food into the inner park, and being in constant contact with people, they will let you almost come among them, particularly if on horseback. But then they have also a thousand peculiarities. They will be sometimes feeding quietly, when, if anyone appears suddenly near them, they will be struck with a sudden panic and gallop off, running one over the other, and never stopping till they get into their sanctuary. It is observable of them, as of red deer, that they have a peculiar faculty of taking advantage of the irregularities of the ground, so that

on being disturbed they may traverse the whole park, and yet you hardly get a sight of them. Their usual mode of retreat is to get up slowly, set off at a walk, then a trot, and seldom begin to gallop till they have put the ground between you and them in the manner that I have described." Lord Tankerville gave a description of them which could scarcely be bettered. He said: " They have short legs, straight backs, horns of a very fine texture, thin skin, so that some of the bulls appear of a cream colour; and they have a peculiar cry, more like that of

A Typical female.

a wild beast than that of ordinary cattle. With all the marks of high breeding, they have also some of its defects; they are bad breeders, and are much subject to the ' rash '—a complaint common to animals bred in-and-in, which is unquestionably the case with these as long as we have any record of them. When they come down in to the lower part of the park, which they do at stated hours, they move like a regiment of cavalry, in single file, the bulls leading the van; and when they are in retreat the bulls bring up the rear."

Lord Ossulston was witness to a curious way in which they took possession, as it were, of some new pasture recently laid open to them. It was in the evening about sunset. They began by lining the front of a small wood, which seemed quite alive with them, when all of a sudden they made a dash forward all together in a line, and, charging close by him across the plain, they then spread out,

A Typical male.

VIII   HISTORY AND THE HERD   85

and after a little time began feeding. It is generally said of other herds of wild cattle that they have suffered from in-breeding, but this does not seem to be the case at Chillingham. In the course of an article in *Country Life* of March 8th, 1913, it was said on authority that " the decrease in size owing to in-breeding is not noticeable, but Lord Tankerville has a pair of cow's horns of the sixteenth century which are somewhat larger and more curved back ; but then the cows and steers have always had longer horns than the bulls." This point was dwelt upon by Mr. Hindmarsh, who visited Chillingham in June, 1838. " It is remarkable," he wrote, " that during the thirty-three years Mr. Cole has been keeper he has perceived no alteration in their size or habits from in-breeding, and that at the present time they are equal in every point to what they were when he first knew them. About half a dozen have had small brown or blue spots upon the cheeks and necks ; but these, with any defective ones, were always destroyed."

In the course of a very full and accurate account of the cattle which Mr. Millais wrote for his " Mammals of Great Britain and Ireland " he makes the remark that " there seems to be but little evidence of the continuous existence of this herd since its beginning." Here is a point that might to great advantage be worked out. In State Papers and other documents it is not unusual to find references to the herd, and, probably, if an antiquarian like the late Mr. Bates had devoted his attention to it, he might possibly have been able to supply a series of references going through the centuries. Many of them were bound to be of an extremely casual character. Indeed, not till recent times has the very great importance of the breed been recognised. Nowadays, the most learned of the zoologists of Germany, Austria, and France have studied these cattle in every minute detail, and many able articles have been written about them in their scientific journals. Little, however, has been added to the data already collected and set out by the writers from whom we have quoted. The man who is no specialist but loves wild life of every kind will be delighted by a visit to Chillingham. It lies on the outside of the wild Cheviots, and the Park has been made a sanctuary of by many wild things in addition to the cattle. The owls hoot there all night, and thousands of birds frequent the rough woodlands by day. It is believed that the ground was imparked early in the thirteenth century, and it remains to-day probably very much the same as it was then.

About six or seven miles from Chillingham is Fallodon, which is likely to be remembered in history because it is the country home of Lord Grey of Fallodon, who, as Sir Edward Grey, was Minister for Foreign Affairs when the Great War broke out. The house, one of the few notable brick houses in Northumberland, was accidentally destroyed by fire while the war was going on, but is being rebuilt in the same style.

Lord Grey is very much attached to the place, where he spent his boyhood. It suited his taste for natural history. The estate consists of about two thousand acres of clay land situated between the sea-shore and the moor, and it has a little stream where the statesman in his boyhood learned to fish. Nowhere could he have obtained better facilities for acquiring his unique knowledge of the birds of the moorland and those of the sea.

À propos of the latter accomplishment, Lord Grey told me a story worth repeating. The previous owner, from whom his grandfather, General Grey, bought the property, was exceptionally keen on horticulture and had built the brick-walled garden which still remains. But Sir Edward Grey, as he was then, put it to a different use. It formed an aviary for his well-known collection of birds. These suffered greatly from the privations of war. Originally they were fed mostly on wheat, but when the food situation became critical the use of good grain was discontinued and the birds suffered from the low diet. *Teal versicolor*, one of the rarest of the teal family, showed the effect of this by breeding only male birds, and extinction was threatened. At only two other places, Hamburg and Kew, were they kept, and the former being of course impossible, the last of the race were sent to Kew in the hope that breeding would take place there. But, alas ! a bomb from Hun aircraft descended on Kew, and male and female alike were exterminated.

Fallodon was the birthplace of Earl Grey of the Reform Bill, but his name is more generally associated with Howick, where he lived with his large family during his mature years and until he passed away.

A mile and a half north of Chillingham on the Till is the pleasant agricultural village of Chatton, which had two old peles. In one of them Edward I stayed in 1291 and 1292. A writ issued from Chatton by him begins : " To the Barons of the Exchequer, Health," and arranges with minute accuracy payments for the annual dress for two Welshmen and a boy at Bamburgh Castle. The frequency with which Welshmen appear in the annals of Bamburgh is due to the political and military connection of the Percies with Wales and the Welsh border. In 1368 the manor was ruined, as appears from an Inquisition of Edward III, in which it mentions " a park with wild animals

Chatton Bridge over Till.

called Kelsowe." It may be that these animals are the same as the Chillingham wild cattle.

In 1634 the tenants of Chatton complained that Sir Ralph Grey was taking and enclosing land on Chatton Common into his park of Chillingham. Robin Hood's bog, where the wild cattle resort when disturbed, is at the point of the park which projects into Chatton Moor. It is conjectured that this may have been the Kelsowe enclosed at that time. About the same date are entries recording the penalties imposed upon two offenders. Ralph Hebborne for stealing wheat was pronounced " a thafe, amerced for his fault 3/4d. and his wife being a scold 3/4d." As she was probably only volubly defending her husband she seems severely punished. Chatton must have been hard

on its poor women, for in 1650 " Jane Martin, the millar's wif
was executed for a wich." How could the millar's sonsy wife
have fallen into the miserable web of rural superstition and
calumny and cruelty ? She was dragged in a cart to Newcastle
Assizes to answer their absurd charges, paying dearly for some
fancied skill in illness or eccentricity of conduct.

Chatton had a poet called James Service, who at the beginning
of the nineteenth century published several volumes. He had
gone to sea, had been schoolmaster of Chatton, and his poems
are mostly retrospective of his loved Northumbria.

> No more I gaze upon my native Cheviot's peaks
> Breaking the soft blue of the summer sky.

His achievement was not very great, and, like John Clare, he
tasted to the dregs the bitterness of failure and poverty. One
of his principal poems dealt with the legend of Dunstanburgh
Castle, " The Wandering Knight." The last record of his life,
written by an unimaginative pen, needs no added word of pathos.
He was far from the sound of Till's subdued murmur and the
watching hills above the village he loved. " From James
Service I had a letter about a year ago wishing me to assist him.
He was then in the poor-house at Sunderland, and sometimes
attended the shop of a bookseller there. I called at the shop
once, but could not see him, as he was at the workhouse. The
bookseller told me he had a wooden leg and disliked extremely
the confinement of the poor house. Very likely he is there still."

Northumberland has few poets, and poor Service loved this
land between the mountains and the sea where he passed his
happy boyhood and, growing up a social soul, had many convivial
hours with the rollicking farmers of the day. Some last lines
to Northumberland we rescue :

> O'er all thy wilds from Tweed's remotest verge
> To where the Tyne rolls blithe to ocean's surge
> No son of thine, how rude so e'er his heart,
> But feels it swell at what thou wast and art !

Bridge over the Bowmont Water.

CHAPTER IX

FROM YETHOLM TO WOOLER

Yetholm the centre of Gipsydom—An anecdote of the gipsies—
Watchers and Setters of the Ford—Kirknewton: its Church.—
The ancient population of Yeavering Bell—Doddington and
the bonny Dod Well—Coupland Castle—Rowting Linn.

YETHOLM is in Roxburghshire, but on the edge of it. Andrew
Lang, in the " Highways and Byways in the Border," confined
himself to discussing whether it or Southdean should be identified
with the Zedon mentioned by Froissart in connection with
Otterburn. But whatever be the truth about that, Yetholm has
very great natural attractions. It consists of two parts separated by the Bowmont—Town Yetholm, new, clean, uninterest-
ing, and Kirk Yetholm, old, dirty and fascinating. They are both
cradled in the Cheviots, and the old town well answers the
description " a churche in a fayre laund." Spring brings
foliage and flowers to Yetholm long before they are to be seen
on the surrounding farmlands.

The place used to have an evil reputation in Glendale as the centre of Gipsydom. A terrace of extremely bad cottages is still called " Gipsy Row." The inhabitants are tame compared with what they used to be. I knew a patriarch there who claimed to be more than a centenarian, and his memory of the manners of the people in old time was summed up in the phrase " If a stranger showed in Yetholm it was oot aik sticks and bull pups I can tell ye." Every spring, at the time when our fore-fathers used to go on pilgrimage, an irregular procession passed out of Yetholm and swarmed over the lanes and farmlands. They were not called gipsies, but muggers, because they sold from their carts or baskets mugs, plates, cups and saucers, all those articles in fact which the hind's wife called her " play-gins." Some tried to sell baskets and some were horsecopers, and all were thieves, rascals, poachers, and dangerous on the road. I remember how the late Mr. George Grey of Milfield used to laugh as he told the story of his grandfather who came in late for dinner one night from a ride on the road from Milfield to Scotland. He apologised and explained that he had been set upon by a Yetholm mugger. Then he went on with his soup. Some member of the family asked if he did nothing to his assailant. " Oh yes, I cut off his thoomb. Here it is," was the unexpected reply, as he extracted the thumb from his waistcoat pocket.

But the road is peaceable now. Practically speaking, the gipsies have melted into the rural population. Commercial travellers have ousted the packman and the pedlar. Fairs have given place to markets and auctions, and the horsecoper who battened on them finds his occupation gone. On a summer day you may walk or drive from Yetholm to Wooler without seeing a human being, unless it be the farm workers in the fields or the zealous fisherman plying his rod on the Bowmont. The charm of the road comes from the bracken-covered hills above it and the glancing river below.

You are in England when you leave the farm called Yetholm Mains and ascend the rise to Pawston. The house encloses an old pele-tower built by Gerard Selby in 1542. Selby is the name of an ancient Northumberland family, and though the branch to which the present owner belongs only goes back to 1512, the lands were held by the same house at a far earlier date. A lake has been formed by damming a little stream. It is well stocked with perch, and at times the blackheaded gull comes here to breed.

A little further on is Mindrum, the nearest station to Yetholm, on the Alnwick to Kelso line. Mindrum, under the name of Minethrum, is mentioned among the stedes or hamlets included with the land on the banks of the Bowmont, or Bolbenda, which King Uswy bestowed on Lindisfarne. In the time of Edward I and Edward II Bolton hospital for lepers had two carucates of land and the mill at Mindrum. Scraps of history these, but they appeal to the imagination. The written chronicle tells of kings and armies, the great men of the Church as well as those of the State, but it affords only an occasional glimpse of those who sowed and ploughed and ground corn under the shelter of these hills in remote time.

A little mention of the place in Raine brings up another picture. Sir John Carey, on June 13th, 1595, wrote to Lord Burghley that Carr of Cessford had twice entered England to murder certain of the Stories, but after lying in wait for them in vain about Akeld and Humbledon, thinking they would take that way to Weetwood Fair, he went to " a town called Newton where he did drinck and to Pawston where he did also drinck and talked with the leird ; and no man asked him why he did so." Carr of Cessford probably knew every foot of this country. Cessford Castle, now in ruins, is just across the Border, almost within walking distance.

An oft recurring scene at these places so close to the Border can easily be realised from official documents of the sixteenth century. They were almost defenceless, for at different times the Scots had " rased and casten downe " the most part of the fortresses, towers and peles, and they had not been repaired, " which is much pittye to se," reported Sir Robert Bowes. He instances the castle of Heton belonging to Mr. Grey, the towne of Twisell belonging to the heirs of Heron of Foorde, the tower of Houtel belonging to one Burrett, the tower of Shoreswood belonging to the colledge of Durham, the tower of Barmor belonging to Edwarde Muschaunce, the tower of Duddo belonging to Robert Clavering.

All the more important was it that watch and ward should be kept. The order of the watch for the neighbourhood of Mindrum is set forth in 6 Edward VI (1551-2). The places are easily recognised, Pawston, Pytmyers, Rye-hare Ford,

Shotton-burn-mouth, Turnchester-bogg, Northside of Myn-drum-bogg, Tenersheughe. These were to be watched " with fourteen men nightly of the inhabitors of Langton, Mylnfield, Edderslaw, Brangestone, Heton, Howtill, Pawston and Myn-drum. Setters and searchers were Oliver Selbie, baylif of Myndrum, and William Selbie the Elder." Lanton, Milfield, Heatherslaw, Branxton, Heaton, Howtel, Pawston and Mindrum are not far apart for men who travelled on horseback, and between them cover the Glen and Bowmont and the Till. Day watchers were set to watch the passes through which the Scots

Kirknewton.

were likely to advance. Hethpool watched Hetheugh, Howtel watched Blacklaw, Pawston watched Pawston Hill, and so on.

In " The Ford," a poem by Marna Pease (Mrs. Howard Pease of Otterburn) printed in the Flodden chapter, the watchers heard only the water rushing in the weeds, a hunting otter, a trapped fox, but what happened when an alarm was signalled can be guessed from the brief notes of Sir Robert Bowes in the Survey.

" Presson-Grey of Chillingham's inheritance. No fortress . . . . . the toun left desolate. Myndrome-Grey of Chillingham's inheritance. In war left to the enemy."

" Continued waste for thirty years " is the report on Shotton—
the Earl of Rutland's inheritance.

It is all a matter of past history and leads only to pleasant
rumination as we wander down by the silvery Bowmont.   Nearly
all the places mentioned are cosy homesteads now and carry
nothing to suggest their ancient troubles.

Kirknewton, a small village, lies at the base of the hills near
the junction of the College and Glen.   In this quiet spot Edwin
of Northumbria married, in 625, Ethelburga of Kent, who brought
in her train Paulinus, whose preaching had a great though

Looking up College Burn from the Railway, Kirknewton.

ephemeral effect.   In the river Glen he baptised his earliest
converts.   The church has claims to be of Saxon origin.
The exceeding lowness of the chancel arch gives a primitive
and unusual character to the building.   A very curious
sculpture discovered in alterations is built into the wall and
may be Saxon.   It represents the Virgin and Child seated on
a rude trough, with the figures of the approaching magi rudely
but vigorously drawn, holding up gifts of considerable weight
as each supports the left elbow in the palm of his right hand.
The artist knew little of the East, as the magi each wear a short-
ened frill garment like a kilt, with uncovered feet and legs.   In

the outer face of the church tower are interesting carved stones.

At old Yeavering is a building described as the palace of Edwin, now a shepherd's house. It has walls of great thickness and may possibly have been a rude pele. At the north of the Glein, or Glen, the legendary Arthur is said to have achieved a great victory over the Saxons. Yeavering is first mentioned by Bede, as Adgehrin, the royal country seat of Edwin. The town was abandoned by later kings for a place called Melmin, sup-

Yeavering Bell.

posed to be Milfield, and at Ewart a Saxon fibula was found; but there are no other remains, as, having been in constant occupation, the past has been obliterated. Yeavering Bell and the surrounding hills formed the principal, and possibly the last, stronghold of the Cymric Kingdom where the advance of the Saxon strangers from the eastern seaboard was opposed. The Bell commands a wonderful range of country, even north past the Eildons.

Arthur and his knights clung tenaciously to this vantage ground from whence alarms and signalling could issue to all the surrounding tribes. Wonderful forts, pastoral enclosures, hut circles, with lines of roadway and the evidences of a very large population, are to be seen on Yeavering Bell and the adjacent hills. Especially interesting are the forts on Harehope Hill and Homildon Hill. An enclosure on the Bell, which has had a wall measuring 440 yards by 200 yards, was possibly a camp of refuge for women and children from the low-lying districts during invasion. On the east summit the hut circles are less frequent, as it had evidently been kept clear for the beacon fire, the presence of which excavations have proved. Every shelf or platform on the Bell and the surrounding hills shows remains of dwellings. On the lower slopes the cultivation of centuries has removed them. Traces of road tracks still exist to show that a pastoral race wandered over these valleys and plains, and in time of danger drove their flocks and herds to the hill forts. They seem to have been able to command the support of a considerable army. Yeavering Bell is conical in shape and separated from the other hills by deep ravines. Its steep ascent from the low flat Milfield plain gives it a solitary grandeur. Below, the Glen winds its way past the base to the Till, which it enters at Ewart. The Doddington hills rise near at hand, and in the distance are the Eildons, Duns Law, and the Lammermuirs, with towns, towers and churches scattered on the intervening landscape. In the field north of the Bell lies a huge monolith blown down in 1890. It is over nine feet long and five feet broad.

About a mile south of Yeavering Bell is Tom Tallon's Crag, which is an outcrop of porphyry on the crest of a ridge. Near to it on a hill looking to the Newton Tors stood a large cairn called Tom Tallon's grave. It is the largest cairn in the district, and on the stones being removed to build a wall, a cist was discovered with bones. The name is supposed to be derived from the Celtic *Tomen*, a tumulus, *Tal*, a forehead or promontory, and *Llan*, an enclosure.

Nearly three miles from Wooler is the village of Doddington, at the foot of Dod Law. It is now only a few cottages, but was once large enough to hold a weekly cattle market and able, according to tradition, to supply forty local lairds to attend the funeral of a neighbour at Belford. It has a wonderful ancient spring, called the Dod Well, which yields seventy gallons a minute. It is now enclosed and surmounted by a cross: The old song of

" the bonny Dod Well and the yea-pointed fern " has not been preserved. The chief object of interest is the castle built in 1584 by Sir Thomas Grey of Chillingham, in whose family it

Pele in a farmyard at Doddington.

still remains. These fortified dwellings were more comfortable than the ancient Border peles, and this one was among the last erected as the Union made them unnecessary. It is about thirty-six feet high, battlemented on the north and south walls, and had three storeys with a spiral stone staircase. Before it was surrounded with agricultural buildings it must have been a prominent landmark, and even now commands the district. The Church belongs to the thirteenth century and has been several times restored. The west end is the mortuary chapel of the descendants of Sir Horace St. Paul, who had an adventurous career in Austria during the Seven Years' War and became a Count of the Holy Roman Empire.

On the hillside below Dod Law, in a prominent mass of red

Coupland Castle.

sandstone, is Cuddy's Cove, to which St. Cuthbert used to retire, according to popular belief, when absent from Holy Island. On Dod Law are two large British camps defended by a deep ditch and with many hut circles, and remarkable rock sculptures are scattered about. Half a mile to the north are two figures on the sandstone. There are three other camps within a short distance. Near one are three standing stones supposed to be remains of a circle. A third one called the Ringses is defended by three ramparts of earth and stone, and in the interior are several hut circles.

H

On Gled Scaur, a platform of rock on the south west of Dod Law, there are more of these cryptic symbols drawn on the rocks by the unknown race who so thickly populated the district. On the banks of the Glen, a mile from Ewart, is Coupland Castle, a place of remarkable strength to be built in the Border in 1619, which is the date carved above a fireplace. The walls are five or six feet thick. At the corners of the castle are pepper-pot turrets and there is the original corkscrew stone staircase.

Lanton Hill, with an obelisk on it, is a conspicuous landmark to the west.

Three miles from Doddington is Routin Linn, a picturesque glade on the borders of Ford Moss, through which runs the Broomridge Burn and falls thirty feet over a precipice into the linn, with sandstone cliffs and lovely woodland making a picture of idyllic beauty. There is another prehistoric camp over the road crossing the glen. On the huge sandstone boulder at the camp is the largest number and greatest variety of sculptured emblems in the neighbourhood. Sixty figures have been traced on it, and very curious it would be to have them explained by an ancient Briton, as it is quite impossible for anyone else to do so. A mile north-west on Hunter's Moor are other incised rocks near which are several barrows.

A thousand years or twenty thousand pass here, and leave as little trace as the shadows of the cloud that rest a moment on the shining slopes and are gone. Unchanging they remain

      . . . . the hills of sheep
      And the homes of the silent vanished races.

CHAPTER X

THE BATTLE OF HOMILDON HILL

FOURTEEN years had to pass before Hotspur obtained his revenge for Otterburn. The latter was fought in 1388, the battle of Homildon Hill in 1402. Humbleton, or Homildon, is a hamlet close to Wooler, and the famous hill of the same name lies to the West of it. The Scots had been long preparing for war, but this encounter was a chance one. The Scots had ridden a foray nearly as far as Newcastle. They were led by that Douglas who was nicknamed the " Tine-man," and he had with him a band of fire-eating young nobles and famous war-worn veterans.

Among the latter was Sir John Swinton of Swinton, concerning whose family one would like to make a little note. During the war with Germany few names were more widely known than that of his descendant, General Swinton. It had long ceased to be a secret that he was the author of some remarkable military stories published after the Boer War, and for a time he was the " Eyewitness " who described our battles in France and Belgium. He does not himself live at Swinton, but has for it the feeling of its being home, the place where his forefathers lived for eight centuries. In 1829 it was sold to another branch of the same family. The village of Swinton is within twelve miles of Berwick on-Tweed by way of Norham and Ladykirk, and Swinton House is a good mile beyond it. Situated in the Merse of Berwick-shire and within a short ride of three formidable English castles, twelve miles from Berwick, four from Norham and six from Wark, the original home of the Swintons was burned

again and again by the raiders.   Its walls never had a chance
of growing old.

Berwick had a tank given it as a war memorial in recognition
of the valour and public spirit of its inhabitants, and naturally
General Swinton, as a neighbour of the old Border Town and
as the military originator of tanks, who had raised and
commanded the first tank unit, was asked to take a leading
part in the ceremony of placing it in permanent quarters.   His
discourse on tanks was highly interesting, but for my purpose
not so much so as his reference to Border life and particularly
to the part played in the battle of Homildon Hill by one of
his ancestors.   It was natural that a soldier should talk of
war at Berwick, " which of all cities except Jerusalem
had borne the record for sieges."   The Swintons of Swinton
played a shrewd part in Border warfare.   Colonel Summers,
who was present, in a speech full of humour recited a few
impromptu lines about the Swintons.   They ran :

> Of old along the Scottish Border
> The Swintons kept us in disorder.
> Their martial ardour they revealed
> By pinching cows from many a field.
>
> Now to the changing mood of time
> Comes to our ears a nobler chime.
> It's mainly due to Swinton's skill
> That we have beaten Kaiser Bill !

On a day in mid-September, five centuries ago, Douglas
and his raiders, laden with booty, were hastening back from
the Tyne to the Tweed and had crossed the Glein, or Glen,
were in fact within an hour's ride of their native land, when they
heard that the Percies were waiting for them at Milfield.   They
had believed the Earl of Northumberland to be following them
and were surprised to find Hotspur barring the road home.

> Then the Percy out of Bamburgh
>   With him a mighty many.
> With fifteen hundred archers bold
>   They were chosen out of shires three.

The Scots decided on a defensive policy and took up a strong
position on the slopes of Homildon Hill, and the English quickly
took ground on a similar position on the hill opposite, called

Harehope. This is how they stood when five hundred English archers, who had been sent out to collect provisions for the army, returned and, seeing the glitter of armour worn by the Scottish knights, sent a flight of arrows among them, and thus the battle began. The archers entered by the Monday Cleugh and shot up hill. Hotspur, as was his wont, would have charged recklessly, but the Earl of March, who was with him and at feud with Douglas, seized his bridle and persuaded him to adopt safer tactics. Douglas trusted too much to his position.

A bit of the Glen Valley.

Knights and men fell to the arrow flight as modern soldiers fall before the fire of machine guns.

It was General Swinton's ancestor who rallied his countrymen. He asked what good would come from standing still and allowing themselves to be shot down like deer in a park instead of grappling with the foe hand to hand as was their brave custom. General Swinton, recalling the incident with pride, asked what would have happened if they had possessed a tank to carry them up the hill. His forebear's dauntless words had an immediate effect. There was one man who seconded his proposal in a remarkable manner. This was Adam Gordon, chief of the Gordons in the days when they lived at Gordon in the Merse of Berwickshire and had not branched off into those

Gordon families that now belong to the North and are represented by the Duke of Gordon, the Marquis of Huntley, and Lord Aberdeen. He was one of the greatest fighters of his time. In his hot youth, the Borders being too quiet for him, he had signed on with John of Gaunt, and legend says he was the hero who, according to Froissart, leaped the barrier gates at Noyon and for love of the fray fought the chivalry of France for more than an hour " alone against them all "— " giving many grand strokes with his lance." When the army began to move and he had to rejoin it, he cleared the way with a thrust or two, sprang back, and mounting, with his page in front, cried : " Adieu, adieu, Seigneurs, grands mercis ! " and spurred away.

At Otterburn he had fought a good fight, and now at Homildon must have become a grizzled warrior of about fifty. It was he who refused to be a passive resister when in the words of the so-called Chevy Chase ballad :

> Yet bides the Earl Douglas upon the bent.

The line obviously refers to Homildon and not Otterburn.

Adam Gordon must have been born with the fighting spirit strong within him. The founder of the family was killed with his sovereign and friend Malcolm Canmore at the disastrous siege of Alnwick Castle in 1093, and three other heads of the house met with a similar fate at different times and in different battles. He had been at feud with Swinton, but forgot the personal quarrel in admiration. He kneeled before Swinton and begged that he would bestow on him the honour of knighthood. This being done, the two, with as many as cared to come, rushed down the hill to get to grips with the foe. But the relentless English archery made their bravery of no avail. The little band was wiped out and there followed a complete rout of the Scottish host. Of the ten thousand originally composing it eight hundred were left dead on the field, five hundred more were drowned in their heavy armour as they tried to cross the Tweed, and the list of prisoners was long and distinguished. It included Douglas with five arrow wounds and a lost eye, Montgomery, Murdack of Fife, the eldest son of the Duke of Albany, and eighty other notabilities.

English archery was at its best in this battle : the chronicles relate that the English arrows sticking in the bodies and armour of their adversaries made the Scottish army look like a gigantic hedgehog with its spines sticking out ; but the victory was the beginning of the end for Hotspur. The Government demanded that Douglas and the other distinguished prisoners should be sent to London, not in order to deprive the victors of such ransom as they might impose, but that they should have pawns in hand when arranging the long contemplated peace with Scotland. But the Percies, father and son, considered Henry IV, the King whom they had made, a stingy paymaster, and they had not been recompensed for their outlay as custodians of the marches. Henry pleaded an empty treasury. " Gold I have none ; gold thou canst not have." He and the fiery Hotspur nearly came to blows in the palace. Percy demanded the release of his brother in-law Mortimer, then in captivity. The King retorted that Mortimer was a traitor. " And thou too art a traitor for shielding him," he added fiercely, unsheathing his dagger. " Not here but on the field " was Hotspur's challenging answer. The quarrel ultimately resulted in the battle of Shrewsbury, where Hotspur was slain. Shakespeare does justice to his fame and his valour in the play of *Henry IV*, although it is his obvious intention throughout to make Prince Hal outshine that hero from the North who with a little guiding and management would have become one of the most useful as he certainly was the most valiant of subjects.

Lord Archibald Douglas cut a figure in this battle which if it stood alone might lead to misapprehension. His nickname Tine-man was not meant to carry the imputation of cowardice. He had only struck one of those runs of ill-luck which come to all. In the battle of Shrewsbury, where Hotspur fell, he was taken prisoner, but not being an English subject was honourably entreated as a prisoner of war. Sir Walter Scott has drawn a virile picture of him in "The Fair Maid of Perth," where he figures as a rugged, domineering soldier who ends by winning the admiration of the reader, but to the Wizard's great and kindly and patriotic mind every member of that house was glorified by the memory of the "Dowglas Dowglas tender and true." In a note, however, he shows that there were good historical reasons for assuming that Douglas shared with the Duke of Albany the guilt of murdering the Duke of Rothesay, his son-in-law, Albany's nephew and heir to the Scottish crown then worn by his father, the weak, amiable, irresolute Robert the Third. The cause of his feud with George Dunbar, Earl of March, is an integral part of this the most exciting of the Waverley novels. After a marriage between Rothesay and March's daughter had been consummated, Douglas forced the weak monarch to bring about a divorce so that Marjory of Douglas should take the place of Elizabeth of Dunbar.

" Rather than this woman had been scorned it were better that the Scots had given her a dower of two hundred thousand pieces of gold." After quoting this passage from John Major, the Pursuivant of the Easter Marches, Captain G. C. Swinton,

The Glen River near Yeavering.

adds : " To the son of Gospatrick the Douglasses, though valiant men, were mushroom upstarts, while the Earl was a bastard at that."

Scott was weaving a romance, not writing history. He sinned in good company, since Shakespeare had already set fact at defiance when he made Hotspur fall to the sword of Prince Hal. After reproducing the Remission or Pardon issued by King Robert and first printed by Lord Hailes, he remarks : " Lord Hailes sums up his comment on the document with words which as Pinkerton says leave no doubt that he considered the Prince as having been murdered, viz., 'The Duke of Albany and the Earl of Douglas obtained a remission in terms as ample as if they had actually murdered the heir-apparent.' "

Scott, indeed, had a sovereign disdain of dates. He makes the great fight on the Inch of Perth take place before instead of after the death of Rothesay in 1402, and Rothesay some time before his death taunts Douglas on the loss of that eye which he was yet to use at the battle of Homildon. Nathless it is not for dates that we read " The Fair Maid of Perth," but for that imaginative genius which makes the old time live again. There is a minor point to which we would draw attention. Hal o' the Wynd is an armourer with an enthusiasm for his craft, and the romance is full of the glory and richness of the war-gear forged and worn. It was therefore in exact keeping with the spirit of the time that Douglas and the nobles and knights who accompanied him should have new armour made for this great expedition when under the most illustrious of Scottish leaders they expected to meet the most renowned English soldier of his day. And it was their undoing, because it was their new and shining armour which first attracted attention and thus proved a target for the deadly bowmen of Hotspur's army.

The Tweed at Berwick.

CHAPTER XI

TWEEDMOUTH, BELFORD, AND GOSWICK SANDS

Crossing the Tweed southward—Ancroft and the Broomie Huts—
Grizzv's Clump and a Scottish heroine—Belford and a story of
medieval justice—Goswick and Cheswick sands and the fishery
of Sandstell— Smugglers and fish poachers—Where King Charles
camped in 1639.

THE romance of ancient Northumberland unfolds before us
as we pass over Berwick Bridge. Many bridges have spanned
the Tweed and led the traveller from the south among the high-
pitched houses of the crowded town that rise above the river
bank. Even now the mouldering pile can be seen in the mud
of a bridge a few yards above the present one, perhaps that
which James VI crossed in 1603 when he found it unstable and
gave orders for a new one to be built. An annual sum for
upkeep continues to be paid from the Exchequer to this day.
Perhaps the stakes are those of the bridge swept away in the

reign of King John when he built the malvoisin or tower to
overlook and intimidate Berwick. The memory of this tower,
which was soon pulled down again by the Scots, is still preserved
by the name of Tower Villa on the high bank overlooking
Tweedmouth Dock. A constant bone of contention was the
ferry which crossed the river here. It was of great importance
in times when the bridge was destroyed, as the Scots claimed
the whole of the river and prevented the English boats touching
the northern bank.

Berwick from the Tweedmouth side must from earliest
times have given an impression of strength. At high tide the
river washed against the walls, and the ships of the busy seaport
rocked in the quay. Higher up the river, on ground now
partly occupied by the railway station, menacing, the castle
stood, an integral part of the great Walls of Edward's day
which still crumble massively among grass and ivy on the
high river bank that faces the flats of Tweedmouth. From
the castle walls the west end of Tweedmouth, with small huddled
houses, looks dull and low-lying. Beyond it miles of cornfields
shine yellow in summer weather where the Low Road leads to
Ord village. But during the last two hundred years Berwick
must have gained in colour, for that is about the date when the
red roofs that enchant the traveller coming by train or road
rose steeply around the eighteenth century town hall. Near
where it is built once stood the Red Hall of the Flemings,
which Edward burnt with its prosperous Flemish merchants
when his wild soldiery reddened with the townsfolk's blood
the gutters that ran to the Tweed.

In Tweedmouth churchyard is buried John Mackay Wilson,
who wrote " The Tales of the Borders," and a well-known
celebrity, Jimmy Strength or James Stuart, noted for his
strength ; he lived to be 115. A stone figure of him by Mr.
Wilson, a former keeper of Berwick lighthouse, stands in the
old bowling green in the Palace at Berwick.

The south road leads from Tweedmouth over Sunnyside
Hill, past Scremerston, a little mining village, the manor of
which belonged to the unfortunate Earl of Derwentwater and
passed into the possession of Greenwich Hospital. The slag
heaps which border parts of the roads after passing Scremerston
were planted about thirty years ago with firs and are now quite
ornamental plantations. But the need of pit props caused many

inroads to be made on the trees during the war. A road to the
right before reaching the Cat Inn, a little bare hostelry, stretches
into middle Northumberland past Lowick and Wooler. Ancroft,
a desolate-looking village, stands on the high ground about
one and a half miles above the turning, and a long, lonely
road through agricultural land leads to Lowick. At Ancroft
is a field called the Broomie huts. There is a curious and
pathetic legend connected with this pretty name. The pretty
name has anything but a pretty origin. In the reign of
Anne a colony of cloggers lived there who made boots for the
army. The plague visited them on its devastating journey
from the south. Those who took the disease were carried out
to the high field where the broom grew, and little bowers were
made over them. When they died, hut and body were burned.
Doubtless they were never visited by the living before death
claimed them, and hunger and thirst would hasten the end of
their pains.

The excellent main road we are on now turns sharply to
the left at Haggerston Castle, where once stood the ancient
tower of the Haggerston family. Leland calls it " a towre
upon the south syde of Lindis ryver." A mile further on
a road branches to the left for Holy Island. The Kyloe
Hills are on our right, and the rugged crags near Belford are
very fine, with trees and heather and many rare plants. On
the height is a British camp with a double rampart, and the
foundations of St. Mary's Chapel of uncertain date and history.
A well near the roadside is called St. Mary's Well and a century
ago still had two ladles fastened by chains to the side to refresh
the thirsty passers-by. From the crags on a clear day the view
of Holy Island and the Farnes and Bamburgh is very beautiful.
On the roadside by the hamlet of Buckton is a plantation called
Grizzy's Clump, where Grizzel Cochrane robbed the mail of
the warrant for her father's execution, who was in prison for
taking part in a rising against James II. A girl of eighteen
dressed in men's clothes, she rode out from Tweedmouth and
awaited the clatter of the postboy's horse :

> The warlocks are dancing threesome reels
> On Goswick's haunted links ;
> The red fire shoots by Ladythorne,
> And Tam wi' the lanthorn fa's and sinks.
> On Kyloe's hills there's awfu' sounds
> But they frighted not Cochrane's Grizzy.

The moonbeams shot from the troubled sky
In glints o' flickerin' light ;
The horseman cam skelping thro' the mire
For his mind was in affright.
His pistol cocked he held in his hand
But the fient a fear had Grizzy.

As he cam' fornenst the Fenwicke woods
From the whin bushes shot out a flame ;
His dappled filly reared up in affright,
And backward over he came.
There's a hand on his craig, and a foot on his mouth,
'Twas Cochrane's bonny Grizzy.

" I will not tak thy life," she said,
" But gie me thy London news ;
No blood of thine shall fyle my blade
Gin me ye dinna refuse."
She's prie'd the warrant and away she flew
With the speed and strength o' the wild curlew.

The delay of fourteen days thus gained by the heroic daughter gave Sir John Cochrane's friends time to plead his cause and he was pardoned. Over the Border at Legerwood her tombstone can still be read, though no mention is made of her exploit at Belford :

Her rests the corps of John Ker
of Moristown who departed this
life the 27 of September 1691
in the thretth year of his age
As also the corps of
Grissell Cochrane his lady
who died the 21 of March
1748 in the 83rd year of her age.

In Wilson's " Tales of the Borders " her story is graphically told.

Belford is a quiet village with an old market cross. It is often mentioned as a stage in the journey between England and Scotland. Queen Margaret stopped here. There are no old houses, as it was very open to raids from the Borders, and even in the reign of Charles I it is described as "the most miserable beggarly town of sods that ever was made in an afternoon of loam and sticks. In all the town not a loaf of bread, nor a quart of beer, nor a lock of hay, nor a peck of oats and little shelter for horse or man." In living memory many Northumbrian houses were roofed with sods of turf, or divots as they were called.

As at Ancroft and many other places, a gruesome tale of the visitation of the plague in the eighteenth century is still remembered. The dead were shovelled hastily out of sight in their

Belford.

wearing apparel on Belford Moor. Afterwards greed recollected the latter fact, and fragments were dug up of dress in the hope of finding money in the pockets of the hapless victims. This was a grimmer body-snatching than that of Burke and Hare, but the ways of our ancestors were not as our ways, as witness the following example of justice that Jeddart might envy.

Cadwallader Bates tells the story as happening near Belford in the thirteenth century. A Scot called Gilbert of Nithsdale was coming over the moor with a hermit called Seman. Why a freebooting Scot, as his name seems to indicate, should be wandering fifteen miles over the Border with a harmless Northumbrian of pious life seems to call for some explanation, which we are unable to-day to give. Gilbert, the stalwart rogue, robbed Seman of his clothes and one penny and beat him soundly. But he had not gone far with his ill-gotten gear when Ralph of Belford, a king's officer, met him, and, judging by appearances in the hasty medieval way, arrested him and took him to Alnwick. Here arrived Seman bleeding and naked to confront the barbarous Scot. The bailiff and townsmen heard the tale of the injured holy man. The singularly appropriate custom of the country makes the heart warm in these days of cold justice by process of law. The injured person must act as his own executioner. So the meek hermit beheaded Gilbert and received his clothes for so doing. He was thus revenged and suitably rewarded in a fashion we cannot help feeling was both original and satisfying.

One other word is gleaned of Belford before the Union of 1603, when it was still a collection of clay-daubed hovels. The Earl of Hertford in one of his retaliatory expeditions against the Scottish borders—the one indeed in which he cruelly burnt the nunnery at Coldstream—was nearly captured as he lay at Belford, but the Scots managed to " lift " his chaplain. Whether he was ransomed or died on the spears of jeering Scots is not recorded.

The local folk-lore preserves a fantastic rhyme which with its hint of a finer poetry is worth remembering :

> In Collierheugh there's gear eneuch,
> In Cockenheugh there's mair ;
> But I've lost the keys of Bowdon Doors
> And I'm ruined for evermair.

This occurs in the lament of the Hazelrigg Brownie. At Cockenheugh Crag, about two miles west of Belford, is Cuddie's Cove, a traditional resting place of St. Cuthbert. Bowdon Door Crags is the name of some rocks on Lyham Moor between Belford and Chatton.

Lying adjacent to the sands over which one crosses to Lindisfarne, and indeed a part of them, are the sands of Goswick—

the picture is easy to make in the imagination—a low and level waste of wet sand with little ridges in it such as the tide always leaves behind and a kind of stipple-work made by the excavations of the lugworm, a wash of little waves far off on the edge, a wreck held fast in the grip of those tiny morsels of sand which separately count as nothing, but when acting in union bury and create.

You see them in the act of engulfing what was once a good ship, and close to the cultivated land arise the dunes which the wind has fashioned, blowing the particles in a stinging shower on dry summer days and heaping them up till the tussock and other wild weeds began to hold them compactly together. Far away to the southwards the hills look down on the sea and are themselves a wall to the horizon.

Goswick and Cheswick were fair game for the Scottish forayers in the old raiding days, and the houses belonging to them were frequently emptied of gear and the harvest fields devastated. In those old days no mention is made of fishermen, and it is doubtful if the craft was carried on there before the days of Sir William Crossman, although in the eighteenth century the coast was haunted by great shoals of salmon. In an account which has been preserved of the produce of the fishery of Sandstell, near the mouth of the Tweed, we get some evidence of the enormous quantity of salmon that must have worked their way along the edge of the coast to the mouth of the river. The accounts were kept by the family of Waite and published in 1831 by William Waite. The accounts begin in 1736 and are carried on to 1818. The best years are those beginning in 1760, which has this N.B. : " Believed the most plentiful season ever known in the Tweed, a great quantity of salmon sold at ninepence, eightpence, and one day at fourpence per stone. One flood on a Monday supposed to produce 10,000 salmon. N.B.— In all these years very few trouts." But the account-keeper had to note on the very next year a new record. It is described as the greatest year that ever was at Sandstell, no fewer than 17,484 salmon being taken, and 13,000 trout. No account was kept of the gilses. Please note the spelling, the " r " is a modern interpolation.

In 1772 a note is made which throws light on the occupation very generally pursued in that quarter of the world. " About this period, the hole in the Meadow Haven began to increase and lowering the beacon rocks for smugglers' ballast—both certainly injurious to the Tweed, but Sandstell particularly." Ten years later, in 1782, occurred two most remarkable floods in May, and for a long time after that the salmon did not seem to come so regularly. But in 1792 the fishery recovered. Sandstell is several miles from Goswick, but undoubtedly the salmon worked their way along the coast towards the river mouth, and those that are taken at Goswick are making for the Tweed. It is much the same on the northern part of the coast. Regular net-fishing is carried on in the sea north of the pier, and it is by no means unusual for the deep-sea fishermen who work from the Greenses Harbour to take salmon out at sea. To return for a moment to the antique character of the people. Those men who are engaged in salmon fishing have at all times been a rude and lawless people. Smuggling was not the worst of their habits; in the sixteenth century they were inveterate wreckers. Probably at that time there was a population on the mainland from Spittal to Scremerston, Cheswick, and Goswick, even as far as Bamburgh, of people who drew part of their livelihood from the land and part from the sea. In the sixteenth century the *Bonaventure*, a ship belonging to Archibald Graham and the Scottish merchants, was driven on the rocks at Sotterburn Mouth; among other receivers of spoil were the townships of Goswycke and Cheswycke, who each received £40. In very recent years many of those salmon fishers, as soon as close time was declared, used to become the most determined poachers, and many are the battles that have been fought between them and the legal guardians of the salmon. On these occasions the women used to figure prominently, and were equally adept at throwing stones and using bad language. But to-day most of this kind of thing has faded away with the progress of civilisation, and the drift-net fisherman now closely resembles his brother of the seine net. He mends his nets and gathers his fish while the season lasts, and when it is closed takes himself to some other vocation. He used to get hold of a ferry-boat or work as an ordinary labourer, for in the course of a varied life he had become, if nothing else, a very handy man. To-day he devotes the energy which he used to give to poaching to working the lifeboat, when he has an opportunity of earning something by salvage, and, if other things have changed, the dangerous sea is the same as it was in the beginning. King

I

Charles I, with an army, camped here on May 25th, 1639, previous to his abortive Scottish campaign. " He lay in a little house belonging to the widow of Sir Robert Hamilton. The camp was pitched neare the sea shore, upon a plain heath ground most part of it, and of a spungie turf which would have been very discommodious to the souldiers had they continued there in rainy weather." Under their vacillating leader, however, they did not stay long anywhere. But one would like to recall, if possible, the sight that must have presented itself to the traveller of those days. There is no old castle or very old house in the neighbourhood. The Scots took care that none survived. Their constant raidings kept the countrymen very poor, and cottages were put together of mud and plaster that would have been flimsy if they had not been made so thick. An old traveller says that the usual roofing of these cottages was not even thatch, but sods of earth laid flat. Indeed, some cottages of this kind survived till comparatively late in the nineteenth century. They had scarcely any walls to speak of, the back one being not more than two or three feet above the ground and the front one perhaps six feet. The doorways were not high enough to admit a man of middle height unless he bowed his head. The windows were very small and the hearths very large. Fuel, at any rate, did not need to be economised, as not only were the coal pits near, but the sea continually heaved up driftwood from the ships that had been engulfed. Some of the cottages to-day are not beautiful ; but those who find fault with them usually know very little of the hard conditions that prevailed on the English Border up to within a very recent period. Not that on the sands cottages obtrude themselves. There are one or two set back among the dunes ; but the eye rests not on them, but on the wide expanse of sand, with its fringe of white wavelets breaking gently on the shore, the dark rocks of basalt that at low tide thrust themselves up out of the water, and at high tide show their position only by the waves that curl and break over their tops. A wreck is always to be seen, and, when the circumstances under which it was lost are forgotten, it becomes a forlorn though picturesque addition to the landscape. Wind and water have cleared away all that was superfluous, and only bare ribs or a broken hull and mast stand as a monument of man's daring and Nature's strength.

Mouth of the Tyne.

CHAPTER XII

" THE LORDLY STRAND OF NORTHUMBERLAND "

The most interesting part of the coast—An unspoiled shore—
Crossing the sands at Holy Island—Looking over Bamburghshire—The Joyous Gard of Lancelot—Tristram of Lyoness,
the great huntsman—The Farnes and their birds—In the
middle of last century—The scene to-day—Northumberland's
heroine, Grace Darling.

THERE is not in Great Britain a more interesting stretch of
sea shore than the seventy miles of Northumbrian coast lying
between a point near Lamberton Toll in the north and Tynemouth in the south. And to the lover of nature and wild life,
as well as to the historian, the most fascinating part of it is
that which stretches from Berwick to North Sunderland. It
embraces Holy Island, Bamburgh and the shore off which lies
a group of black rock islets, the Farnes, in summer gleaming
with the plumage of multitudinous sea birds, in storm almost
lost among the crashing waves, and always with turbulent water
boiling through the narrow channels, rushing when the tide is
flowing and rushing again when it is ebbing.

This portion of the coast retains its ancient and natural charm. No polluted river flows into the sea, no commercial town is near it. Its wild beauty has not been exchanged for the sophisticated attractions of a popular watering place, nor is there any bungalow town erected on its clean sands. It remains exactly what it was in pre-civilised days. History gave it many a crowded hour of glorious life in England's morning ; but the long day passed and Nature re-asserted her old calm mastery and assumed the relics as her own, adding her charm to those it had inherited from the ages. Therein lies a something peculiar and supreme belonging to this portion of the coast and this only.

This is not said in disparagement of the rest. Viewed from another angle, the commercial achievement of Newcastle and its neighbourhood commands unstinted admiration. Modern Northumberland is a great energetic county of which not only the inhabitant but the nation is proud. But Tyneside has paid for material prosperity by the sacrifice of natural beauty. To realise what has been lost, imagination must rebuild the scene as it was when the Venerable Bede was alive. Shorthose had not yet built the first wooden fortress, anterior to that of Henry II, which gave the town its name of Newcastle. On its site was a settlement of monks, but it was still *Pons Ælii* close to the end of the Roman Wall. Tyne, not the murky smoke-and-mist-shrouded waterway of to-day, but a pure and limpid stream, flowed between wild banks of heather, bracken and scrubby wood. It ran past the Wall, too—that eloquent relic of imperial Rome. Bede could see it from his cell at Jarrow, and his accurate measurements show that he pondered over it and wondered.

What does the very name Wallsend suggest to-day ? Not the end of the Wall, but coal, the mother of industry, indeed, but mother, too, of smoke and soot and huge factories and general squalor. What beauty is attached to Newcastle and the mouth of the Tyne is what belongs to the useful and efficient, the beauty of an engine or a battleship. Newcastle and its mighty business extensions form a Titanic workshop.

What a contrast between all this and our eighteen or twenty miles of coast ! Look at it from Halidon Hill. You can, on a clear day, follow the coast from Spittal to the Farnes. There is Berwick still engirdled with walls, but carrying little to suggest its description by the monastic recluse who wrote the Chronicles of Lanercost, as " the Alexandria of the North, whose riches were the sea and the water its walls." Its " staitelie tours and turatis he on hicht " have disappeared. The Tweed flows past unstained, and fishermen with seine net and little black cobles pursue the same antique method of catching salmon as did their distant forefathers. A fine pier bends to protect the harbour, and a few miles south of it lies Holy Island, always dark and mysterious, with its castle-crowned rock and ruined Priory—a picture of wistful, dreamy beauty.

Cross the old Border Bridge at Berwick, follow the irregular broken coast line and you will find " no change " written everywhere. The way lies through an alternation of beach and cliff, the Spittal sands yielding to the rocks at Scremerston and they give place to a low beach, with a setting of bent-grown sandhills, and so till you eventually arrive at " the haunted sands of Goswick." Here the tide ebbs from a shore that is almost flat and leaves behind a vast area of " ribbéd sand." Over it the sea fowl have held sway from time immemorial. There is an old place rhyme which gives an explanation of the local names and appears to show that Lindisfarne Priory drew its supplies from these shore farms and that it was no uncommon experience for the collector to find that he had been anticipated by the raiding Scots.

> From Goswick we've geese ; from Cheswick we've cheese ;
>   From Buckton we've ven'son in store ;
> From Swinhoe we've bacon, but the Scots have it taken,
>   And the Prior is longing for more.

Extensive as are the sands of Goswick and Cheswick, they are not so spacious as those of Holy Island. Usually the visitor first catches sight of them when he arrives at the sea shore after a mile and a half's drive through purely agricultural country from Beal station. His first impression will vary with the state of the tide and the condition of the atmosphere. On a sunny June morning, when a foreground to a gently heaving and still more gently murmuring sea is made by the shimmer from wet sand, still pool and trickling stream, the white-winged sea-gulls hover above the " low-lying shores of a beautiful land " fringed with " tender curving lines of creamy spray." Should the weather change and bring a haar from the sea, a new charm of mystery is added as the cloud of fog opens and closes over the scene.

It has been proposed more than once to make a bridge across the sands, but it is to be hoped that such a project will never be carried out. It would reduce a romantic feature of the island to commonplace, and there is no excuse of commercial necessity for this undertaking. Every crossing, whatever be the season of the year, is new. On a summer night when the sky is flecked with clouds and the moon is sailing through them, now obscured, now brightly shining on the dimpling water and the far-reaching sands, patterned with castings of the sand eel, one thinks of the " far countree " to which Kilmeny was carried or repeats such lines as :

> On such a night
> Stood Dido with a willow in her hand
> Upon the wild sea banks, and waft her love
> To come again to Carthage.

Did the meek-eyed, sandalled monk ever turn his thought to the exquisite and tender loveliness revealed by his island mother in her intimate moments ? No, is the probable answer. He was but a sojourner here, who preferred the hardships of life because through them alone might he win eternal happiness.

The external features of the island are easily apprehended. At the south are rocks of black basalt, part of Northumberland's great Whin Sill, hardened lava, formed when Cheviot stump was a volcano. On the top of one of them sits the castle, like a bird on its nest. Away to the north is a barren, but beautiful, region of blown sand, wind-woven into dunes and hollows. Between these two are lands of great fertility and a little lake, much haunted by the wild birds indigenous to the island. Let there be added a hag or moss where grow many beautiful wild flowers, among them the grass of Parnassus, of which so many poets have sung. In order to obtain a satisfactory view of the neighbourhood it is best to mount to the castle battlements from which Bamburghshire, " the richest coontie in England," as the natives used to call it, stretches out. Its county town is Bamburgh, shorn of its ancient importance, but with a castle which, by the lapse of time, has become more interesting than ever it was before. " King Ida's castle huge and square " still bears the majestic appearance it must have presented when rebuilt in the twelfth century. Ida, first of the Saxons to become King of Bernicia, is said to have noticed the strength of the basaltic rock and built a tower and surrounded it at first with a hedge and then with a wall. But it must have been a modest edifice in comparison to what it became afterwards. It is interesting as a royal palace, and, in Freeman's phrase, the cradle of Northumbrian history ; but the light of romance falls on it too. For surely it was the Joyous Gard of Lancelot du Lake. " Some say it was Alnwick and some say it was Bamburgh," Mallory remarks when telling how Lancelot came hither to die. What a delightful expression that of the Bishop : " I saw the angels *heave* Sir Lancelot up to Heaven ! "

On a sunny day, when the cloud shadows chase one another over the widely diversified country which stretches from the sea to the Cheviot ranges, one likes to think of Tristram of Lyonness and La Beale Isoud riding out with hawk on hand from the gateway of Bamburgh. If the Northumbrians of that day were the true progenitors of those who inhabit its district now, they must greatly have delighted in Tristram. He was a master of venerie, who hunted the deer with as much zest as the members of the North Northumberland hunt the fox. Mallory says he was " the noblest blower of the horn of all manner of measures." It is not altogether an idle or an impossible fancy that the thanes and villeins of Bamburgh, of Wooler and Milfield, of Mindrum and Yetholm, knew the sound of his horn as he blew the uncoupling, the seeking, the rechate, the flight, the death, the strake, and many other blasts and terms. King Arthur and Lancelot and Tristram, Guinevere and La Beale Isoud may have been familiar figures, and there are many legends connected with the shadowy company.

The Farnes lie almost direct east from Bamburgh. In old times they were closely connected with Holy Island, as they formed part of the patrimony of the church in Lindisfarne, passing afterwards to the Priory and Convent of Durham. In the troubled times of Border fighting every island was looked upon as being safer than the mainland. Until the middle of last century there was a population on the islands and a certain amount of agriculture carried on. To-day they are tenanted by birds only, since the modern lighthouse does not demand the constant presence of a keeper. It is remarkable that the curious names of the islands were nearly the same in the twelfth century as they are to-day. In all there are over a score at low water and fifteen in all tides. Northumberland is a county rich in bird life and nowhere richer than on the coast. The Farnes, under the care of an association, are now kept as a sanctuary for sea-birds. The nesting species are eider-duck, puffin, razorbill, guillemot, cormorant, roseate tern, Arctic tern, common tern, Sandwich tern, lesser black-backed gull, kittiwake, herring gull, ring dotterel, and oystercatcher. The ornithologist finds here one of his best hunting grounds, and the lover of nature could desire to see no more delightful picture than is presented by the feathered nations in the middle of the breeding season, say, early in June. Tern, soaring and dipping into the water, guillemots crowded on the rocks so that they can scarcely find standing room, the gulls in their swinging flight, odd-looking puffins and a black crowd of cormorants make a living picture of bird life such as can be seen in very few other places.

It is not necessary here to dwell on the individual islands, though the mind lingers over the quaint old names—the Knoxes, the Wawmses, Megstone, Longstone, Crumstone Farne, and the rest. The most delightful way of exploring them is by sailing from Holy Island.

That was how Miss Turner, the famous photographer of flying birds, went, and no words can describe the vivid, wild beauty of bird and breeze and rock so graphically as her pictures. She was on a first visit to Holy Island, and both sides of her personality were kindled to enthusiasm—the ornithologist discovered an ancient yet fresh and fair world teeming with the life in which she is most interested : the artist found the sea-birds in a natural and most picturesque setting.

Before crossing to the Farnes she had been engrossed in the quieter but perfect loveliness of the larger island. She had made pictures of the winged visitors to a little fresh water pool near the sand dunes. In photographing the visitors to it—a common tern " standing on one of the stones and talking to his own reflection," an eider duck alighting, a ringed plover, a stockdove, a sheldrake—she contrives to get into the picture the mounds of sand and the scanty vegetation slowly beginning to appear on them, till those who know and remember almost exclaim : " Here is ' all the charm of all the Muses flowering in '— a photograph ! " It carries us at once to the wind-swept shore.

The little island lake, changing from its winter aspect of

ruffled water framed in withering reeds to a summer wilderness
of water plants, is a wonder and delight to the lover of nature,
as it must be to the birds that haunt and nest there.   It is best
seen what time the strifes and loves of the coot and waterhen
are being transacted when the jack snipes are on the bank,
fishermen heron wading in the shallows, and the wanton lapwing,
having got himself another crest, flies and pipes.

   From the sedgy mere and the sand dunes of Holy Island to
the bare and jutting rocks of the Farnes is a short but glorious
sail. Most of the islands are of the dark basalt which occurs
at intervals on this northern coast as far south as Cullernose
Point, a magnificent cliff from which the Whin Sill turns inland.
Stern and forbidding in winter, the Farne Islands are scenes of
life and gaiety in late spring and early summer, when the sea-
birds gather from the quiet creeks and far distant lands of their
roaming. They have arranged themselves in some appearance
of order—cormorants on the Megstone, guillemots and kittiwakes
on the Pinnacles, puffins in the rabbit-holes of the Wawmses
make their simple nests. No addition to the number of tribes
appears to take place. In 1856 Prideaux Selby, the famous
and exact Northumbrian ornithologist, prepared a catalogue,
which stands good for to-day, of the birds which inhabit or
resort to the Farne Islands. Selby did not include migrants or
strangers blown on the rocks during a storm. His list, however,
tells the visitor exactly what birds are to be looked for in the
breeding season. A different story is that of the immense
crowds of small birds that alight on the Farnes and Holy Island
during the migratory period. George Bolam, in " The Birds of
Northumberland and the Eastern Borders," gives a fine account
of the innumerable thrushes, the ring-ouzels, meadow pipits,
finches, linnets, warblers, wrens, buntings, stonechats and other
species that rose from turnips, stubble and grass of Holy Island
on a day in mid-October.

   Although the bird nations remain very much what they were,
the population has grown tremendously since protection was
organised and the islands transformed into a sanctuary for sea-
birds. How they were previously kept down was told by William
Howitt, who visited the Farnes about the middle of last
century. His description of the Pinnacles has never been
bettered : There were the guillemots " sitting erect as close as
they could crowd and waving their little dark wings as if for

joy." And "on the sides of the cliffs on little projections sate gulls, looking very white and silvery against the dark arch." He ascended "wrinkled hills of black stone and descended into worn and dismal dales of the same ; into some of them when the tide got entrance, it came pouring and roaring in raging whiteness and churning the loose fragments of whinstone into round pebbles." And "over our heads screamed hundreds of hovering birds, the gull mingling in hideous laughter most wildly." He goes on to say that between May and July thousands of eggs are collected and sold, many being sent to London. Gathering samphire on Dover Cliffs was child's play in comparison with egg-collecting on the Farnes—" the fowlers pass from crag to crag over the roaring sea and even from one to another of these perpendicular isolated rocks, the Pinnacles, by means of a narrow board placed from one to the other, and forming a bridge over such horrid gaps that the very sight of it stills one with terror."

No sights such as this harrow the visitor of to-day. Peace reigns except for the internecine bickering of the birds, their rivalry, thieving and revenges. On the rock, in the sea and in the air, fowl in multitudes innumerable hatch their eggs, hunt their prey, and disport themselves without molestation. The visitor watches in the same spirit that inspired Cuthbert when he surrendered to them the little crop of barley grown for his own use. In each he finds a separate grace to admire—as the tern or sea-swallow for the elegance of its flight and the skill of its fishing, the puffin for his oddity, the eider duck for her tameness and confidence, the gulls for their wild shriek born of the ocean and its thunder. Even the ghoulish cormorant, despite its noisome, insanitary home, evokes reluctant admiration when, with wide dark wings, it floats rather than flies above the surface of the water.

An advantage of Holy Island is that frequent visits may be made to the Farnes ; the bird lover and the naturalist, indeed all but the mere sightseer, will want to go again and again. You want to see the Crumstone covered at high water, but a resort of seals at ebb ; to study the uproarious channels between the islands. It was in Staple Sound, where there is a deep passage between the Ox Scaurs on the north and the Crumstone on the south, that the *Pegasus* struck.

Northumberland's heroine, Grace Darling, is associated with

the Harcar Rocks, on which the *Forfarshire* struck at three
o'clock on a wild tempestuous September morning in 1838.
Nine people escaped in a boat, which drifted miraculously through
the only possible passage. The stern, quarter-deck and cabins
were swept down the furious channel called the Piper Gut, while
the other half of the vessel remained on the rock. Such of the
passengers as survived clung to the swaying vessel as the waves
dashed over it, threatening death at every crash. On the Long-

Seahouses.

stone Lighthouse Grace and her father heard their cries, and the
rescue has often been described in prose and verse.

After a sunny, windy day on the Farnes one returns to Holy
Island with a mind surcharged. Within it there goes on a rever-
beration of colour as well as sound, flashing white wings, birds
speeding across the water and the air, screaming fowl and beating
wave commingled. There is added an intense longing to realise
that past of which we know so little. Something of it is revealed
on the land, but the sea carries no outward mark of its history,
and its worst tragedies can only be surmised. How much

romance lies buried under the waves of that coast between Berwick and the Farnes! Some hint of it may be disclosed by a study, however imperfect, of the records preserved no less in stone than on sheepskin, by which we can piece together a story of the central part, Lindisfarne. It will carry us through the noblest period of Northumbrian history and cast a ray of light on that of Early England.

CHAPTER XIII

ST. CUTHBERT AND HIS ISLAND

OSWALD, after the brilliant victory over Cadwallon, at Heavenfeld, under the standard of the Cross, determined to establish
Christianity in Northumbria and appealed to Iona for help in
635. Aidan was asked to choose the seat of his Bishopric.
Already he had made acquaintance with Bernicia, the northern
part of Northumbria, having, with Oswald as his interpreter,
taught the Gospel there. It stretched from the Tees to the
Firth of Forth. Deira, the southern part of the Kingdom, had
embraced Roman Christianity and was ecclesiastically ruled
from York. Aidan was a man of the ancient apostolic type,
who took no thought of earthly rank or riches, but who believed
with deep enthusiasm in that eternal Treasure which is found
where neither the moth nor the rust doth corrupt. We must

try to look through his eyes to understand why his choice lighted upon Lindisfarne. Probably the greatest consideration was that it reminded him of Iona. A modern writer has described the latter in words that might almost be applied to Holy Island : " It is but a small isle, fashioned of a little sand, a few grasses salt with the spray of an ever-restless wave, a few rocks that wade in heather and upon whose brow the sea-wind weaves the yellow lichen. But since the remotest days sacrosanct men have lived here in worship. In this little isle a lamp was lit whose flame lighted Pagan Europe."

In Lindisfarne the evangelist monk beheld a new Iona like the old one, but with one or two different and remarkable features. It lay closer to the mainland, from which it is divided by a tract of flat sand that the flowing tide conceals and the ebb lays bare twice every day, an occurrence first described by the Venerable Bede and afterwards by nearly all subsequent writers who in prose or verse have recorded their impressions of the famous isle. Aidan must also have seen a great bare hump of basaltic rock that formed a centre round which the rest of the island landscape is naturally grouped.

There was more to see. We can imagine the young Bishop climbing this bare crag—it is that on which the castle now stands—and gazing at the objects which interested him as he listened to the water sobbing among the rocks or watched it flowing over the sands. On the friendly shore within an hour's sail rose the Royal vill of Bamburgh, not as we know it, but as it was built by Ida and dwelt in by Oswald. Further off were the Farnes, dark and, according to the belief of the time, devil-haunted rocks rising ominously from a dangerous sea. The monk of that period was convinced that the way to Heaven lay through self-imposed penances. For such austerities Nature might have purposely brought forth these bleak and melancholy isles.

In this spirit the See of Lindisfarne was founded, and with little essential change it existed for two centuries and a half. Were it possible to form a picture of the primitive church built upon the island, it would help us to realise the life of that early monastery. No vestige of it remains to-day, but from chance hints and allusions it is known to have been first built of wood and roofed with thatch, made most likely of the reeds that still grow plentifully in the island mere. As preachers of the Word the early monks of Lindisfarne soon became famous, and great crowds came across the sands to hear them. They were also active missionaries. Boisil, from Iona, had founded the monastery of Mailros, or Old Melrose, very shortly after Aidan's establishment.

There were in all sixteen Bishops of Lindisfarne, and of these the most famous was Cuthbert. He was a shepherd boy on the Lammermoors when Aidan died, and the Venerable Bede says that on that night he saw stars falling. " Behold a servant of the Lord ! " exclaimed Boisil when the comely " herd laddie," spear in hand, rode up to the monastery door of Melrose. In those lawless times even the godly dared not go unarmed. Comely in appearance, thoughtful in habit, and of an inborn piety, Cuthbert soon attracted the notice of great ecclesiastics. Joining the monastery of Melrose, he received the tonsure from Eata, and quickly surpassed the other monks in prayer and labour, reading and discipline. He subsequently accompanied Eata to Ripon, at which King Alchfrith had built a monastery. This was when the great struggle was taking place between the Celtic and the Romish parties. At the time of Eata's appointment, King Alchfrith was on the side of the Irish missionaries ; but under the influence of his mother, Eanflea, he passed to the side of the Romans and made Wilfrith Abbot of Ripon. In consequence, Cuthbert and the other Melrose monks were driven out. He returned to his old home at Melrose, and, after recovery from an attack of plague, gave himself to preaching the Gospel, visiting places so wide apart as Coldingham and Nithsdale, and everywhere making converts and winning renown as an eloquent and persuasive preacher. The struggle between the Romish and the Celtic monks was brought to a close by the victory of the former in the decision of the Synod held at Whitby in 664, and Cuthbert obediently followed his leaders. Eata, now Abbot of Lindisfarne, made him prior in order that he might teach the Romish usages to those monks who still persisted in following those taught at Iona. It was a great step upward when the erstwhile shepherd lad was made prior ; but humility was of the very essence of the man. He continued to wear the simple garment, made of undyed wool, which was that of the ordinary brother, and in chapter was distinguished for the sweetness of disposition with which he subdued the wrangling that was ever breaking out between the new school and the old. For twelve years he seems to have shared fully in the activities of the monastery, which continued to send forth preachers and teachers to the wild places of Northumberland, while many individuals, as we shall see, kept alive the tradition of art and beauty which they had acquired with their Celtic origin by way of Iona. No doubt a worthy fane had been reared for worship; we hear incidentally of vessels of silver and gold, of treasure accumulated through the offerings of the

The Farne Islands.

faithful, and there is visible proof that among the monks were artists skilled to produce the beautiful. At first he shut himself in a natural hermitage which tradition associates with a cave at Howburn, near Lowick, and then, as if his hope of ultimate glory depended on intensifying his suffering, he, as Aidan had done, turned his eye on Farne, the name island of the Farne group, which is now identified with House Island. A reference to it by Hutchinson, who wrote in 1776, is worth quoting as an expression of the older view of such scenery: " He built a cell with a small oratory and surrounded it with a wall which cut off the view of every object but heaven. He could not have chosen a place better adapted to a life of mortification and severity than this island : the ancient description of it is horrible, seated near a stormy coast surrounded by rocks over which the sea breaks incessantly with great tumult, destitute of fresh water, without tree for shelter or fruit-bearing shrub, or wherewithal to sustain human life ; and worse than all, said to be possessed of devils." On a rocky slope Cuthbert built his cell. Outside it was about the height of a man, but inside it was so hollowed out that through the single window only the sky could be seen. Here for nine years Cuthbert lived the anchorite's life, and though the King came in person, accompanied by Archbishop Truman and many powerful followers, lay and ecclesiastical, and begged him on Eata's transference to Hexham to accept the See of Lindisfarne, he yielded with the greatest reluctance. But they insisted, for the report of his holiness and miraculous power had now spread over Christendom, and with the due ritual and solemn pageantry of the Church he was consecrated at York. The event was treated with the importance now reserved for a coronation. King Eagfrith himself was present. The archbishop was assisted by seven other bishops in the perform-ance of the ceremony. But Cuthbert knew it impossible that he should hold the office long; sickness and self-mortification were bringing him close up to the Great Shadow. Two years after-wards he was departing from Lindisfarne to the Farne. A monk asked when he would return. " When you bring my body hither," he replied.

The body of Cuthbert was taken from the Farne, where he died, to Lindisfarne and laid in the Church of St. Peter in a stone coffin. This church must have been architecturally a great advance on its primitive predecessors. The wealth of the monastery had already begun to accumulate, and we hear of great possessions in silver and gold.

The history of the body was stranger than that of the living man. In those early times reverence for the dead, especially the holy dead, was carried to its utmost limit, and the bones of the saint, resting in their stone sepulchre, were the proudest possession of the monks. They did not leave them very long undisturbed. After nine years, on the anniversary of his burial, April 20th, the sepulchre was opened with the permission of his successor, Bishop Eadbert. On the authority of Bede

K

and Reginald it is said that the body was found unchanged and the joints still flexible. Even the clothing had suffered no decay. The object in opening it had been to place it in a smaller coffin, on the assumption that it would have been reduced to dust. The body was reverently replaced, and when Bishop Eadbert died, a fortnight later, a burial place for him was found beneath that of Cuthbert. It must have been opened again at the death of Bede, whose remains were placed beside those of the saint. So Cuthbert slept in that island church, with the voices of the choristers singing round him and mingling with the noise of those sea waves over which were to come the Vikings to disturb the peace of the quiet, religious settlement. Cuthbert died in 687 and Lindisfarne was laid waste by the Danes in 793. But they did not disturb the tomb. In 875, however, they came over again and the monks fled in alarm, carrying with them the remains in a temporary wood coffin. They took away also the famous Gospel of Lindisfarne and journeyed to Cumberland with the intention of crossing over to Ireland, but they were turned by a storm, during which the precious Gospel was swept into the sea, which miraculously returned it to the land.

It would take too long to recite in detail the further adventures of the body, which, after many wanderings, rested in Chester-le-Street, where it remained for a hundred years, until under the terror of another Danish invasion it was carried to Ripon. A few months later an attempt was made to bring it back to Chester-le-Street, and thus occurred the legendary incident which is said to account for the image of a cow familiar to all who have ever looked at the main entrance to Durham Cathedral. Supposedly by the saint's directions, they followed a cow until it stopped. Then they first erected a chapel made of boughs and afterwards built a little wooden fane to cover the coffin, and on September 4th, 998, it was removed to Ealdhun's Church of stone. But when William the Conqueror swept over the north like a devastating storm, in 1069, the monks of Durham fled back to Lindisfarne, where they concealed Cuthbert's remains for a year, after which it was carried again to Durham and placed in the new church built by Bishop William.

Many interesting and valuable relics of Cuthbert are still in existence. There is first the Lindisfarne Gospel, of which something will be said anon. Then when the tomb was opened in 1104 it was found to contain, among other things, a sixth-century manuscript of St. John's Gospel. This is now at Stonyhurst. In 1827 the coffin was opened for the last time by the cathedral clergy, animated, it has been assumed, by no higher motive than that of curiosity. They found in it, among other things, a little Pectoral Cross of dull gold, with a loop, at the top, of bright pure gold. It weighs fifteen pennyweights and twelve grains. There was also a little portable altar made of embossed silver, attached by silver nails to a slip of oak about a third of an inch in thickness and about 6 ins. by 5 ins. in area. But perhaps the most interesting of all are the robes found on his body. Among them was a stole and maniple, with an inscription wrought into them : *Ælflæd fieri precepit pio episcopo Frithestano* (" Ælflæd caused to be made for the pious Bishop Frithestan "). Ælflæd was the queen of Edward the Elder, Alfred's son, and Frithestan was the contemporary Bishop of Winchester. Dr. Browne suggests that after the death of Frithestan his robes might be at the disposal of anyone who wished to make a special gift, or they might be Palace property. Athelstane, after his successful invasion of Scottish territory in 933–4, made rich gifts to the body of Cuthbert, then lying in Chester-le-Street, among them a stole and maniple. Dr. Browne, the authority already quoted, says " both the stole and maniple, now at Durham, have the inscription given above worked into them in worsted work. The substance of these robes is narrow gold tape, woven with self-edges for the insertion of the lettering, the prophets, the floral ornamentation, and all parts of the subjects, in worsted. It is a marvellous piece of work, just a thousand years old, with an unusually clear and convincing pedigree."

There is a strange ironic contrast between the living Cuthbert, abjuring luxury in dress during life and choosing to go about in a cloak of undyed wool, skin leggings and boots that were not taken off from year's end to year's end, and the same body after death, sheathed in a royal garment that has not wholly lost its beauty after a thousand years, and furnished with rich and precious religious symbols, making the splendour of the tomb utterly unlike the simplicity of the man. On each occasion when his sepulchre was changed, magnificent clothing was found for the poor remains. It was all in keeping with the religious spirit of the age which attached miraculous power even to the bones of a saint; and the belief was widespread that his body was incorruptible.

When the time came for the body to be removed from its island resting-place to Durham, new robes were provided. They were after the fashion of the gorgeous presents which Leopold III made to Charlemagne, describing them as " two robes of Syrian purple with borders of cloth of gold wrought with elephants." A circular medallion of silk was found in the tomb of Charle- magne when it was opened in the presence of William II. The elephant, which is their outstanding feature, may possibly be connected with the Emperor's favourite elephant Abulabas, which accompanied him in his great progresses. Expert opinion is that these robes were woven in Syria and Mesopotamia. Cuthbert's robes, Dr. Browne writes in his " Life of Bede," " were presumably made between 1085 and 1104 to be ready for the translation of the saint's body to the new Cathedral Church of Durham." If the conjecture that they were produced by women of Syria and Mesopotamia be correct, the monkish artist from Lindisfarne must have sent to the Arab weaver sketches and verbal directions for giving the local colour. Of the more beautiful of these robes Dr. Browne says " it was of stout silk, ornamented with circular medallions two feet across, containing a vase symbolic of an island floating on the sea. The floating vessel was laden with fruit and the whole was en- closed in a circular border of fruits." The rippling sea, the fish and fowl, indicate Lindisfarne clearly, and the fruits may represent those of a holy life.

Of the portion of another robe of thin silk the same authority says " the medallions were less artistic. They had a very rich border of incurved octagons fifteen inches across enclosing a man on horseback with hawk in hand and a row of rabbits below." He suggests that the falconer may be intended for King Ecgfrith, who was at the head of the Synod, all the members of which, on bended knee, besought Cuthbert to accept the Bishopric of Hexham. There was no anachronism. Falconry was already a sport in Anglo-Saxon England. Alchfrith, Ecgfrith's brother, is represented, hawk on fist, on the con- temporary memorial cross at Bewcastle.

The story of the Lindisfarne Gospel as told by Sir Edward Sullivan was that, " having reached the West Coast, they (the monks) took ship for Ireland ; but the frail vessel in which they sailed was driven back by a furious tempest, during the raging of which their treasured manuscript was washed overboard. When they regained the English shore the holy volume, to their great amazement, was already there before them, lying in safety on dry land in the box in which they had packed it, the illuminations, according to the chronicle of Symeon Dunelmensis, being quite uninjured by the sea-water. For more than a century after this the successors of the exiled monks wandered to and fro through the land before they found a final resting-place for St. Cuthbert's remains in the Minster which they founded at Durham. The Book of the Gospels was then laid on the coffin of the saint, and there it remained till early in the twelfth century. It was removed at the time when St. Cuthbert's body was exhumed, and, shortly after, it was sent back to Lindisfarne, where a monastery of the Benedictine Order has been established by some monks of Durham on the spot once occupied by St. Cuthbert's ancient abbey. Here it was safely housed until the dissolution of the monasteries in the reign of Henry VIII, when its original gold cover was torn from its sides and melted down. The manuscript itself was fortunately unharmed, and was afterwards, early in the seventeenth century, bought from Robert Bowyer, then Clerk of the Parliaments, by Sir Robert Cotton, from whose possession it passed, together with many other volumes that belonged to that noted collector, to the British Museum."

On the last page of this celebrated book is a note, apparently written in the tenth century. Incidentally it shows what pious occupations were followed by the monkish recluse, and it will serve better than any description of the lovely Gospel of Lindisfarne. It has been translated by Mr. Warner as follows : " Eadfrith, Bishop of the church of Lindisfarne, he at the first wrote this book for God and for St. Cuthbert and for all the saints in common that are in the island. And Ethilwald, Bishop of those of Lindisfarne Island, bound and covered it outwardly as well as he could. And Billfrith the anchorite he wrought as a smith the ornaments that are on the outside and adorned it with gold and with gems, also with silver overgilded, a treasure without deceit. And Alfred, an unworthy and most miserable priest, with God's help and St. Cuthbert's, overglossed it in English. . . ."

" The Holy Isle which was the mother of all the religeuse

places in that part of the realm " now became, in the words of Flambard, " a hand-mayde to Durham." In 1082, Bishop

Ruins of the Priory.

William Carileph by charter bestowed on his newly-established cell of Benedictine monks, *inter alia*, " The Church of Lindisfarne which had been originally the Episcopal

See, with its adjacent vill of Fenham, and the Church of Norham, which had been rendered illustrious by the body of St. Cuthbert, with its vill of Shoreswood." Until now the island had been known as Lindisfarne, but under Benedictine rule it was called Holy Island, " in consequence of the sacred blood shed upon it by the Danes." The Benedictines cleared

A Study in Durham Cathedral.
(Compare with The Priory, Lindisfarne.)

away the decayed remains of the old cathedral and built upon its foundation the priory whose ruins still remain. The foundation was probably laid in 1093 or 1094. Reginald, the Durham Monk, records that it was built by one of the monks, named Edward, whose " main anxiety was to increase the possessions and improve the buildings of the church," and that it was "new from its foundation." He modelled it on the lines of Durham Cathedral.

The ruins are the most beautiful and picturesque in Northumberland. Anyone looking at them to-day must share in the

The Parish Church of St. Mary.

admiration so eloquently expressed by Sir Walter Scott. Elsewhere, ruins might in themselves be as lovely, but nowhere have they a setting so appropriate. In other cases decay has gone so far as to obliterate the outline of the original; or shop and factory have invaded what were once the garth and precincts of a house of religion. Here there is nothing in the surroundings to jar with the ancient masonry, for the ruins have the same companions as the old building. The sea and the rock, the flat sands and the dunes, are more ancient than any work of man. Nor have the dwellings of the inhabitants altered materially. When the village was at its prime, thatched cottages greatly prevailed over all others. The thatch has disappeared, but still they are the homely old cottages, and inhabited by the same types of men and women. The sun and the sea breezes produced the same complexion a thousand years ago that they produce to-day, and an island preserves mental as well as physical characteristics. If the old monks were to come to life again, they would indeed see their church in ruins, but there would be nothing to startle them elsewhere. They would still find the same raving, restless sea—the same dark Beblow. They would find the people, save for an alteration in dress here and there, were the same as those among whom they ministered. It is this persistence of old environment that makes the ruins not only beautiful, but the most picturesque in a county rich beyond the average in memorials of the past.

The parish church of St. Mary, Raine tells us, was built before the year 1145. He tells us that in his day it was " very respectably pewed with old black oak. The pulpit is even ornamental. One of its decorations is a shield, upon which is carved, ' 1646. T. S. May 3.' " But in the restoration of 1861 the old church furniture was ruthlessly swept away. The most interesting memorial left is a slab over the grave of Sir William Read, an Elizabethan governor of the island and a " character " who warded off death longer than most—a fact alluded to in the epitaph :

> Contra vim mortis
> Non est medicamen in hortis.

The second period in the history of the island lasted from 1082 till about 1538. The last inventory of the church is dated 1533, or just before the dissolution of the monasteries. Holy Island for four centuries was ruled from Durham, and the annual accounts transmitted to the treasury of the mother church show that fasting and penance gave place to good living. The Saint had been content with pulse, and sometimes gave that to the eider ducks. But oxen, sheep, and porkers, capons, ducks, and geese, malt for strong ale and store of wine " for the solace of the brethren and strangers " formed the diet of those who followed.

The Lindisfarne Gospel appears in every new inventory as part of a very small library ; but there is nothing to indicate that the monks gave their time to making other illuminated works. In these same inventories are included a few guns and pieces of rusty armour, and we know that the priory was crenellated or loop-holed and had other defensive fortifications, but the monks never were assailed. Yet of "insight," as the Border robbers named household gear, there was more in the priory than in any of the villages. The last inventory enumerates treasures and embroideries, cloths of "whitte and rede sattin " and cloths of gold, images and pictures, robes and relics and altar-cloths.

It was not till after the dissolution of the religious houses that the need of a fortress in the island was urgently felt. The castle owed its existence to the Order in Council (1539) that "all havens should be fensed with bulwarks and blockehouses." But the work was not immediately begun. What forced the island upon military attention was the preparation for Hertford's tremendous raid in 1543. Things had not settled down after Flodden. Surrey, instead of carrying his advantage home by an invasion, had disbanded the army, and hostilities were conducted by riding forays into the Merse and Lothians—a policy that had the effect of exasperating the Scots to the last degree. In 1543 they had renewed the old alliance with France, and this accounted for the expedition under Edward Seymour, the Earl of Hertford.

The main embarkation took place at Berwick, but on the way to it two thousand two hundred troops were landed on Holy Island, and in October 1543 ten English line of battleships were in the haven. In the previous year was made the first attempt at a serious fortification of the island, under the direction of " Robart Rooke of Barwik." The plan was to make two bulwarks, the one to be set in such place as would command the roadstead, the other in the most favourable situation for defending the island. In the report of the master mason and Robart Rooke, it was said that " there is stone plentie and sufficient remayning of the olde abbey lately dissolved there to make the bulwark that shal defend the eland all of stone if it maie so stand with the good pleasure of the kinges said majestie." We find the castle mentioned for the first time in the Border Survey made by Sir Robert Bowes in 1550. He writes exactly in the manner of one looking at a newly-built fortress : " The Fort of Beblowe, within the Holy Island, lyeth very well for the defence

The Castle from North-West

of the haven theire ; and if there were about the lowe part thereof made a ring, with bulwarks to flancke the same, the ditch thereabout might be easily watered towarde the land. And then I thinke the said forte were very stronge, and stood to great purpose, both for the defense of the forte and annoyance of the

enemies, if they did arrive in any other parts of the Island."
Later, in 1675, a second fort was built upon the east end of the
Heugh, but it was soon allowed to fall into ruins.

For objects of her own, which we need not go into here,

The Post Cart crossing the Sands.
With the ebb and flow its style
Changes from continent to isle.

Queen Elizabeth had a survey made in the third year of her
reign. It gives a vivid picture of the Holy Island of that time:

"The Holy Iland is scituate within the sea, and yit at every
tyde of lowe water men may passe into the same on horseback or

foote, and it is in compasse about iij^{oa} myles by estimat or more, and hath in the same a little borowgh towne, all sett with fishers very poore, and is a markett town on ye Satterday, howbeit it is little vsed, and yit by reason thereof all the townes of Norham and Ilandshyre ought theire to receive y^r measors and wights, and are in all things to be directed by thassisse of the said towne of Iland. And there was in the same Iland one Cell of Monks of the house of Durham, which house hath the personage of the said parish as before is declared, which mansione howse was build in fovre square of two Courts, as appeareth by the platt theirof, and nowe the same howse is the Quene's Maties storehouse, and also another howse in the towne called the Pallace, which is the newe brewehouse and bake-

The Village.

house, and other offices in the same for the said storehouse. And in the same Iland is also one forte builded vpon an hill called Beblawe, which serveth very well for the defence and saveguard of the haven, the which haven is a very good and apt haven both of the harborowe and landinge. The inhabitants there have baylifs and all other officers of their owne elections yerely, charged at Michmas, and have certeine men which be burgesses and fremen, of wch companie the sayd officers be always chosen. And everye burgesse payeth certen borrowe rent, save xij and xiij, which clame to be so free that they never payd anye burrowe fearme. The moreparte of the towne is nowe decayed in howses, and yit the tofts and crofts where the howses did stand remayne, of which the burrowe rent is nowe for the most part collected and raysed, as hereafter doth appeare."

The Elizabethan surveyor paints a scene of desolation. Only a few emblems and remnants remain to tell of the importance of Lindisfarne during days when it was a famous seat of learning and the home of a powerful monastery. St. Cuthbert's shrine, not only in ruins, but abased into the uses of a storehouse for the garrison ; the market of the island town still claiming precedence, but little used ; the main houses decayed, but still showing the " tofts and crofts," the land " set with fishers very poor " ; the castle armoured with

The Castle and Village.

culverins and demi-culverins, sakirs and falcons, but never assailed—its history since Aidan's day is being obliterated. In the reign of Elizabeth's successor, when Scotland and England became united under James, the island lost importance even from the military point of view. The castle, it is true, remained a Government fortress, and the parish register shows, by the frequent entry " a soger died," that a military garrison was maintained, the soldiers being probably strangers to the fisher community. During the tragical reign of Charles I we obtain

an unexpected peep at it. This is to be found in the diary of
John Aston, a younger son of the ancient family of Aston, of
Aston in Cheshire, who was attached to the suite of Charles I
on his expedition through the counties of York, Durham and
Northumberland, in the first Bishops' War of 1639. His diary
is published with five others by the Surtees Society, under the
editorship of Mr. J. C. Hodgson of Alnwick. On May 25th,
1639, the King's Army was encamped at Goswick, the place being

Holy Island to-day. A Famous Inn.

chosen because " it should seeme the king's designe was to have
set downe with his army heere, it beeing neare the Holy Island,
and to have had the command and pleasure of his shipps for his
security upon any exigent."

Charles did not, as a matter of fact, join the camp at Goswick,
but Aston went to the place, and from it made an expedition, the
account of which shows exactly what the island and fortress were
like in 1639 :

" Hence wee went to view the Holy Island, and about 10 a clock,
when the tyde was out, wee rode over to it and divers walked on
foote into it. It is about 5 mile in compasse, a levell ground with a
short greene swade upon it, noe part of it tilled nor affoording any
thing but conies. Just at our comming those shipps wee sawe last

night, beeing 20 sayle under the command of Marquisse Hammilton (having beene with him at Dum Fryth with 5,000 land souldiours), heere landed 2 regiments of foote. Sir Simon Harecourt's, and Sir Tho. Moreton's 24 ensignes, who in the island stood to their armes and musterd, and soe soone as the tyde was a little more withdrawne, marched away towards Barwick. . . . In this island is a small villadge, and a little chappell. There is yet remaining the ruines of a faire church very like the cathedrall at Durham, both for the stone and manner of building. It was consecrated to St. Cuthbert, who, for his holy life, obtained a miraculous gift to the island, that about 9 a clock every Sonday the water should bee soe

A Holy Island Fisherman.

lowe that the inhabitants of the countrey that paris to that church may come dry shod to prayers and retourne before it flowe againe, and it happens soe noe day of the weeke besides : but upon enquiry I was tould it was but a superstitious tradition, and noe truth. This church and buildings were demolished by the Earle of Sussex since the beginning of King James his reigne, to whom the government of the isle was given. There is a pretty fort in it, which upon this occasion was repaired and put into forme. There are 2 batteries on it, on the lower stood mounted 3 iron peeces and 2 of brasse, with carriadges and platformes in good order. On the higher was one brasse gunne and 2 iron ones with all ammunition to them. There are 24 men and a captain kept in pay to man it, the common souldiours have 6d. per diem, and the captain (*a space is left here*). The captain at our beeing there was Captain Rugg, knowne commonly by his great nose.

The castle, after its many vicissitudes, was beautifully restored by Mr. Edward Hudson, with Sir Edwin Lutyens as architect, in the first decade of the present century.

Budle Point.

CHAPTER XIV

THE ROYAL CASTLE OF BAMBURGH

The Royal Castle of Bamburgh—From Belford to Bamburgh—
The Laidley Worm of Spindleston Heugh—Early History of
Bamburgh—From Ida to Eadwine, the first civilised King
of Northumbria—Description of Paulinus, its first missionary
—Oswald of the Fair Hand, its first Christian King—The great
Penda : his rise, reign and overthrow—Later Saxon kings—
The tragedy of Nechtansmere—Athelstan's visit to Northumbria
—The last King of Northumbria—Rufus, Edward II, Mar-
garet of Anjou—Henry's nine months' reign at Bamburgh—
The Battle of Hedgeley Moor—Forster of Bamburgh—Castle
and Church in modern times—Joyous Gard and Lancelot.

BAMBURGH CASTLE is without doubt the noblest in Northumberland, its huge dimensions, crowning the cliffs, making an
instant impression of grandeur. The level sands below, where
the waves curl and break along the spacious bay, with the Farnes
rising darkly in front, complete a picture of unassailable dignity.
The village, with its " sweet Auburn " air of peace and prosperity,
stands probably where Ethelfrid strengthened Ida's citadel and
called it fondly after Bebbah, his wife. Proud Eadwine rode
out and in here in royal state, pious Oswald offered his almost
hourly prayers beside the mocking voices of the sea, humble

146

Cuthbert walked among the country folk teaching them by example as much as by precept. Then was the golden age of Christianity, when the tides of faith beat full around rocky Bamburgh. Robes of magnificence, too, rustled here—to contrast with the humility of Cuthbert—when Wilfred, after a simple training on Lindisfarne, became Bishop of Northumberland. The world called to him, and his fortunes fluctuated between York and Hexham, where he founded the glorious church. But robe of noble and prelate at this, the greatest period perhaps of Bamburgh, can be seen in the illuminated wonderful gospels of Lindisfarne, and the high state of Bamburgh's civilisation is shown in the furniture drawn by the artist from what he had seen in the palace.

On the road from Belford to Bamburgh there are several places tempting one to linger. Budle Bay, a large sandy stretch of coast, is two miles from Belford, and the Budle Hills rise above the little hamlet of that name. Where the Waren stream runs into the bay stood a town called Warnmouth, long since covered by the sea. It must have been a port of some size, for a charter was granted to it by Henry III, but little else is known of it. About a mile inland to the south lies the well-known Spindleston Heugh, the scene of the ballad of the Laidley Worm (loathsome snake or serpent) :

> Word went east and word went west
> Word is gone over the sea
> That a Laidley Worm in Spindleston Heugh
> Would ruin the North Countree.

This was a princess of Bamburgh Castle who, by a wicked stepmother, had been transformed into the worm until her brother, "the Childy Wynd," should come from oversea and rescue her. On hearing of his sister's misfortune he embarked in a ship "with masts of the rowan tree, and fluttering silk so fine." The queen, seeing the ship approaching, sent her witch wives to destroy it. This turned out to be beyond their power, as the rowan tree of which the masts were made was charmed. There is an old north country saying : "Witches have no power where there is rowan tree wood." Then the sorceress tried a boat of armed men, who were likewise unsuccessful in the attempt to break through the rowan's spell. Childy Wynd landed on **Budle Sands** after passing " the banks of Bamburghshire."

L 2

> When he met the Worm
> He sheathed his sword, and bent his bow
> And gave her kisses three ;
> She crept into a hole a worm
> And stepped out a ladye.

So he wrapt her in his mantle and hastened to King Ida's castle, where the queen grew pale as she watched their approach. In just wrath he addressed the trembling queen and, with three drops from the well, turned her into a most horrid toad.

> The virgins all of Bamburghtown
> Will swear that they have seen
> This spiteful toad of monstrous size
> Whilst walking on the green.

The cave where the Worm lived and the trough "out of which she did sup the milk of seven stately cows" were shown at Spindleston sixty years ago, but were destroyed in the making of a quarry.

An isolated pillar of whinstone still standing is said to have been used by the brother to throw the bridle of his horse over when he went to meet the Worm. It is unreasonable perhaps to ask why he needed a horse for the short distance from his ship to the cave. It is a wild and rugged spot where this strange adventure is placed, with the Cheviots to the west, a beautiful view. To the north are lonely sands, with a number of streams winding slowly and circuitously to the shining sea. Over Beal Sands is that little thread of a river, the Low, where the Celtic King Urien was treacherously killed when he had almost succeeded in wresting Bernicia from Ida's son. Urien was king of a Celtic State called Reged, afterwards probably Redesdale. It was in the moment of triumph, when he had driven the English across the sands to Holy Island, the Celtic Medcaud, that he fell on the banks of the Aber Llen. His heroic exploits and those of his son, called "The Chief of the Glittering West," was sung by the bards.

To the south, dunes of blown sand lead the eye past the Harkness Rocks to Bamburgh.

From remotest times its position must have made it desirable, and the eyes of the early English invaders turned to it as the most promising fortified place for securing the domination of the country. Ida, in 547, in his appointed task of uniting under one rule the scattered States, seized and strengthened the Celtic fortress of Dinguardi, which had probably been raised on a Roman one. It is hardly likely that the Roman would have left such a splendid position untenanted. The summit of the Whin Sill is here about eighty feet thick and a

Bamburgh Castle.

hundred and fifty high, and forms an impregnable and glorious situation for a castle. The castle takes us back, as does no other in this country, to days before the Conquest, and before the Dane. Here Ida reigned, and his six sons followed him as rulers of Bernicia.

Northumbria had been growing rapidly as the various newly-founded States of the English battled for power, and to Eadwine, who mounted the throne in 617 on the death of Ethelfrith, Bamburgh became the chief city in a kingdom which extended from the Humber to the Forth. He succeeded in defeating the East Anglians, East Saxons, and West Saxons, and the south country became subject to Northumbria, now at the height of her greatness. Eadwine was a ruler whose talents were notable as much in peace as in war, and in his kingdom of Northumbria began a settled and civilised government embodied in the proverb : "A woman with her babe might walk scathless from sea to sea in Eadwine's day." He was the first great Northumbrian. His northernmost city was called Eadwine's burgh, the romantic Edinburgh of later days. As he rode through the villages of his domain a standard of purple and gold floated above him, and a banner formed of globes of feathers, the Roman tufa, preceded him. Thus he is said to have ridden, in imperial pomp, through the wild northland. In places where he saw clear springs near the highways, he caused stakes to be fixed, with brass dishes hanging from them for the refreshment of travellers, and so strongly were Eadwine's laws administered that none injured the dishes. He married Ethelburg, a Kentish princess, who brought with her Paulinus, a follower of St. Augustine. The Venerable Bede, who died in 804, has preserved an impression of the first great missionary of Northumbria, given to him by a monk who had talked with an old man baptised by Paulinus in the presence of King Eadwine. He remembered the tall, stooping form, slender aquiline nose, black hair round a thin, earnest face—a picture truly of the resolute man whose pilgrimages have left a trail of legend across the north country. As no mention is made of any inability to make himself understood by the Northumbrians, it has been suggested that Paulinus may have been among those English slaves in Rome who, according to the famous story, attracted the notice of the benign and punning Gregory and were Christianised by him in order to return to their native land to convert their pagan but handsome brethren. Paulinus had a struggle to convert Eadwine, who, although abandoning idols, hesitated about the worship of Christ. A wise and thoughtful man, he debated long the new religion. The Pope wrote him an able letter and sent him a shirt, a gold ornament and the blessing of Peter. Also, with worldly guile, he wrote Ethelburga, pointing out her peculiar opportunities to influence her husband and supplementing his advice with a silver mirror and an ivory comb inlaid with gold—wonderful intuition in femininity in a celibate ! But it was years after this that the king, evidently an obstinate, questioning, cautious north countryman, made the great decision that throws glory on Northumbria. Bede's account of this acceptance of Christianity has surely no equal for beauty and wisdom in all the stories of conversions. The wise men of Northumbria gathered together to hear the doctrine that was to replace the pagan worship. We would like to think that it was in the hall at Bamburgh, the waves whitening the giant rock amid all the passionate declamation of winds and clamorous sea-birds—the voices perchance of Thor and Woden— that the voice of an aged Ealdorman broke on their ears.

" So seems the life of man, O king, as a sparrow's flight through the hall when you are sitting at meat in winter-tide, the fire on the hearth, the icy rainstorm without. The sparrow flies in at one door and tarries for a moment in the light and heat of the hearth-fire, then flies forth into the darkness whence it came. So tarries for a moment the life of man in our sight, but what is before it. what after it, we know not. If this new teaching tells us aught of these let us follow it."

A wholesale conversion and baptising of the Northumbrians followed. Seven years after, Eadwine's wonderful reign ended, when he was only forty-seven. Penda, King of Mercia, the champion of the deserted gods, allied himself with Cadwallon, the Welsh king, and slew Eadwine at the battle of Hatfield, in Yorkshire.

Oswald, who succeeded him, became a champion of Christianity and won the great battle of Heavenfeld.   Cadwallon fell in flight where the Rowley Burn runs into Devils Water, near Hexham. Oswald may be regarded as the first great Christian king who inhabited Bamburgh. Paulinus had fled from Northumbria after Eadwine's death, although his memory still survives in a few place-names.

It was at Bamburgh that the king and bishop, one Easter day, were at dinner when the thane whom he had set to give alms to the poor came in to say a great multitude still fasted outside. The king at once ordered the untasted meat on the table to be carried out and the silver dish to be distributed among them. Aidan seized the royal hand and blessed it. " May this hand," he cried, " never grow old." Oswald received the surname of Langwyn or Fair Hand, and after his death and mutilation in a battle against Penda, in 642, his " white hand " remained uncorrupted. Bede saw it still fresh in a silver case at Bamburgh.   As Oswald died he prayed, and the memory of him was preserved in an old couplet :

> " God have mercy upon their souls ! "
> Quoth Oswald as he fell to the ground.

Thus died the greatest and gentlest king of Northumbria. The country was given over to the savage Penda for the next few years. All England bowed before him, and the Christian faith was almost overthrown. Only the dour Northumbrians refused to yield. Once he even reached royal Bamburgh, impregnable and steadfast on its rock. Assault would not take it, so he pulled down the surrounding cottages and, piling the wood against the walls, fired it, and Bamburgh seemed doomed. Aidan, on an isle of the Farnes opposite, saw in anguish the coming triumph of the barbarian. " See, Lord, what ill Penda is doing." The wind changed and the smoke lifted from the fair city and drove the flame in the faces of its persecutors. But in spite of Penda's victories, when the rest of England was " swithering " in its new alliance with Christianity, in Northumbria the Cross stood firm, held up by the brave band of missionaries who wandered on foot from Holy Island all down the coast. The gentle Aidan died leaning against the west end of the wooden church in Bamburgh, and that night a vision came to the shepherd boy Cuthbert, who saw Aidan's soul carried heavenward by angels as he lay praying on the hills. On him descended Aidan's mantle. Oswi, brother of Oswald, was now king, but Penda still lived, old and indomitable, to disturb the peace of the harried Christians. His son became converted, and this perhaps aroused the wrath of the great pagan, who, indeed, said he hated " those whom he saw not doing the works of the faith they had received." The Northumbrians offered him costly gifts ; Oswi offered his son as a hostage at Penda's Court ; but they were contemptuously refused. Penda laid waste Bernicia, and all that was left of the church and village of Bamburgh was the wooden stay against which Aidan had leant in his last hours.   It was probably on the banks of the

Tweed, dark and swollen with autumn rain, in November 655, that Penda and his forces had to halt. They were destroyed by the rushing waters as much as by the swords of the Bernicians, and with his death the cause of the ancient gods was lost for ever. A wild but not ignoble figure, he strides across the early history of Bamburgh, a man of blood and iron, a constant and perhaps fanatic opposer of the pale Galilean whose doctrine he would have stamped out ferociously.

Oswi, after reigning twenty-eight years, was succeeded by Ecgfrith, and he raised Northumbria to its highest glory, for in his continued campaigns against the British he extended his kingdom to Carlisle. But, attempting to conquer the land north of the Firth of Forth, he and his army perished at Nechtansmere in the dim moorlands where the Picts dwelt. After that disaster Northumbria never again had any real chance of becoming a reigning power in Britain, in spite of heroic efforts of later rulers. Lindisfarne, after being the centre of English Christianity for a century, saw the spiritual headship of the Church transferred south. By the middle of the eighth century the glory of royal Bamburgh departed, when Corbridge on the Tyne became the capital.

Bamburgh's greatness in the past was nearly forgotten in the anarchy that became the lot of Northumbria. A chronicler in the eighth century thinks it necessary to describe the ancient capital :

Bebba is a most strongly fortified city, not very large, being of the size of two or three fields, having one entrance hollowed out of the rock and raised in steps after a marvellous fashion. On the top of the hill it has a church of extremely beautiful workmanship, in which is a shrine, rich and costly, that contains, wrapt in a pall, the right hand of St. Oswald the king, still incorrupt, as is related by Bede, the historian of this nation. To the west, on the highest point of the city itself, there is a spring of water, sweet to the taste and most pure to the sight, that has been excavated with astonishing labour.

For over a century Northumbria had been a scene of terrible anarchy, and king after king came and passed in murder or battle. Eventually Athelstan, the grandson of King Alfred the Great, came north in 926 and took the inviolate fortress of Bamburgh and Northumbria after that was practically incorporated in Athelstan's domains. There is a record of the latter's victorious campaign in the rhyming grant he is said to have made of Roddan and Heddon to Paulan :

> I Kyng Adelstan
> giffs here to Paulan
> Oddan and Roddan,
> als gud and als fair,
> as evyr thai myne war,
> and thar to wytnes
> Mald my Wiffe.

In 954 Eric Bloodaxe, the last king of Northumbria, perished by the hand of a traitor on the wilds of Stainmoor. It was now weak and open to attack from Scots and Danes, and the latter sacked Bamburgh in 993. The kingdom had shrunk to about the size of the modern county and become an earldom. Bamburgh continued to lose prestige. From the ruined church a monk of Peterborough stole the right arm of St. Oswald, and nothing could mark the degradation and the neglect of Bamburgh more completely in medieval eyes. Reginald of Durham thus laments its fall : " The city renowned for the splendour of her high estate is in these latter days burdened with tribute and reduced to the condition of a handmaiden. She who was once the mistress of the cities of Britain has exchanged the glories of her Sabbaths for shame and desolation. The crowds that flock to her festivals are represented by a few herdsmen. The pleasures her dignity afforded are turned to naught." When the Norman Conqueror received the fealty of the great nobles of the North, Earl Oswulf of Bamburgh was the only one who did not bend his knee, and his earldom was given to a henchman of William's, who never enjoyed it, as at the feast of welcome, at Newburn, Oswulf managed to kill the intruder. However, a few months later he himself was killed in pursuing a robber, and thus obscurely perished the last descendant of the great house of Bamburgh whose forty kings had reigned. When William came north to quieten the rebellion against him, he left a desert from the Humber to the Tweed, the lurking-place of wolves and robbers only. York, Durham, and Bamburgh were the only inhabited towns left, and for nine years cultivation ceased. Later on Northumberland was parcelled out amongst William's friends, and only the native proprietors continued on the small estates.

In 1095 Rufus marched north to Bamburgh to chastise the comparatively new Earl, Robert de Mowbray, who refused to

appear at Court when commanded. The Earl had taken refuge
in the Castle with his young bride. Finding it impossible to
take the castle, William built a Malvoisin. The nobles in his
army who had promised to assist Robert's rising, William
maliciously bade help in the erection of the Bad Neighbour.

Bamburgh Village.

Mowbray, from the ramparts of the castle, shouted taunts to
them on their broken oaths, and their confusion and shame
greatly amused Rufus. However, the siege was unsuccessful
and William returned south. A promise from Newcastle that
its gates would be opened to him induced the Earl to escape
from Bamburgh. It turned out false. He had to fly to

Tynemouth, where the castle and monastery made a brave defence for two days ; but he was at last taken prisoner. His brave young countess continued to hold out in Bamburgh, which was still besieged. William ordered that Mowbray should be taken in front of the castle, and the lady was told that his eyes would be gouged out unless she submitted. She saved him that torture ; but little light he saw, poor rebel, in those adamant days, for a dungeon held him for the rest of his life.

Another unfortunate, Edward II, after Bannockburn, arrived in a small boat at the gates of Bamburgh. A miserable time followed for Northumberland after that battle. Safety was only found under the shadow of a castle—and that was dearly bought at Bamburgh, for the Constable would only allow them to purchase a truce from the Scots if they paid him a similar amount of blackmail. He also charged them heavily for storing their goods in the castle, while the porters would not let their chattels out or in without more payment. In addition the garrison robbed the villagers of their provisions. For years the country suffered unspeakable misery, and the land even down to the Tyne was desolate except where the owners paid blackmail to the raiding Scots. For instance, at Dunstan-burgh Castle only one horse was lifted from the " garniture "— a piece of fortune due to Thomas of Lancaster's dealings with the Scots.

At Berwick three little boys who had gone out to play in the Magdalene Fields were coming back through the Cowport, when one found he had forgotten his song-book and went back to look for it. They were immediately seized for trafficking with the Scots. The suspicion and fear were terrible. It was North-umberland's blackest hour. A century or more earlier it was said that " Northumberland was then so renowned that right down to the Pyrenees there was no country so well provided with the necessaries of life nor inhabited by a race more univer-sally respected." There is little to record of importance after those years until the Wars of the Roses sent the tumult of opposing factions against the grey walls of Bamburgh. It was seized in 1463 by the Lancastrians. Margaret of Anjou tried vainly to take Norham, but it proved too wary. In July of that year the royal fugitives at Bamburgh were in such straits that for five days they lived on one herring. On St. Margaret's day, the 20th, her namesake had nothing to offer at mass. In desperation she begged a Scots archer to lend her something, and ruefully he gave her a groat! Ten days after that, on the approach of the Yorkists, she set sail with her French supporters for Flanders. One headstrong French drummer refused to go, and remained tabouring and piping on a sandhill near the castle till Warwick came up. Prince Henry, in the castle, was strong enough to defy the besiegers, who retired southward, and he was left reigning over Bamburghshire. The

Hedgeley Moor.

Scottish allies of the Lancastrians decided to sue for peace. As their envoys had to pass through troubled Northumberland, and the Lancastrians now held Norham, Lord Montagu, with a force, set out for the Border to convoy them. On April 25th he found his progress barred on Hedgeley Moor by the Duke of Somerset and a large body of Northumbrians.

Sir Ralph Percy fell, crying: " I have saved the bird in my bosom." The poignant allusion is probably to the faith he had kept so bravely—courage and faith, " vain faith and courage vain." In a small enclosure of trees, now fenced, on the side of the road near Wooperton Station, can be seen two large stones, twenty-seven feet apart, which are said to mark the leap of his dying fall. Further down the road on the way to Alnwick, but on the opposite side, behind some cottages half hidden by sombre trees—they seem melancholy—is the Percy Cross, weather-stained and carved with the arms of Percy and Lucy. An ancient grief surrounds the spot :

> 'Tis of the Percy's deathless fame
> That dark grey cross remains to tell ;
> It bears the Percy's honoured name,
> For near its base the Percy fell.

The only place Henry was safe at was Bamburgh ; for at Bywell Castle, shortly after, he was nearly surprised by Earl Montagu. " How and whither the King himself escaped," says the chronicler, " God only knows, in whose hands are the hearts of kings."

Bamburgh, besieged by Warwick, was valiantly defended by Sir Ralph Grey ; but Henry, alarmed at the fall of Dunstanburgh, had escaped. With the courage of despair, for he was exempted from the general pardon offered, Grey replied to the heralds who demanded its surrender that he had determined to live or die in the castle. The heralds then laid the blame of further bloodshed on Grey, and said that, if it took seven years to win, they would capture it. " If ye deliver not this jewel the which the King our most dread Sovereign Lord hath so greatly in favour seeing it marcheth so nigh his ancient enemies of Scotland, and especially desireth to have whole, unbroken with ordnance ; if ye suffer one great gun to be laid unto the wall and be shot, to prejudice the wall, it shall cost you the chieftan's head . . . and the last head of any person within the place." From the battered castle Sir Ralph was taken and executed at Doncaster, and Bamburgh never more had her walls assailed in all the sub-sequent rebellions and invasions that swept over Northumberland.

In Elizabeth's reign the governorship of Bamburgh passed into the hands of the Forsters, and in 1715 the name of Forster became notorious through the incompetence of General Forster, who was chosen to lead the Northumbrian Jacobites from the mistaken idea that a Protestant would rally many more to the cause. He was taken prisoner, and according to tradition his sister Dorothy rode up to London in the company of John Armstrong (whom she afterwards married), and, obtaining an impression of the key of his cell in Newgate, contrived his escape. The whole story is to be found in Sir Walter Besant's romance of " Dorothy Forster." Her beautiful aunt married Lord Crewe as a second wife. He had long been enamoured of her. He was Bishop of Durham, and after her death, when the Forsters were ruined through extravagance, he bought the estates and Bamburgh Castle. He left a large sum of money in the hands of trustees to found the Bamburgh Trust, the most eminent of whom, Dr. John Sharpe, Archdeacon of Northumberland, conceived the idea of restoring Bamburgh Castle and adapting it for the famous Crewe Charities. He repaired it at his own expense and left a sum to maintain it, and founded the library and collected the tapestry and pictures. The humane archdeacon wisely interpreted Lord Crewe's desire to benefit the manor and coast to which his loved wife belonged. He used to spend hours by her grave at Stene, where she was buried in 1715, a comparatively young woman, and when he followed her, in 1722, he was nearly ninety.

The castle occupies an area of eight acres, enclosed by great battlemented walls. At the south-east angle are the remains of St. Peter's chapel, which was discovered in 1773 when the sand was removed under which it had long been buried. At the north front is the castle windmill. The castle is entered through the barbican on the south-east and through the sally-port on the north-west approached by a flight of steps.

The Norman keep is within the bailey and the walls are of great strength. The original roof was only the height of the second storey. It is now raised to the height of the battlements. There are no signs of chimneys at any early date, and the room believed to be the guard-room has burnt stones on the floor. In the large vaulted room on the ground floor is the ancient well the virtues of which have been already quoted. It was rediscovered in 1770. It is 145 feet deep, cut through the solid rock. At the bottom is said to lurk the queen of the ballad of the Laidley Worm in the form of a great toad. It is of unknown antiquity, perhaps the work of Ida. In the entrance hall hang two huge chains formerly used for raising sunken vessels, now facetiously known as King Ida's watch-chains.

The passages in the upper part are very narrow gulleys in the thickness of the wall just wide enough to pass.

There is a Court Room and Armoury, Banqueting Hall (now partly used as a kitchen), and a library that contains many interesting relics and portraits of the Forsters and others. Nothing remains of the Saxon church, and the fine Norman church that succeeded it, dedicated to St. Aidan, is large and impressive and has been often subject to alteration. In the chancel is a recumbent effigy of a cross-legged knight locally called Sir Lancelot du Lake. The name reminds us that Bamburgh Castle, the only

Bamburgh Church.

pre-Conquest castle in Northumberland, is supposed, as has already been said, to be the Joyous Gard of Mallory, where Lancelot came home to die. " So, when he was housled and eneled, and had all that a Christian man ought to have, he prayed the bishop that his fellows might bear his body unto Joyous Gard . . ."

" And now, I dare say," said Sir Ector, " that Sir Lancelot there thou liest, thou were never matched of none earthly knight's hands ; and thou were the courtliest knight that ever bare a shield ; and thou were the truest friend to thy lover that ever bestrode horse ; and thou were the truest lover of a sinful man that ever loved woman ; and thou were the kindest man that ever struck with sword ; and thou were the goodliest person that ever came among press of knights ; and thou were the meekest man, and the gentlest, that ever eat in hall among ladies ; and thou were the sternest knight to thy mortal foe that ever put spear in rest."

"Then there was weeping and dolour out of measure."

In the north transept is a figure chivalrous and devoted as that of Sir Lancelot, the Northumbrian heroine, Grace Darling, resting with an oar by her side. Her name lives for evermore here, where the sea boils around the rocks that witnessed her daring, and in all lands where the English tongue is spoken.

Underneath the chancel is an Early English crypt, the most remarkable feature of the building, which was rediscovered in 1837 and contained the bodies of members of the Forster family. Among them is the famous Dorothy, and Ferdinando, who was shot in the streets of Newcastle by Sir John Fenwick, and whose helmet, gauntlets and sword hang on the wall of the chancel. General Thomas Forster had two dates on his coffin ; the first, 1715, referred to the mock burial which the intrepid Dorothy carried out when he escaped from prison.   This ill-fated Jacobite died in France in 1738 and his body was brought back to rest under the shadow of the great castle which he once owned, and is the pride of every true Northumbrian "though mountains divide him and a world of seas."

CHAPTER XV

THE RUINS OF DUNSTANBURGH

Barony and Manor Purchased by Simon de Montfort—Building by
Thomas of Lancaster—Queen Margaret at Dunstanburgh—
Saddle Rock and Rumbling Churn—Dunstan and Duns Scotus.

LEAVING North Sunderland, we pass the fishing village
of Beadnell, with a fine sandy bay, and the rocky shore of Newton-
by-the-Sea, and, turning the bold headland of Newton Point,
Embleton Bay, two miles in extent, stretches before us. At its
southern extremity magnificent basaltic cliffs are seen crowned
by the ruins of Dunstanburgh Castle, the most imposing in
Northumberland. It rises a hundred feet above the shore, and
Turner's genius was hardly needed to idealise a position wherein
the grandeur of nature is added to the romance of human history.
On the north and east the sea dashes against the frowning cliff
and in stormy weather batters it with gigantic waves. Water
and wind have combined to wear away the walls. In the
thirteenth century the Manor of Dunstan and the adjacent
Barony of Embleton were bought by Simon de Montfort,
doubtless attracted by the extraordinary fitness of this
part of the coast for a fortress, as he was anxious to extend his
influence in the north. After his death, at the battle of Evesham,
his forfeited lands were given by Henry III to his own son
Edward, Earl of Lancaster. Thence they came to Edward's son
Thomas, a grand-nephew of Simon de Montfort, who had married
Henry's sister and succeeded in 1294. He began to build the
castle in 1313, and in 1316 the earl obtained a licence to crenel-
late it. It is interesting to note here that many of the masons'
marks are the same as those at Alnwick Castle, which about that

time was being rebuilt by the first Lord Percy. In 1322 the earl
was executed at Pontefract, either for dealings with the Scots
or for organising rebellion against the weak favouritism of
Edward II. Later on, his forfeited estate was restored to his
brother Henry, and in the deed of gift it is remarked that Earl
Thomas " had gone the way of all flesh " ! He was, however,
regarded as a martyr and was canonised ; the hill on which he was
beheaded was called St. Thomas's Hill. Later on, Dunstanburgh
came again into the possession of the Crown, as Henry Wryneck,
son of Earl Henry, had a daughter, Blanche, his heiress, who
married John of Gaunt and became the mother of Henry IV.

During the Wars of the Roses the castle was a great stronghold of the Red Rose in Northumberland. After the battle of
Towton, when the Lancastrians were defeated, Queen Margaret
attempted to retrieve her fortunes in the north, which was well
disposed to her, and in 1462 seized Dunstanburgh, but had to
surrender it after a short siege. In 1464 Margaret, still bent
on restoring her husband to the throne, again captured it. But
after the battle of Hexham, and her total defeat, the castle was
delivered up to the Earl of Warwick. The chronicle says he
slept in it on the Feast of St. John the Baptist in June 1462, a
month after the fatal field of Hexham. Warwick took the captain
of the castle, John Gosse, to the King at York, where he was
beheaded with a hatchet. The south-eastern tower is called
St. Margaret's Tower, as tradition says the Queen occupied it
when she stayed there. But it is loosely called either St.
Margaret, after the Scottish saint, or Queen Margaret tower.
A creek below it is called Queen Margaret's cove, where she is
supposed to have embarked in a fishing-boat for Scotland when
her hopes were ruined, but this is an unconfirmed tale. We
know she retired to France after Henry's death, where she died
after many sorrows.

Dunstanburgh had been much injured by the artillery in these
sieges, and its strength was gone for ever. Henry VII's survey
in 1538 pronounced that it was a "very reuynus howsse and of
smaylle strength," and in 1550 Sir Robert Bowes, in his "Book
of the State of the Marches," said it was in "wonderfull great
decaye." It was never repaired, and its further ruin was augmented by the stones, etc., being used for other buildings in the
neighbourhood. Sir Ralph Grey became its owner in 1625, and
it remained with his descendants till it was sold by the late

Earl of Tankerville to the Eyres trustees of Leeds. It has
been sold again recently.

The ground plan of the castle covers about eleven acres. There
was no wall on the north side as the perpendicular cliffs supplied
a natural defence. On the east was a wall about six feet
thick ; on the west side a wall and towers and also a deep

Dunstanburgh Castle from the North.

ditch eighty feet broad. On the south there were walls, towers,
and a great gateway, and the traces of a rough stone rampart
which show that it was probably fortified in prehistoric times.
A recent writer (J. E. Morris) says : " Its military engineering is
hardly more ingenious than that of the neolithic Britons who
constructed the existing ramparts round the top of Yeavering

Bell. Each started with a site of such singular natural strength
that the most that they accomplished, or needed to accomplish,
was merely to accentuate existing conditions."

The chief building left is on the south, and consists of the
entrance gateway and two semi-circular towers which, when
entire, rose to a height of eighty feet. This may have been the
keep. At any rate there is no other to be traced.

On the west side the most remarkable feature is the Lilburn
Tower, rising grandly above the black basaltic cliffs. It was
probably built by Sir John Lilburn, Constable of the Castle,
about 1325. Its walls are six feet thick. At each angle rose
four smaller turrets, which completed at about sixty feet from
the ground this noble and commanding tower. In storms,
whitened with spray, it stands a sentinel looking over the wild
surge. No hamlet creeps up to its base supplying a softer and
humbler note as in the other great castles of Northumberland.
Untouched by Border warfare and its battles and feuds, the
spirit of loneliness and majesty finds expression in its weather-
beaten walls.

Below the tower a small postern gate with a round, decorated
arch leads down the slope to Embleton. A few yards further on
the castle walls cease abruptly on the Gull Crag, a precipice a
hundred feet above the sea. In this headland is the famous
Rumble Churn, a perpendicular chasm hollowed out by the
crumbling of a column of the basalt. Just here the columns,
are so distinct as to resemble the more regular forms at
Iona and the Giant's Causeway. The sea rushes up this gully
with a great noise in a storm. The stones roll together violently
and a column of water spouts up. This commotion and foam,
suggestive of the movement in a gigantic churn, is the reason of
the name. In the cove beneath the castle are the quartz
crystals, locally known as Dunstanburgh diamonds. On the
shore there is a contorted limestone called the Saddle Rock.
The theory regarding it is that in a remote age two molten
streams of rock collided with each other and made this curious
formation, but there are other theories interesting to geologists.

Two miles from Dunstanburgh lies Embleton, which is reached
by taking the path by Embleton Burn and the farm of Dunstan
Steads.

The visitor to Dunstanburgh coming to Christon Bank Station
passes through this village. The church, part of which is early

Norman, was rebuilt in the thirteenth and fourteenth centuries and has much to interest the antiquarian. In the entrance porch are several grave covers ornamented with crosses and swords, and one has shears, which indicate the tomb of a female.

The vicarage has a pele tower after the manner of Elsdon and Witton, mentioned as existing in 1415.

About a mile and a half from the castle, near to Craster, is the interesting hamlet of Dunstan, near which is a Jacobean building called Proctor Steads, with an ancient pele tower attached. The lowest storey of the tower is much older than the two above, and was probably built at the same time as Dunstanburgh, as the masonry is of similar character. The walls are four feet thick. The mansion beside it was probably built by the owner of the tower when he wished a more comfortable dwelling. The dismantled castle of Dunstanburgh evidently supplied most of the stones. The name of the original owner is unknown, but on the lintel of the doorway are the letters J.P. and the date 1652, very indistinct.

Dunstan has long been the reputed birthplace of Duns Scotus, the great medieval schoolman and theologian. But, equally with Duns in Berwickshire, it sues in vain for fame, as there is no proof existing of his birthplace. As Embleton was and is in the gift of Merton College at Oxford, it is believed that he went there from Dunstan. But his name is not mentioned in the rolls at Merton either as student or professor, and the apocryphal manuscript often quoted as in the library at Merton College, which states that " this is the lecture of Duns Scotus of the hamlet of Dunstan in Embleton, sometime known as the Subtile Doctor," has never been verified at Merton.

CHAPTER XVI

FROM CRASTER TO ALNMOUTH

Howick and Howick Haven—The Longhoughton copyholders—
Bondagia and Bondager — A curious burial custom — An
irascible 18th-century vicar and his register—Boulmer and its
smugglers—Old importance of Alnmouth.

FOLLOWING the coast from Dunstanburgh's caverned shores,
fine cliffs continue rising from the sands for two miles till we
come to the little fishing village of Craster. Crab fishing is
very prosperous here, and there is a large herring-curing business.
Craster Tower, the seat of the Craster family, is a short distance
from the village. In it are incorporated the remains of an ancient
pele tower which has been from Norman times in the possession
of the Crasters. The station for Craster is Little Mill, 2½ miles
off, so that at any point the pedestrian can get the convenience
of the railway. About 1½ miles from the station is Howick
Hall, built in 1782 for Earl Grey. Originally it was a pele
tower.

A mile from Craster, Cullernose Point shows again the magnificent basaltic cliff 120 feet high. The Whin Sill, the great
igneus rock that bestows the wonderful grandeur on Dunstanburgh Castle, here cuts the coast for the last time. Its
columns do not occur again on the coast, but we shall see how
the practical ingenuity of Rome turned it to account.

About two miles further on is Howick Haven, with sands,
fine rocks and caves, where there is another Rumbling Churn.
A high tide in 1849 laid bare near Howick boathouse a submerged
forest which revealed remains of oak, hazel and alder, both
rooted and lying prone.

Before reaching Boulmer we can turn inland and visit Longhoughton, now a small agricultural village, but a place of importance in the Middle Ages. In 1569 it had no fewer than forty-seven copyholders. It may be interesting to-day, when so much is said of small-holders, to give their standing and estate. Thirty of them were the old Bondagia, for which we have no equivalent word, although the word " bondager," now meaning

Craster.

female out-worker, is probably derived from it. These holdings are described as containing a house and a husbandland of thirty acres of arable, meadow or pasture land and paying the lord thirty shillings yearly. In Longhoughton, at a very early period, the villan's services on the baron's land had been commuted to a money payment—a great stride from the times when he had to work a certain number of days on the lord's demesne. The remaining seventeen holders, called "cottagia," had a croft or garden and a selion of land with a rent varying from 2s. 2d. to 3s. 4d. The selion varied in different parts of the county, but here it was a ridge of from half an acre to an acre and a half. The names of the small proprietors are given in the Elizabethan survey, and in 1863 Mr. George Tate, to whose researches I am indebted, records that one man called Elder was still a tenant farmer in the village where his forefathers had held land. A few descendants in the female line are yet to be found.

In those early days a weekly market was held, and tradition points out where the market cross stood. Round it every corpse was carried before burial. The cross, after being lost for many years, was found in a smugglers' cave, and now crowns the east wall of the church, which was probably built soon after the Conquest. It shows early Norman work, but its most notice-able feature is the strong Early English tower, with walls five feet thick, which was erected for defence as well as for religious purposes, as there was no pele tower in the vicinity. In 1567 Longhoughton Church was still a refuge for the inhabitants against Scottish marauders. Clarkson's survey says: " The Church and steple is the great strengt, that the poor tenants have to draw to in tyme of warre ; wherefor it is ever neadfoull the same be for that and other causes kepid in good reparations."

But the student of the human document will be more intrigued by the Register kept by the Rev. George Duncan from 1696 to 1719 than in looking at a church which has little architectural beauty. He seems to have been a very irascible parson, but the characters of the villagers are stamped with true Northumbrian aberrations and pieties. The vicar spares neither dead nor living in his comments, which are sometimes in Latin, sometimes in English. To take the old name of Elder he remarks : " Henry Elder (infelix valde nuptiis) an ingenious smith of an ancient race of Longhoughton." Anne Wilson, " a poor mendicant widow," is stigmatised as " vilis ebriosa peccat." William Gray is " a hind, valde ignorans et obstinatus peccat." He buried Robert Pringle, a day labourer, in 1712, and notes, " malus filius mali patris."

In the English tongue he remarks : " Married 1706 Thomas Story (a very brutish and wicked fellow) herd of Sharplee." Another herd is even worse, married in the same year : " William

Morton is a gross, ignorant and wicked herd of Scrablees "; another herd is " very wicked and obstinate, hardened." This plays havoc with the illusion entertained by literary people of the blameless pastoral lives led by the man of the crook as he follows in solitary ways his bleating flock !   In a later register it is a relief to this dark picture to know that in 1723 he buried Barbara, the serious, good wife of James Gustard, an old and good herd. Another Gustard was also " a knowing good man."   Nicholas Davison is " a serious and religious herd."   In 1711 he buries " Mary the wife of a very honest herd and an old and long oat-meal maker."   Belief in darker powers is evinced when he records the burial of " Jinie, wife of William Grey, a quack and warlock doctor."   The fishers of Boulmer and Seaton get very bad characters.   They are all very ignorant, obstinate, profane, careless and brutish people.   At their marriages these terms are employed, but he notes, at the burial of a bachelor, " George Grey, an old innosent and fortunate fisher."   He shows a natural elation when a dissenter is brought to reason, no doubt by his own efforts.   " Buried John Egden, a very dissenter in his life, and yet (note the yet) very good charitable man ; he was some years before his death brought to be a sincere member of the Church," and his wife is called " the good widow of the good dissenter."

But dissenters are badly treated indeed by the vicar.   A webster of Longhoughton is called " a wicked knave and a dissenter," and a dissenting herd is called " a tergiverse Janus whig."   Dissenters in Northumberland are still jeeringly called whigs.   To the eccentric vicar we owe a debt for a little light on the occupations and habits of the past, but his lack of humour led him mostly to fasten on the shortcomings of his flock.   When the labourer's task was o'er, the vicar acidly recites with a black recording pen the sins that kind oblivion would cover.   If only the maligned villagers had left a retort in their candid and jocular Northumbrian style it would be deeply appreciated now.   But, alas ! few among their busy hands ever held pens, and the vicar's judgments are written above the silent dust.

About a mile from Longhoughton Station is Ratcheugh Crag, the grand basaltic columns eighty feet high and finely overhung with trees.   An observatory crowns it, from which splendid views of the coast are seen.   Two miles to the south is the beautiful Cawledge Dene, which can be followed south till coming to the road which leads to Alnwick.

Returning to the coast we reach the old fishing village of Boulmer, notorious once for smugglers, very pretty now with old cottages and the cobles on the sands and the fine background of cliff scenery and its old-fashioned fisherfolk, the descendants of those whom the irate vicar found so troublesome. He does not mention smugglers, but many a cask of spirits was landed in his day. The Border and all parts of Northumberland patronised Boulmer. An old rhyme discloses the distances

Alnmouth from the Golf Links.

travelled by farmers. The Forest is the ancient Forest of Rothbury :—

> Awd Bob Dunn o' the Forest,
> He's ridin' te Boomer for gin,
> Wi' three famed horses fra' Bushy Gap lonnin',
> But ' Kate o' the West ' is the queen o' them aa'.

Bushy Gap farmhouse had a double gable, and in the space between the walls the gin was concealed till distributed.

Three miles further south we come to the sand-dunes of Alnmouth, standing at the mouth of the river Aln, the ancient port of Alnwick. It is called Alemouth, and has undergone much

change in its spelling, but has always kept the soft " ae " sound.
Standing at the mouth of a river that was navigable by the small
craft of the day, it was early of importance as a seaport. The
bailiff of Alemouth had by royal command in 1316 to send
ships munitioned and victualled to Gascony, and in 1333 he had
to give up all ships capable of carrying fifty tuns of wine for the
defence of the realm. Two years later the town was actually
required to send three or four trustworthy men to Norwich to
take counsel for further measures. Before the Union a beacon
was maintained on the Watch Hill or Wallop Hill at the west end.

During the eighteenth century and the early nineteenth

An Alnmouth Caddy.

Alnmouth was a very flourishing
place, exporting corn, which was
kept in large granaries now used
as dwelling-houses. But it did
not evade the fate of many similar
places on the east coast. These
high, gaunt buildings with small
windows look very curious. The
export trade declined after the end
of the French wars and became
extinguished with the growth of
the railway. Now the trade of
Alnmouth has departed, and only
the fishing industry remains. In
recent days it has been best known
for its famous golf course.

The mouth of the Aln is interesting owing to the change of its
course. Formerly the Aln reached
the sea south of the Church

Hill, which was united to the town, and the Cheese Hill by a
low sandy ridge. Current and storm bore on it so strongly
that in 1806 a breach was made, and since then the river has
run into the sea on the north side. The tide flows up for a mile,
sometimes going as far as Lesbury's beautiful old bridge. On
the Church Hill was an ancient Saxon chapel dedicated to St.
Waleric, but wind and wave and wanton spoliation hastened its
decay. Probably the remains, which were blown down by a
great gale in 1806, were of an early Norman building. That there
was a Saxon foundation is proved by the discovery in 1789 of

the shaft of a Saxon cross. The sandstone slabs have a crude representation of the Crucifixion. An inscription reads : " Myredeh meh wo "—Myredeh me wrought. The other name resembles Eadulf, who seized the throne of Northumberland in 705, and Myredeh is probably the name of an Irish sculptor. A few tombstones remain of the eighteenth century.

On the Northumbrian coast, Alnmouth holds with Berwick the distinction of presenting to the traveller's eye, from the railway, a charming picture of river and sea. At Berwick the huddled red roofs rise steeply above the mouth of Tweed, but, with beauty born of murmuring sound and wide skies flashing in keen sunlight, or misty in the haar, Alnmouth sits close to the water's edge—with an intimate grace that suits its quiet history—thirty miles and more from the Walls at Berwick.

Alnmouth from the North Eastern Railway

CHAPTER XVII

THREE miles south of Alnmouth, within a short distance of the
sea, stands Warkworth. Its Hermitage is far famed and equally
so its Castle. We enter it from the north by the well-known
fourteenth-century bridge over the river which almost encircles
the little town. At the southern extremity are the remains of a
tower where gates had guarded the bridge. Passing over, on
the left is the church, and we come to the ancient village cross,
round which in the Middle Ages great markets were held.
Facing us is the wide main street with its high irregular pavements climbing up to the proud ruins of the castle which crown
the height. The village is thus hidden, and only the intimida-
ting tower of the castle surveys the immediate surrounding
country.

We first hear of Warkworth in 737, when Ceolwulf, King
of Northumberland, granted his manor of Wercerwode to
Lindisfarne, to which he himself retreated, tired of wars
and of defending his country. A hundred years later it
was seized from the monks by King Osbert. The next
notice is about 1145, when Henry II granted it to Roger,
son of Richard, the Constable of Chester. This Roger is supposed
to have been the first builder of the castle, but there is considerable uncertainty on the point, as in 1174 William the Lion did
not deign to stop there, for " weak was the Castle, the wall, and

the trench and Roger, the son of Richard, a valiant knight had it in ward but could not guard it." But Earl Duncan, with a division of the Scots, burned the church and did much damage. So that it is probable the castle is of a later date, as one would judge by the present strength of the ruins. The manor continued in the same family until the reign of Edward II. It is to be noted that at this time surnames appeared, and John Fitz Richard took the name of John de Clavering, Clavering being the name of a property acquired earlier by the family. He, it seems, was no believer in blood being thicker than water, for to the discomfiture of his relatives, being childless, for a life estate of £400 per annum he made over to Edward III the reversion of Warkworth. Thus it was that the Percies became owners of Warkworth from 1329. The King granted the barony to Henry de Percy in lieu of the hereditary custody of Berwick and an annuity of 500 marks from the port customs. It was thought that the strong castles of the north would protect the royal interests there and be a wall against the Scots. But when the Percy influence grew strong, Alnwick and Warkworth, instead of sustaining the peace in the north, grew to be centres of ambition and intrigue. In 1403 Hotspur fell at the Battle of Shrewsbury, and Warkworth, with other castles, was ordered by Henry IV to be placed " in safeguard and good governance." Warkworth and Hotspur's father refused to be reduced to submission, and Sir Henry dared to imprison a royal messenger. After further fruitless orders the King came north, and Warkworth capitulated after a brief siege. The unfortunate Sir Henry was killed at Bramham Moor in 1408. In 1415, after having been in the possession of both Sir Robert Umfraville and John, Henry IV's son, it was restored to Henry Percy, the son of Hotspur. He fell at the Battle of St. Albans, on the side of the Red Rose. His dust rests there in the noble abbey that rises on the height above the sluggish Ver, far from the lovely banks of Coquet.

The next owner died on the field of Towton. None of the later possessors seems to have died in bed. I do not know if fate was kinder to the fifth earl, surnamed the Magnificent, who was so remarked upon by the chronicler of the marriage of Princess Margaret, Henry VIII's sister, to James of Scotland.

In 1670, on the death of Josceline, the eleventh earl, without male issue, Warkworth, with the other estates, devolved to

Algernon, eldest son of the Duke of Somerset through his marriage
with the heiress, with remainder to his son-in-law, Sir Hugh
Smithson, who in due course succeeded and whose descendants
are the present family.   The castle appears to have fallen into
decay about the middle of the sixteenth century.   The lead was
removed from the towers, and permission was obtained by a man

The Coquet and Warkworth Castle.

called Clarke to take the materials from the keep to build himself
a mansion at Cherton.   Clarke actually employed 272 " waynes,"
and the forced labour of the tenants at Warkworth and elsewhere,
to carry out his wanton spoliation.   It is only by the loving
labour of later possessors that the ruins still retain part of their
magnificent original effect.

The outside walls and towers are for the most part considered to be the earliest work, probably begun by Roger Fitz Richard. We now enter the quadrangle by the postern gate, but the principal entrance was by the gatehouse, from which the court-

The Lion Tower, Warkworth Castle.

yard was seen as an irregular triangle terminating in the keep. " A marvellous proper donjon " of which Grose says, in his antiquities, " nothing could be more magnificent and pictur-esque." In the foreground are the remains of a mysterious unfinished church, or college, of unknown date. Masons' marks

N

may be traced on every stone and are worth observing.   On the
right hand, on the east of the curtain wall, the most distant tower
is called the Grey Mare's Tail.   A brewhouse and bakery on the
eastern gable are connected with it.   At the south-east corner is
the Montagu Tower.   On the south-west is the Lion Tower, with
mutilated blazonings of Percy, Lucy, and Herbert, and the fragment of the grim lion which has given the name to the tower.
To the west of the gatehouse are the remains of a chapel which
adjoins the Crakefergus Tower.   It had been part of the defensive system of the first builder, but in later times was used as a
place of residence.   From the chapel a stairway leads to what is
known as the Great Chamber, and thence by a passage to
Crakefergus and to the adjoining pantries and kitchen.
This range of buildings lies between the little postern gate
and the gatehouse.   But the chief object of interest is the
remarkable keep, which is regarded as a perfect model of
architectural skill, particularly in its domestic convenience.   It
is situated on rising ground considerably above the level of the
other buildings.   Freeman finds it "a good study of the progress
by which the purely military castle gradually passed into the
house fortified for any occasional emergency."   Its value is in
its unaltered contour and the internal domestic arrangements so
interesting to the mind that would construct the past
and the figures that peopled it.   The interior is a most
wonderful example of medieval domestic architecture.   On
the ground floor is the dungeon, and cellars with stone
tanks for collecting water, which was led from the roof
by conductors fixed in the impluvium, which an ancient
survey calls " a lantern which both receyveth and hath convey-
ance from the same, and also giveth light to certain lodgings in
some parts."   From this the staircase then leads to the great
chamber and the chapel and banqueting hall, forty-one feet long,
and rising to the top of the keep.   At the west end, doorways
lead to the kitchens and pantries.   A central slender turret or
look-out rises thirty-two feet above the roof, consisting of three
floors, and is a noticeable feature in distant views.   From other
sources, particularly the minute description of Mr. Bates in the
" History of Northumberland," the visitor can reconstruct the
interior of this marvellous "donjon."   It was probably built by
the first Earl of Northumberland when Warkworth became the
favourite residence of the Percies.   Several scenes in " Henry

IV " are laid at Warworth Castle, which Shakespeare calls "this worm-eaten hold of ragged stone"—probably a true description of it in his day, but inapplicable to the castle as Hotspur must have known it.

Half a mile up the river, on the north side, is the famous Hermitage. It is a lovely walk. Crossing by the ferry, a flight of steps, roughly cut out of the sandstone, leads into the rock-hewn retreat, which is entered by a little porch with stone seats. Above the entrance is a weather-beaten sculpture of the Crucifixion. Just inside, looking up, is the worn inscription : " Fuerunt mihi lacrymae meae panes nocte ac die "—" Tears have been my bread day and night." Ineffably poignant these words always are, but doubly so when we picture the solitary grief immured there :—

> The long mechanic pacings to and fro.
> The set grey life and apathetic end.

The first decoration the eye rests upon is an altar with two crosses and an aperture in the wall above for the pyx, and on the wall is also the faint outline of a head surrounded with an aureole. In the recess is a three-quarter length figure of a man with upraised hand kneeling at the feet of a reclining female figure and separated from him by a rudely designed bull's head. To the left of her is a cherub or child. Facing them is a traceried window of the fourteenth century which lights the inner apartment, to which we pass through a doorway over which, on a shield, are the emblems of the Passion, " the cross, the crown, the spear," and also nails and a sponge. The inner chapel is merely a tunnelled chamber with steps to an altar now demolished. It has a recess for a seat or bed. The chamber was probably a dormitory, but the use of the three rooms must be conjectural. The two altars may be accounted for by the supposition that one was used as a private oratory and one as a public chapel, and the traceried window may have been for purposes of confession.

Outside are a mill and an orchard, and in modern times fruit trees have been said to have grown in it. But the only early record about the Hermitage is in 1531, when the Earl of Northumberland made a grant to George Lancastre, a priest, of " myn Armytage belded in a rock of stone within my Parke of Warkworth." The story which has popular favour on its side is that told by Bishop Percy. Bertram of Bothal (who was a friend of Hotspur's father) loved Isabel, daughter of Lord Widdrington.

The lady wished to test his devotion, and sent him a helmet which he had to prove "where sharpest blows are tried." He of course rode out with Lord Percy to make a raid on their ancient enemies over the Border. Being wounded, cleft through the precious casque, he was taken to Wark to recover. Isabel, possibly reflecting that " 'twas not love but vanity dealt Love a blow like this," hastens to nurse him. Near the Cheviots she is taken captive by an enamoured Scottish chieftain and carried to his stronghold. Bertram, quickly recovering, starts with her brother to rescue her, they taking different directions. He finds the place, and, waiting for an opportunity to enter, he sees one night his love descend a rope ladder with a youth in Scottish garb. He shouts out and, rushing forward, confused with jealousy, attacks the youth. The lady calls out, recognising his voice ; but too late. Flinging herself forward to avert the blow, she also is fatally wounded, and he hears from her dying lips that she had been rescued by her own brother. So, filled with penitence and grief, he hews out the Hermitage to pass his remaining days.

Warkworth Church was founded by Ceolwulf. During excavations a Saxon cross was discovered, which is preserved in the chancel. The present building dates from the twelfth century and stands on the south bank of the Coquet. Later a tower was added which was finished by a stone spire, the only other medieval example in Northumberland of one being at Newbiggin. The porch also was an afterthought, and the room above was used until a century ago as the village school. The vestry is worth inspecting. It was probably once the habitat of an anchorite, as a window was opened out which may have been a confessional. In the south aisle lies the figure of a knight with hands clasped, clad in armour of mail and plates, probably fourteenth-century. He is supposed to be Sir Hugh of Morwick, who gave the common to Warkworth.

In 1174 a division of William the Lion's army burnt Warkworth and, with shocking barbarities, put to death three hundred men, women, and children who had taken refuge in the church. An excessively large number of human bones, thought to be those of the victims, were found inside the building during alterations. The chronicle of Fantôme records the intention of these northern Huns.

> Let us allow our Scots to waste the sea-coast.
> Woe to them if they leave standing a house or a church.

Possibly this church was the old Saxon one, and after such desecration was rebuilt, as the beautiful chancel which formed the original church nave is supposed to date from a year or two later.

About two miles from Warkworth is Morwick Hall, formerly a property of the Greys of Howick. Going through a field to the east and descending to the Coquet by a steep bank midway between two ancient fords, the lower one still being called Paupersford, a perpendicular cliff of sandstone is seen. On it are engraved strange circles and spiral characters similar to others in the county, as at Old Bewick, Doddington, and Rowting Linn. These, however, occur on rocks on moors, but the Morwick drawings are just above sea level. Over the ford is the road leading to the south, on which was stationed a camp to guard it. At a bend of the river stands Morwick Mill, which has been painted on many canvases.

The Hermitage on the Coquet at Warkworth.

CHAPTER XVIII

AMBLE TO CULLERCOATS

The Song of Amble—Coquet Island—Its eccentric hermit—Hauxley
—Druridge Bay—Widdrington—Hero of Chevy Chase—Wid-
drington Tower—A French landing—Chibburn Preceptory
—Newbiggin—Seaton Sluice and the Delavals.

THROUGH fertile fields the Coquet pursues its course to the sea
from Warkworth. On the south of the wide estuary stands the
busy town of Amble, and at high tide the gleaming waters and the
shipping make a fine picture, whilst beyond on the heaving sea
is Coquet Island with its conspicuous whitewashed lighthouse.

Amble is of ancient origin as a township. On the links have
been found a prehistoric burial place, and at Gloster Hill, adjoining,
some traces of Roman occupation. The Priory of Tynemouth
was endowed with the tithes of Amble in 1090, one of the earliest
records of its existence. It possessed a Benedictine monastery,
and the remains of the interesting pre-Reformation manor house
are still to be seen. Now it is encircled by collieries, to which it
owes its prosperity and shipping. The town claims a song which
is usually associated with Falmouth, but the reference to the
north certainly gives Amble a strong claim to it, and the tune is
called a characteristic Northumberland one, although, apart from
Tyneside and its many ballads, we are not aware of much tune-
fulness in our northernmost county. The first verse goes :

> Oh, Amble is a fine town, with ships upon the bay ;
> And I wish with my heart I was only there to-day ;
> And I wish with my heart I was far away from here,
> A-sitting in my parlour and talking to my dear.
> And it's home, dearie, home ! Oh, it's home I want to be !
> My top sails are hoisted and I must out to sea.
> For the oak, and the ash, and the bonnie rowan tree
> They're all a'growing green in the North Countree.
> Oh ! It's home, dearie, home.

A mile off shore is Coquet Island, sixteen acres in extent, where from very early times had been a cell for Benedictine monks. Some Saxon relics have been found on it, which point to remote civilisation—a coin of the Emperor Valerian, a ring with an old English rune, possibly ninth century, a bronze buckle, and an enamelled ornament. In Elizabethan days it became the resort of lawless folk and money-coiners, and during the Civil War was taken by the Scots. Leland says that " The Isle of Coquet standeth upon a very good vayne of secoles ; and at the ebbe,

The Pier at Amble.

men digge in the shore by the clives " ; and a writer in 1747 describes it : " Coquet Island lies at the mouth of the River of that name where was anciently a castle with a Monastery but both have been long demolished, and here are no habitations but Hutts for the Diggers of Sea-coal. Vast flocks of wild fowl continually harbour and lay their eggs on this island, by the sale of which the fishermen make great advantages as well as by the fish which they catch here in abundance." After storms coal is often washed up on Amble shore. At the building of the lighthouse (in which is incorporated the vault of the old tower) the terns and eider duck disappeared and the seals which used to inhabit the north end of the island were shot down.   The light-house is eighty feet high and the intermittent light is visible four-teen miles off, whilst an explosive fog signal warns the mariner in thick weather on this dangerous coast.   Two picturesque incidents Bates records about Coquet Island.   In 684 Elfled, Abbess of Whitby, asked St. Cuthbert to meet her on the island

Coquet Island, from Amble.

to discuss her brother King Egfred's affairs.   He told her that the King had only a year to live and would be succeeded by another whom she would also regard as a brother.   " Thou seest this great and broad sea, how it aboundeth in islands.   It is easy for God to provide someone out of one of these to be set over the Kingdom of the English."   Elfled thought he referred to a reputed son of her father, Oswi.

At a later date Robert Fitz-Roger, at Warkworth, had a curious dispute with an eccentric hermit of Coquet Island called Martin.

The latter built a windmill, which infuriated the lord of the manor, and he sent men with mattocks and axes to destroy it in the sight of the terrified Martin, but the chronicler adds that it was a strange fancy for a professed hermit to indulge in, as mills, like shows, were apt to harbour promiscuous society. So poor Martin, enlivening his solitude with a little worldly speculation, was quickly chastened by the jealous knight who reigned at Warkworth.

The fishing village of Hauxley is a little to the south of Amble. It has a lifeboat station above the rocky entrance to its harbour, and beyond it are the Bondicarr Rocks and Druridge Bay. There is now a flourishing coalfield near it. Until the beginning of the nineteenth century the only industries were fishing and the burning of kelp, which was made from the seaweed in summer. The kelp was dried in the sun, and after being treated by fire was sold to glass and soap manufacturers. On the links, where it was dried, one of the latest smugglers is commemorated by a hill called Tom Forsyth's Hill. Forsyth operated even in the nineteenth century, and forty horses have been seen there awaiting the arrival of the lugger. In those days too it was thought to be an ill winter that brought no wrecks, and within memory is the story of the old fishwife who, after a suspension of shipwrecks, shut her cat up in the cupboard to bring luck.

In the village street is a cottage with a moulded window and a doorhead with the date 1600—all that remains of the original mansion of the Widdringtons. At Hauxley Hall, a hundred years ago, lived one of the Surtees, a partner in a Newcastle bank that failed. He was so afraid of arrest that he never came out except on Sundays, and had a shuttered lattice in the outer door so that callers could be observed and interrogated from it. The Whitehouse sands at Hauxley preserve the recollection of the white-painted hut where a lieutenant and a few bluejackets lived during the Napoleonic Wars watching for the advance ships of the disturber of European peace.

From the Bondicarr rocks extends the fine half-circle of Druridge Bay, with beautiful white sands rich in shells.

Turning inland from Amble or Warkworth, or by following a road leading from Druridge Bay, about two miles from the coast, is the village of Widdrington. The station is on the main line, but the village is a mile and a half off. Chevy Chase has handed down to us for ever the memory of Widdrington, the doughty

" Squyar of Northumbarlonde Ric. Wytharyngton was his nam."

> It shall never be told in Sothe Ynglonde, he says
> To kyng Henry the fourth for sham.
> I wat yone byn great lordes twan
> I am a poor squyar of lande ;
> I wyll never se my captayne fyght on a fylde
> And stande myselfe and loocke on.
>
>   .   .   .
>
> For Wytharyngton my harte was wo,
> That ever he slayne shulde be,
> For when both his leggis were hewyne in to
> Yet he knyled and fought on hys kni.

The splendid tower of Widdrington, built in 1341, with lofty battlements, was ruthlessly levelled in 1777, and the shooting box which replaced it has also been demolished.   The Widdringtons were devoted to the Stuarts, and taking part in the ill-fated rebellion of 1715, their estates were forfeited to the Crown. Robert Carey, in his hasty ride to Edinburgh to take the news of Elizabeth's death to the least admirable of the Stuarts, stopped at Widdrington and proclaimed King James.   He had left London after nine in the morning and reached Widdrington the next night.   It was the first place the King drew rein at after leaving Berwick in April 1603, and he was entertained there by Sir Robert Carey and "his virtuous ladye."   Less than a hundred years ago there was a curious tradition that Widdrington had at one time been devastated by a foreign invasion.   It has been proved that the French landed on the coast by the following extract from the parish book of Billingham, in the county of Durham :

July 31st 1692.   Collected in ye parish church of Billingham in ye Countie pallatine of Durham, for a briefe for ye inhabitants of Druidge, Widdrington, Chibborne, for a losse by ye French landing there, three shillings, seven pence.

No history book refers to this, and it would be interesting to know if any remembrance of a two-centuries-ago panic in these hamlets was awakened with the threat of the German invasion recently, and if particular precautions were taken at Druridge Bay.   The lieutenant and his bluejackets at Whitehouse sands must surely have hastened to the assistance of Widdrington. What a pity no local chronicler or letter-writer mentions it, or the garrulous pen of Longhoughton's vicar, a century later, might have preserved some story of this historic and unnoticed incident.

Widdrington Church stands on a knoll within the same field where the tower once was, and dates from the latter part of the twelfth century. The chancel and south aisle and south door are fourteenth-century, and in the wall is a piscina of a date no later than 1200. On the north side of the chancel are two recesses which have evidently contained effigies of the Widdringtons ; over the arch of one is the Widdrington arms. There are two old grave covers with crosses engraved in the church. The learned John Horsley, the first historian of Northumberland, was the Nonconformist minister of Widdrington at the beginning of the eighteenth century. The romance of the name Widdrington is attached solely to the family of that name. After hundreds of years' possession they lost all through loyalty to the Jacobite cause. The village is not very interesting.

About a mile from Widdrington is Chibburn Preceptory, a house of the Knights of St. John of Jerusalem, standing in rich meadows where the Chibburn runs to the sea about half a mile off. This Order originated in the twelfth century, and Chibburn was probably founded by a Widdrington in the fourteenth. The buildings originally enclosed a courtyard and were defended by a moat, of which there are remains on the west and south sides. Part of the interior, which was the chapel, is now a stable, and behind the manger at the east end are the traces of a piscina. On the west side is a block still inhabited. This had been used as a dower house by the Widdrington family. There is much speculation about the dates of the various parts and the uses of the buildings, and it is all of extraordinary interest. There are several ornamented doorways, and some old woodwork. It is unfortunate that it has been adapted now for labourers to live in; but even so, the chants of the Knights Hospitallers, antique, pious figures, still echo for the solitary listener across the fields.

Towards the southern extremity of Druridge Bay is the fishing village of Cresswell, and looking out to sea from among the trees is the old pele tower of Cresswell. Druridge Bay terminates in the reef at Snab Point, a dangerous rocky coast and the scene of many shipwrecks and brave rescues. Walking along the coast to Newbiggin we pass the Lyne sands, where is a small hamlet called Lyne, and a stream of the same name enters the sea. The large fishing village of Newbiggin, now also a popular watering-place, is only interesting

for the prominent position on the promontory of Newbiggin
Point of the Church of St. Bartholomew. It is the sailor's
notable landmark here. Part of the churchyard has been
crumbled away by the waves and the bones of the dead scattered
much in the same way as the sea has undermined Dunwich on
the Suffolk coast. South of the mouth of the Wansbeck,
with Cambois and North Seaton on either side, the sandy coast
stretches to the busy town and harbour of Blyth, where the
Blyth enters the sea after a short course of twenty miles. It

Blyth Harbour.

flows past Belsay and then, uniting with the Pont, winds through
the lovely vale of Stannington and the " sounding woods " of
Plessey referred to in " Marmion." A stretch of sand dunes
swept and torn by the wind continues to Seaton Sluice. A
feature of the coast between the Blyth and Tyne is the common
occurrence of landslips, usually after heavy rainfall. Seaton
Sluice used to be an important harbour and bears witness to the
enterprise of the Delaval family in the past. One of them
placed large sluice gates on the burn which the incoming tide

closed. When the tide retreated, the strong current opening
the gates carried all before it and thus twice a day washed the
haven clean. A later Delaval made a great cutting to the
harbour through the solid sandstone cliff. All along the coast-
line are prettily wooded denes bordering the streams which
rush to the sea. They form a welcome break in these dreary
colliery districts. The Abbess in " Marmion," as she sailed to

Seaton Sluice.

Lindisfarne, " marked amidst its trees the hall of lofty Seaton
Delaval." This magnificent mansion was built by Sir John
Vanbrugh, the great architect of Blenheim. The first castle,
long razed, was begun by Hamon de Laval, one of the companions of the Conqueror, who obtained these lands as reward
for his services in subjugating England. Vanbrugh's house
suffered from two fires and is now partially ruined.

The little chapel to Our Lady, near it, possibly built in the twelfth century, has a claim to be considered of Saxon origin. This is the opinion of J. E. Morris, who calls it the most interesting ecclesiastical structure in Northumberland. Another authority regards it as a pure and perfect specimen of Norman architecture. Above the west door are six shields with the arms of the Delavals, and the walls are decorated with armour, tattered banners, and escutcheons. There are two recumbent figures, one of a knight in armour, the other a female figure, each with a dog at its feet, Delavals, possibly, of the fourteenth century.

High cliffs from Seaton Sluice continue past Hartley, a quaint village with red-tiled roofs, and beyond it is a continuous stretch of popular coast resorts.

At Whitley Sands, a great resort of trippers, are fine table rocks. All the sea-front here has assumed a suburban aspect, although at Cullercoats the picturesque fishwives strike a primitive note. It is singularly refreshing amidst the bustle of Newcastle Station to see one of these brown-faced, hatless women, largely petticoated, with her creel giving out as she passes the too distinct smell of fins and scales.

Cullercoats.

CHAPTER XIX

SEVENTY miles stretches the changing, picturesque, historic
coast from Lamberton to the mouth of the Tyne, where, on a high
cliff, stands the last goodly tower of Northumberland. The
Magnesian Limestone which forms the headland here rises a
hundred feet. The arrangement by which castle and priory
adjoin speaks to-day of ancient invasion, the wild pillaging
Norseman, the frightened Saxon monks, and the joy with which
after much tribulation they saw rising the embattled walls of
warrior protectors. Their thankful praises may also have risen
many times when another potent ally, the sea, pounced in
wrath on the pirates' galleys. Between them and the fishermen's shiels (now the black coal district, North Shields) lay
the treacherous reef of the Black Middens, where many a
brave ship has met its doom.

It was in 627 that Edwin selected this bold promontory for
a site for a timber chapel, and his daughter, who had the sweet
name of Rosella, took the veil. Oswald rebuilt it with stone about
ten years later, and here was buried the body of King Oswyn,
who became the patron saint in 651. The Danish marauders
burnt it in the reign of Egfrid, who restored it. Then in 865 they
appeared again. The terrible rumours of their doings drove
hither the poor nuns from St. Hilda's Convent at Hartlepool in a
panic, hoping for refuge. They, alas ! were " translated by mar-
tyrdom to Heaven." But the monks clung to the sacred spot.

It proves no common test of courage to live defenceless in such a conspicuous position, for it was devastated again in 870 and 876. During the next two centuries it was probably unused. In 1075 it was given by Earl Waltheof to the monks of Jarrow, and the monastery was rebuilt some years later. However, Robert de Mowbray, the succeeding Earl, quarrelled with them and travelled to St. Albans for monks to fill it, a signal proof of the high-handed methods of the Norman barons. Until the Dissolution in 1539 the Priory of St. Mary remained a cell of St. Albans monastery, which caused much dispute and annoyance to the great Durham establishment. The principal ruins now are of the church, for, after the dismantling, the monastic buildings perished with the exception of a part that was either the prior's or the guest house. Apparently the church was allowed to decay, and this neglect has deprived us of one of the finest examples of ecclesiastical architecture in Northumberland. It was used for service as late as 1668. In it was buried, in 1093, Malcolm Canmore and his son Edward, killed at the siege of Alnwick.

In a previous raid into Northumberland, in 1091, Malcolm so reduced the country that, even when he was driven over the border, the lack of provisions continued acute, and the victorious force had to hasten to Tynemouth, which was the storehouse for the unfortunate Northumbrians, as it enjoyed the Peace of St. Oswin. The monks went out to meet their countrymen bearing the shrine of St. Oswin and praying them to respect his Peace. One of the knights, piously conscientious, called Nigel de Wast, was in the act of vowing he would not eat of the rich store till he was assured of the saint's forgiveness, when another, annoyed at his scrupulousness, cannoned into his horse, and both it and the rider vanished over the steep cliff. But St. Oswin was watching, for they both miraculously escaped unhurt. That he was a dangerous saint to trespass against had been also proved in the previous year, when the Conqueror was returning from Scotland, where he had forced Malcolm to do him homage. The new castle was not then built further up the Tyne, but he stopped at Pons Aelii, the old Roman fort where now Newcastle hums. The river was in flood. There was little food, for Malcolm never left much behind him. Fodder was urgently required, and a band of warriors was sent to pillage Tynemouth, to which, as usual, the stores had been removed. But by the time the leader saw the

church on the cliff he had discovered that a miserable fate
stalked those who violated St. Oswin's patrimony. In spite
of warnings, some of the soldiers took the forage, and madness
attacked the horses who ate it. Even the knight's charger had
unwittingly brought the curse on itself. But its master offering
his best cloak at St. Oswin's shrine, the faithful quadruped
recovered its reason.

Robert de Mowbray was glad to seek sanctuary in St. Mary's
after his futile rebellion against Rufus. Here also Edward
II's favourite Piers Gaveston sought sanctuary from the
triumphant barons. To Tynemouth, when Herebald, the friend
of Bede, was Abbot, we owe the early portion of Symeon of
Durham's history of the kingdom. A notable scholar was the
monk John of Tynemouth, who lived during Edward III's reign
and was vicar of the parish church. The treasures of the library
which he had probably helped to collect were scattered at the
Dissolution, and only one fragment of it is authenticated now, a
Latin psalter in the British Museum, known as the " Book of S.
Oswyn." There were also sixty-two ounces of gold plate, and
1,827 ounces of silver in the monastery when it was closed and
Robert Blakeney, the Prior, and his eighteen monks left it for
ever. Its importance can be judged by the yearly value,
returned as £309 15s. o½d., a great income when Henry VIII
ruled.

Leading from the ruined Priory at the east end of the presbytery
is the Oratory or Percy Chapel, built early in the fifteenth century,
and the only part that is in complete preservation. It has an
image of the Virgin over the west doorway and an extremely
complicated ribbing on the vaulted roof, with decorations of a
circle of angels blowing trumpets and the Saviour in the midst,
and also figures of the Apostles. There are sculptured heraldic
bearings of the Percies in this chapel, which was probably built
as a memorial to a Percy. The castle had been vested in the
Priory for the latter's protection since the fourteenth century,
the gatehouse being built by John of Wheathampstead, the well-
known Abbot of St. Albans. During the Civil War it was visited
by Charles, and was then well fortified. The Royalist garrison
had to surrender to the Scots in 1644 and Colonel Lilburn was
left in charge. He, however, declared for Charles, and a force
was sent to capture it. Lilburn was slain and the castle was
carried by storm. In 1681 it was in a ruinous state with a small

O

garrison. The defence of the Tyne is a different matter now. At Tynemouth during the war one wondered what Haldane the Viking would have done had he come up against the wire-netting erected to stop the landing of Germans.

Old Tynemouth with its wide old-fashioned street is a pleasant countrified village and in great contrast to the towns with which it is surrounded. It looks like the cool green spaces amidst the roar of London. Over seventy years ago Harriet Martineau lived and wrote there for a time. Behind the Spanish Battery and looking across the terrible Black Middens is a monument to Lord Collingwood with four guns of the *Royal Sovereign*, one of Northumberland's great sons and Nelson's friend. There is also the fine monument to him in St. Paul's and in St. Nicholas's Cathedral in Newcastle.

There are two magnificent piers, four hundred yards apart, with two lighthouses. One hundred and fifty years ago a coal fire burned in Tynemouth's old lighthouse instead of a lamp. The north pier is nearly a mile long and the south pier rather longer. There are three other lighthouses, the Groyne on the Herd Sands, visible for seven miles, and the High and Low Lights of North Shields, visible for thirteen miles. They show the danger to shipping at the Tyne entrance. It is related that St. Cuthbert, as a lad, had wandered to North Shields (in early times a collection of fishing shiels, hence the modern name) and had the courage to rebuke the heartless heathen dwellers there who were hilarious at the spectacle of five boats manned by monks who had almost got to the opposite bank of Tyne being swept to sea by a sudden westerly gale. Opposite Tynemouth, where stood a small oratory belonging to the priory, is St. Mary's Island. There is now a magnificent lighthouse, 120 feet high, built on the site of the old chapel, from which it is said the monks showed a light to guide mariners. We can fancy the offerings made at the shrine of St. Oswin by the grateful seamen who had navigated in bad weather this dangerous river mouth. Whilst the rude population that dwelt on these shores even entreated the Deity with raised hands to send them wrecks, the monks ceaselessly preached love and mercy. On this bitter coast they must have led a hard, toiling life in the days before riches and ease came to enervate them. The population would be apt to be hostile, and they were defenceless against alien foes. On that cliff those noble walls must often have sheltered the wet, exhausted sailors escaped from the icy sea that beats against the last massive cliff of Northumberland's changeful coast.

The legend of the Monks' Stone near the Priory would give scoffers another picture of monkish life. This is a sandstone

Doorway at Tynemouth Priory.

pillar, the remains of an ancient cross, at the base of which used to be the words so familiar in the neighbourhood :

> O horrid dede
> To kill a man for a pigg's hede.

The explanation is as follows. A monk from Tynemouth went once to Seaton Delaval, and in the kitchen a pig was roasting, the favourite food apparently of the master. The monk wanted the head and the cook represented the impossibility of his desire.

O 2

When his back was turned the monk cut off the head—was not the smell and crackling irresistible, as Ho-ti found out when he had to burn his house to get it ?   He ran off with it, hoping to get to the monastery, six miles away, before the theft was known to the master.   At Monkseaton a house is still shown where he rested.   Delaval came home from the hunt and was furious at the loss of his titbit.   He mounted his horse, and, galloping, came up to the monk, whom he belaboured so hard that he could not reach the monastery.   The brethren going in search found him half dead.   He was carried, poor lover of good things, to the Priory, and his death taking place within a year and a day, it was asserted that the beating caused it.   Delaval was charged by the monks with the murder, and before he could receive absolution, was obliged to make over certain lands to the monastery and to set up this cross, always known as the Rode Stane, in expiation of his violence.   Thus the holy men got their own back, and this curious stone remains for posterity to ponder on the frailties that linger in the dedicated soul.

Tynemouth Priory from Cullercoats.

CHAPTER XX

NEWCASTLE-ON-TYNE

A great commercial city—Present inhabitants and old times—The famous monastery of the Black Friars—The Cathedral—The eye of the North—History of the Castle—The Black Gate—Neglect in eighteenth century—The old walls—Mr. Grainger, Mr. Clayton and the modern streets—The Hancocks and natural history museum—the genius of old Newcastle as seen in its "characters" and song writers—Still "Canny New-cassle."

NEWCASTLE'S paramount claim to attention is that in the whole world there is not a more stirring monument to human energy than is presented by the town and its river, the Tyne. It has been shown that distinction has been achieved at a price, but the price has not been too great. To say otherwise would be to reverse the highest praise bestowed on " Men, my brothers, men the workers." The fitting eulogy of Newcastle would be a recital of the names of the great shipbuilding and other works on the Tyne, the array of inventions and discoveries which trod hot on the heels of Stephenson's first locomotive, and the bulk of goods manufactured by those armies of labour which man the innumerable works. To do that adequately would necessitate the production of statistics easily accessible and not very suitable for these pages.

Newcastle is not a creation of yesterday. Its merchant princes were famous in the Middle Ages, only its advance was enormously accelerated during the latter half of the nineteenth century. It was not until 1850 that the River Tyne Commission was formed as an outcome of a feeling that improvement was possible and indeed imperative. Before that was the hour of the keelman and his local anthem :

> Oh weel may the keel row, the keel row
> Oh weel may the keel row
> The boat that my lad's in.

The keel was a barge used for loading ships where there were few docks and the quays lacked the mechanical facilities. To-day the occupation of the keelman is gone. Until 1850 or thereabouts the Tyne retained much of its ancient character. Wilderness and moorland had given place to agricultural land on its banks, but the stream itself was shallow and in other respects unfit for navigation. The magnificent harbour of Tynemouth with its Black Middens remained as dangerous as it was when, according to Bede, Cuthbert performed the miracle of saving the men on a sinking ship. The North Pier was begun in 1854, completed in 1893, destroyed in 1897 and since rebuilt. During the same period the channel was deepened, the banks straightened, docks built, the first being the Northumberland and Albert Edward Dock, and the difficult, dangerous river mouth was transformed into a magnificent harbour in which a navy could ride in safety. Newcastle at length was in a position to take full advantage of the illimitable resources which nature had provided on either bank of the Tyne. " Men, my brothers, men, the workers " had conquered the apparently insurmountable obstacles to progress. It was regrettable but inevitable that much of historic value should be swept aside in the process. Many traces of the Roman Wall and even of the City Wall disappeared. Yet much remains to recall the city's dramatic and stirring history.

Newcastle is a pleasant town for a ramble. Long ago when I used to go there from the country it impressed me only as a welter of streets full of people in a hurry. Then during a prolonged visit there came an understanding of the reason why the inhabitants are so proud of it. By the by, if any reader wishes to explore it methodically he will find an abundance of literature to assist him. The local guide-book published by Reid is excellent, and so is the chapter on it in Tomlinson's Guide to the county. I must be content to record a few personal impressions. One of them is that the manners of the place have changed much and for the better since the time of John Wesley. In his Journal he says of the population of the Sandgate : " So much drunkenness, cursing and swearing even from the mouths of little children do I never

The Friary, Newcastle.

remember to have seen or heard before in so short a compass of time." It is getting on for two hundred years since that was written, and it holds good no longer. North country people have not the polite manners of the south. They do not " sir " you or touch their caps. With them the bob and curtsey have long gone out of fashion. But they make up for it in genuine kindness and intelligence. I remember once asking a Lincoln-shire rustic if Oliver Cromwell had not fought a battle near Somersby, and his answer was that he " did not know the name—it must have been afore my time." But along the Roman Wall, any day, labourers can talk to the point about the Romans in Britain, and in the slummiest part of Newcastle

Half-timbered Houses in Newcastle.

I have been astonished at the knowledge of local history. Once, indeed, a tatterdemalion showed me to the old stone steps leading to the upper story of the Guildhall in the Sandhill, and spoke of John Wesley's visits to Newcastle. Nor did he hang about afterwards for a tip. One can go nowhere in Newcastle without meeting someone able to perform a similar office.   The same man showed me the house near the Guildhall from which Jack Scott, afterwards Lord Eldon, carried off Bessy Surtees— a very consenting party, who had let herself down with a ladder for the purpose of eloping.   She was the daughter of Aubone Surtees the Banker, and this happened in 1772.

Doorway, The Friary, Newcastle.

Nothing is pleasanter than to hang about the old streets near the quay and river and peer up the narrow entries called " chares."   If their glory has departed it has left no melancholy behind, any more than there is in the modest villa which a man advancing in the way of prosperity forsakes for a mansion. Up to a hundred years ago the notabilities still lingered by the Tyne and had private residences and public offices there. They left only because quickening trade made demand on

the shore. In a street called the Side—a real Northumbrian
name—is the house in which Lord Collingwood was born. Only
a public-house now, it is remembered for the sake of Nelson's
friend and a national hero. In Low Friar Street is a building

Doorway and Friary, Newcastle.

of the greatest historic interest. It is the Smiths' Hall, and
bears over a door the motto :

By hammer and hand
All Artes do stand.

John Balliol, in 1334, as King of Scotland, did homage here to Edward I as his overlord. For this was part of the famous monastery of the Black Friars.

As interesting as the Wynds and closes of old Edinburgh are the corresponding " chares " of Newcastle. They are a lasting joy to those who like to dawdle where chance leads in the

Castle and Cathedral, Newcastle, from Gateshead.

knowledge that they must inevitably hide something with the charm of antiquity or interesting association attached to it.

The church of St. Nicholas was made a Cathedral in 1881 when the Bishopric of Durham was divided in two. It is certain from internal evidence that it stands upon the site of an older church, perhaps on that of the Saxon monks of Monkchester.

The previous edifice was destroyed by fire in 1216. In all likelihood its replacement began immediately, since there is

St. Nicholas Cathedral.

a thirteenth-century capital of a pillar embedded in part of the masonry, and there are other relics of the ancient building.

At any rate the present church was finished in 1350, except the famous steeple.

The latter was put up by one of the earliest of the many

Newcastle from Gateshead.

public men connected with Newcastle, Robert de Rhodes, lawyer and member of Parliament. Original and beautiful, the lantern spire stands on a well-built tower. It was erected in 1435 and was imitated in succeeding churches such as St. Giles in Edinburgh, the church at Linlithgow, and the College Tower in Aberdeen. Wren copied it also in St. Dunstan's-in-the East.

History records many dramatic scenes in St. Nicholas, but they are too well known to bear repetition. Some of them show that war has always been very much the same. Sir John Marley, who was Mayor in 1644, when Newcastle offered so sturdy a defence to the Scottish under General Leslie, was the prototype of those gallant mayors of Belgian towns whom the Germans could not intimidate. When Leslie threatened to blow the lantern steeple to bits he retorted by putting his Scottish prisoners under it. Newcastle's motto refers to her gallant defence at that siege. It was originally " Fortiter defendendo triumphat "—" she glories in her brave defence," but it was watered down, or at least changed, to the present form : " Fortiter defendit triumphans."

Another scene, that between King Charles and a Scottish minister, must ever find a place in the records of the church. The ill-bred minister, insulting the captive, gave out the fifty-second psalm :

> Why dost thou tyrant boast thyself
> Thy wicked works to praise ?

Whereupon the King rose and called for the fifty-sixth :

> Have mercy, Lord, on me, I pray,
> For men would me devour.

This the congregation sang with fervour. A regrettable incident in the history of the church occurred in 1784 and 1785, when, in pursuance of a plan for turning it into " a sort of a Cathedral," much that was ancient and venerable was destroyed. Such tombstones as were not claimed, or belonged to families then extinct, were sold by the churchwardens to a postmaster who was building a house in Hew Street, in the foundations of which they are buried. It was an outcome of the time rather than of the locality, and could be paralleled with very similar occurrences in other parts of the country. Only in recent times have people come to value such survivals and monuments of the past.

On the other hand the town has always been proud of its great church—" the eye of the North," as Grey called it in his Chorographia. It has been enshrined in a very popular Tyneside song, one that used to be sung over the whole county.

Div you mind of St. Nicholas Church ma pet
And the clock with the fiery fyece.

The Bigg Market.

This is a variant due probably to a lapse of memory. A correct version will be found in "Allan's Illustrated Edition of Tyneside Songs and Readings." The southerner who can give the proper pronunciation of " fyece " has advanced a long way to the understanding of English as she is spoken at Newcastle. The

origin of the song is explained in the following note to it :
" The dial of the clock in St. Nicholas Church first lighted by
gas Dec. 5th 1829.   The dial blown out by a violent storm of

The Black Gate.

wind October 19th 1862 ; relighted November 15th 1862."
Other ancient churches in Newcastle are those of St. John and
St. Andrew.   The former stands at the foot of Grainger Street

and the latter at the top of Newgate Street. St. John's Church is said to have been built towards the end of the thirteenth century, but it has from time to time been partly rebuilt or

Norman Postern, Castle Garth Stairs.

repaired. St. Andrew's is the more interesting and claims to be the oldest church in Newcastle, having been built by King David, whose name is treasured in Melrose Abbey.

P

Two heritages from antiquity tower above all others in Newcastle. It owes its name to one of them, the Castle. "And so the said vill from that time began to be called New Castle," says Simeon of Durham, referring to the fortification put up by the Conqueror's son Robert Curthose in 1080. But probably nothing remains of this structure. It has indeed been surmised that it was of wood. William Rufus began the building of the

The Old Town Wall.

great Norman Keep, and the work was concluded by Henry II between the years 1172 and 1177. The purpose in view is tersely explained by the old metrical historian Hardyng :

> He buylded Newcastell upon Tyne
> The Scottes for to gaynstande and to defende.

The circumstances are very well known. Within two years of the Battle of Hastings the Conqueror was taken unawares by a revolt in favour of Edgar Atheling and the slaughter of 3,000 Normans at York. His vengeance was delayed but terrible. He bribed the Danes to withdraw their navy, he dealt with

Old Town Wall.

his enemies in the west, and then with fire and sword so devastated the county that for more than half a century it lay bare and desolate for sixty miles north of York. But even this did not end the terror. Malcolm Canmore of Scotland had married the Athelings' sister Margaret, and he again and again attempted the conquest of England till he met his death before Alnwick in 1071.

The castle occupied an area of three acres, enclosed by a curtain wall through which the chief entrance was by the Black Gate. This was built or renewed by Henry III in the year 1248, and is a most interesting and impressive piece of late Norman. The upper portion was restored by the Newcastle Society of Antiquaries, and is now very appropriately used as a Museum of Antiquities, most of which are Roman and from the Wall.

In a county so full of historical associations as Northumberland it would make a notable advance in education if a museum exclusively devoted to local antiquities were established in each local centre. There are already many museums in the smaller towns, but they are too miscellaneous, and often contain articles brought home by travellers that would find a more appropriate habitation in a great central museum. Northumbrians are born antiquarians, and young people especially delight in that kind of history which enables them to compare the village or town in which they live with the same place as it was in the days of their forefathers.

From the historical point of view the most important part of the castle is this entrance gate to the bailey—it gets the name of Black Gate from an occupant in the time of James I named Black—one of the three postern gates, and the great Norman Keep. Like the rest of England in the eighteenth century, Newcastle was careless of her antiquarian heritages. After the castle had been put to many mean uses, when it was no longer needed as " the bridle of Scotland," it was in 1782 advertised to be let as a windmill. Here is the notice :

" To be let, the old Castle in the Castle Garth, upon which with the greatest convenience and advantage, may be erected a wind-mill for the purpose of grinding corn, and bolting flour, or making oil, etc. There is an exceeding good spring of water within the Castle, which renders it a very eligible situation for a Brewery, or any Manufactory that requires a constant supply of water. The proprietor, upon proper terms, will be at a considerable part of the expense. Enquire of Mr. Fryer, in Westgate Street, Newcastle."

It was not till 1848, or fifty-six years after this, that the Newcastle Society of Antiquaries succeeded in obtaining a lease of the old Castle from the Corporation. At that time the Society, now the oldest of its kind, had already been thirty-five years in existence.

There is little left of the famous Walls and their Gates. There seems to have been a very early wall which was superseded by

Grey Street.

that built in the time of Edward I. The funds for this enterprise were according to Grey found by a rich citizen who had been "taken prisoner out of his house and carried into Scotland." How Newcastle has expanded outwards may be inferred from the fact that in 1745 the length of the Walls was 2 miles, 239 yards. They were gradually demolished, and what is left of them may best be seen between Westgate Street and St. Andrew's Church, a distance of about a quarter of a mile. They bring an air of antiquity into busy Newcastle. So do the names of the old streets. Pilgrim Street, High and Low Friars Street, The Close, and many similar names point to a time when monks formed an important part of the population. Jesmond, the Mount of Jesus, forms a natural centre to these surroundings.

Modern Newcastle owes its reconstructed streets almost wholly to two men. Richard Grainger, who was responsible for the building of Grey Street, and Grainger Street, as well as many other scarcely less important parts of modern Newcastle, was a self-made man of a type not uncommon among the Novo-castrians. Born of poor parents, educated at a Charity School and afterwards apprentice to a carpenter and builder, he succeeded in attaining a high position and securing the respect and affection of his fellow townsmen. His disposition can best be described by the kindly old Northumbrian phrase " a canny man." Shrewd but good-hearted and unassumingly religious without ostentation, persevering to the highest degree but no hustler, he seems to have satisfied his ambition without making enemies. Grey Street and Grainger Street form his best monument. Their solid, substantial stone houses will compare favourably with those of any other provincial English town. The monument to Lord Grey—the Reform Minister—is not unworthy the memory of Northumberland's most distinguished statesman. Grainger's most ardent desire was the improvement of his native town and the realisation of his projects, the building of Grainger Street and Clayton Street, Nun Street, Nelson Street, Hood Street and so on, in which he had the assistance and advice of Mr. Clayton, who came of good substantial Newcastle stock and had the welfare of the town as much at heart as his friend.

Apart from banks, theatres and other buildings devoted to business or amusement, the greatest interest attaches to the Museum of the Natural History Society at Barras Bridge. The county has a bird list of exceptional length, and every Northumbrian town and village possesses a naturalist or two. Consequently the work of the brothers Hancock is known far and wide. John Hancock took a prominent part in getting this museum built, and in it are housed the great collection of birdskins made by him and his elder brother, Albany Hancock. They afford the very best material on which to build up a knowledge of Northumbrian ornithology.

John Hancock lived from 1808 to 1890. His greatest predecessor in the same field had been Prideaux John Selby, of

Dean Street, Newcastle.

Twizell House, who was born at Alnwick in 1788. A careful observer and voluminous writer not only on birds, but trees, he was a great friend of Sir Walter Scott, who used to send him each of his books as it was published. Those first editions were in Twizell House during the time of Lord Redesdale, not the Lord Redesdale who died a few years ago, but the previous

holder of the title. Afterwards birds and books were scattered
and the house passed into other hands.

The founder of the Berwickshire Naturalists' Club, Dr.
Johnstone, did not specialise on birds as much as on some other
branches of natural history; and James Hardy, for many years
its secretary, had equally wide tastes, but he wrote many interesting papers on migration and kindred topics.

These are the outstanding names, but it would be possible to
find in any Northern hamlet someone whose special delight it
is to watch and remember the proceedings of the feathered folk.

It must be very difficult for a stranger to get into the atmosphere or recognise the true spirit of Newcastle. The first
barrier in the way is the dialect, and the dialect is more formidable
in print than in speech. The late Mr. Swinburne gave up all
hope of writing poems in it, and used the braid Scots tongue for
his Northumbrian ballads. To take a simple example, it is
easy to indicate the pronunciation of " stone," by spelling it, for a
southern ear, or " stane " for the Scottish, but the equivalent in
Northumbrian defies the alphabet. If spelt as is usually the
way, " styen," few except natives would recognise it was
pronounced as a monosyllable which, roughly speaking, rhymes to
" gin." But for this difficulty, any stranger could learn much
about the manners and traditions, habits and humours of
Newcastle by reading " Tyneside Songs." They take you into
what may be called low company, but it is a company of real
men and women. Though they are closely akin to the *dramatis
personæ* of the Jolly Beggars of Robert Burns, a very considerable
portion of the poets were ne'er-do-weels, eccentrics, wastrels of
one kind or another; and here a peculiarity of Northumberland
in general and Newcastle in particular may be noted. In other
parts of the kingdom the rich are the leisured class who find
time to write verses, and the poor are the horny-handed who
have no leisure. But in Northumberland these conditions are
reversed. The city merchants have always been too much
immersed in the great projects of their generation to cultivate
the Muses. But the poor sprang largely from the raiders
of Reedsdale and the like, men who closely resembled that
Robson who, like a good canny man, depended for his livelihood
on lifting cattle. There is something of the outlaw lingering
still in the families of those who form the " characters " of
Newcastle. One consequence is that they break into rhyme

very easily and the rhyme is steeped in local tradition and expressed in the local dialect.

A glance at the frontispiece of the revised edition of " Tyneside Songs," published in 1891, will show what the makers were. Their very names are sufficient to do so : awd Judy, Jenny Ballo, Whin Bob, Jackie Coxon, Pussy Willy, Cull Billy Donald, Bugle-nosed Jack, Hangie, Bold Archie, Blind Willie, Shoe-tie Anty, Captain Starkey, Doodem Daddum, to which are added the dog, Timour, a stodgy, short-legged, bull-headed piece of impudence. These, in their day, were eccentrics and well-known characters in Newcastle-upon-Tyne. Some were the singers, and some the heroes of the songs. It may be worth while to give a brief glance at the contents of the book in order to show how it expresses an aspect of Newcastle which is really collected from the whole of Northumberland. In miniature every little town used to have a group of similar characters. Examples still survive, though modern progress is tending towards their ultimate extinction. The songs open, as was right and proper, with the authorised version of the Newcastle anthem :

> As I went up Sandgate, up Sandgate,
> As I went up Sandgate I heard a lassie sing
> Weel may the keel row, the keel row, the keel row
> Weel may the keel row that my laddie's in !

" Bobby Shaftoe " is a local song which has attained the very widest favour and deserves it :

> Bobby Shaftoe's gone to sea,
> With silver buckles at his knee ;
> He'll come home and marry me,
>   Bonny Bobby Shaftoe.
>
> Bobby Shaftoe's bright and fair
> Combing down his yellow hair ;
> He's my ain for ever mair,
>   Bonny Bobby Shaftoe.

" My Eppie " makes one sure that many of these Newcastle minstrels drifted in from the country :

> There was five wives at Acomb
> And five wives at Wa'
> And five wives at Fallowfield
> That's fifteen o' them a'.

" Sair fail'd hinney " is an old favourite, but the pathos is too much accented for modern taste. " A new song made on Alice Marley, an alewife at Pictree near Chester-le-Street," has been sung for the best part of two hundred years at sheep-shearing gatherings, harvest suppers, and barn dances, where the chorus resounded among the bare roof joists :

> Did ye ken Elsie Marley, honey !
> The wife that sells the barley, honey ;
> She wont get up to serve her swine
> And do you ken Elsie Marley, honey.

" Canny Newcassel " is a celebrated song which sings the true glories of the Tyne by contrasting them with those of the Thames. The chorus runs :

> Bout Lunnun then divn't ye mak' sic a rout,
> There's nouse there ma winkers to dazzle :
> For a' the fine things ye are gobbin about,
> We can marra in canny Newcassel.

Naturally the glories are sung of the various public houses where these characters disported themselves, and the way to their haunts carries us into many a curious chare and street since destroyed by the improvements of Mr. Grainger.

" Ma canny hinny " is a good example of this kind of ditty. It is too long to quote, but begins :

> Aw went up the Butcher Bank and down Grundin Chase,
> Call'd at the Dun Cow, but aw cuddent find thee there.

The wanderings end where they ought to end—at home and in a manner very distinctly Northumbrian :

> Hing on th' girdle, let's hev a singin' hinny.

How often in the traditions and songs of old Northumberland we find a reference to the " singin' hinny." It is sometimes called a knead cake and is a product peculiar to the county. The pitman and his dog are inseparable, and many dogs appear in these songs. Here is the first verse of one about " Cappy " :

> In a town near Newcassel a Pitman did dwell,
> Wiv his wife nyemed Peg, a Tom Cat, and himsel ;
> A Dog, called Cappy, he doated upon,
> Because he was left him by great Uncle Tom.
>   Weel bred Cappy, famous awd Cappy,
>   Cappy's the Dog, Tallio, Tallio.

In the list of eccentrics already given there is one called Blind Willie. He was an unfortunate but happy soul who spent the last days of his life in the poorhouse of All Saints, but even then travelled the streets, which he could do as well as many a man who had the use of his eyes. There is a song about his singing of which one verse may be quoted for the sake of the local colour :

> It's fine to hear wor Bellman talk,
>   It's wond'rous fine an' cheerin
> To hear Bet Watt an' Euphy Scott
>   Scold, fight, or bawl fresh heerin ;
> To see the keels upon the Tyne,
>   As thick as hops, a' swimmin',
> Is fine indeed, but still mair fine
>   To hear Blind Willie singin'.

Blind Willie appears in the " Lamentation on the Death of Captain Starkey," another of the worthies. He, with Cuckoo Jack, Bold Archie, and others make an unconventional elegy of their departed comrade in which occurs this serious question :

> Then what'll poor Newcassel dee, deprived of all her
>   ornamentals ?

When poor Willie's own turn came, the grief was expressed with the same genuine feeling and disregard of the ordinary proprieties. Whatever the faults of this company there can be no doubt of their affection for one another.

> " As aw was gannin up the Side,
>   Aw met wi' drucken Bella ;
> She rung her hands, and sair she cried,
>   He's gyen at last, poor fellow !
> O hinny, Bella ! whe is't that's gyen ?
>   Ye gar my blood run chilly ;
> Wey, hinny, deeth hes stopt the breeth
>   O' canny awd Blind Willie."

Although only one or two of these rhymers touch the high-water mark of poetry, they are homely and friendly, they are full of spirit and they reproduce with good humour the prize fights and cock fights, the drinking habits, the racing, the practical jokes and quips of the tap and bar. In this way they make themselves essential to a sympathetic understanding of that old Newcastle out of which the present one came.

We cannot take leave of them in terms more fitting than are

to be found in William Watson's "Thumping Luck to yon Town":

> There's native bards in yon town
> For wit and humour seldom be't ;
> And they sang se sweet in yon town,
> Gud faith, I think I hear them yet :
> Such fun in Thompson's Voyage to Shields,
> In Jemmy Joneson's wherrie fine—
> Such shaking heels and dancing reels,
> When sailing on the coaly Tyne.

> Here's thumping luck to yon town,
> Let's have a hearty drink upon't,
> O the days I've spent in yon town,
> My heart still warms to think upon't.

The Start of the High Level 'Bus from the Newcastle side.

CHAPTER XXI

THE ROMAN WALL

An ancient " Hindenburg Line "—Stations near Newcastle—Segedunum—Pons Aelii—The " Notitia "—Chesters : its remains
and museum—The Roman bridge across Tyne—Borcovicus
and the Northumbrian Lakes—A sportsman's description—
the worship of Mithras on the wall.

THERE is no other ancient relic in Northumberland to compare
with the Roman Wall. Yet imagination is needed to realise
its full impressiveness. The remains have in many cases to be
sought for diligently, and nowhere do they arrest attention by
gigantic proportions or towering height. The Wall stretched
from the mouth of the Tyne to the Solway, passing over a rich
variety of scenery—rivers and rich meadows, wild craggy moorland, farms and woods—with Roman directness and Roman
disregard of obstacles, dipping into the hollows and climbing
heights of the rugged whinstone. But in the centuries elapsed
since its building, so many changes, wars, movements have
surged over the country that, in times of desperate fighting and
amid revolutions that shook old faiths as well as governments,
its origin and purpose have been forgotten. Camden, in his
" Britannia," called it the Murus Picticus, and it used to be
described as a defence against the inroads of the Picts and
Scots who inhabited the northern part of the Kingdom.
This view is no longer tenable, for reasons which have been stated
with convincing force by Dr. Collingwood Bruce. They
are that (1) every station and mile-castle along its course seems
to have been provided with a wide portal opening towards the
north ; (2) there are stations situated far to the north of the

Wall on the line both of Watling Street and the Maiden Way which can be proved to have been garrisoned by Roman troops until near the end of the Roman occupation.

An ancient " Hindenburg line " may serve as a rough description. The reader will readily make a liberal allowance for the differences in fortification rendered necessary by the substitution

The Roman Villa, Chesters.

of poisonous gas and high explosives for the arrows, catapults, balistæ, and other engines employed by the Roman legions.

It may be regarded as a series of fortifications linked together so as to enable the occupants to assemble promptly at any given point either for attack or defence. Those wishing to explore it cannot do better than take Dr. Collingwood Bruce as a mentor. His famous Handbook has, since his death, been edited and kept up to date by a most competent successor, the well-known archæologist, Mr. Robert Blair, one of the secretaries of the

Newcastle Society of Antiquaries. Dr. Bruce was very far indeed from being a Dryasdust. He was a charming and versatile writer with many sympathies as well as great learning, who had the gift of explaining a difficult subject simply and lucidly. There are few more agreeable ways of spending a Northumbrian holiday than with his book as company, exploring the Wall from start to finish. Between Wallsend on the Tyne and Bowness on the Solway is rather less than seventy-four miles, so that the pilgrimage along it presents no formidable task to a moderate pedestrian who is able to take his ease at his inn when fatigued with the rough going. He will see more than one interesting aspect of the country.

It is not easy for fancy to reconstruct the country round Wallsend as it must have appeared to the guardians of the Wall. The houses, wharves, offices, stores, must give place to moor and forest, and the dark, sombre Tyne bearing endless traffic on its bosom make way for a pellucid sparkling river so shallow as to to be no defence from attack. The reason why the building started at Wallsend—the Segedunum of the Romans—was probably because here the river widens to its mouth and forms a natural frontier. Little has been left of the Wall in the neighbourhood of Newcastle. The Venerable Bede, who lived at Jarrow, has left a record of what it was like in his day. He, the most accurate of ecclesiastical writers, gives the height as twelve feet and the breadth eight feet, but the dimensions probably varied with the locality, and Dr. Bruce reckons that the average height was about twenty feet and the breadth eight. Jarrow is almost opposite Wallsend, so we may assume that Bede measured the portion which daily met his eye. Newcastle-on-Tyne had not come into existence when the Wall was built. There was only the Pons Ælii Station, opposite the Pons Ælius, so called by Hadrian in commemoration of his family. Coal must have been known and used by the Romans, as cinders have been unearthed in the works, but its paramount value as fuel was not realised till the thirteenth century. There were no pits, so the town and the buildings and the tall chimneys of the mines must be wiped out in order to get a picture of the landscape as it appeared to Roman eyes or to those of the Venerable Bede.

There was a third station at Benwell, about two miles from Newcastle, but the development of the collieries has caused

this also to be obliterated. Where the first three stations
of the Wall were, you see to-day the busy industrious side of
Northumbrian life. But the Wall has a long way to go, and
presently there will be unfolded to the pilgrim who perseveres
all the wild beauty of the Northumbrian moors. And the
wilder the region the more complete and interesting become the
remains of the Wall. Where the scenery is tame the Wall was
an easily accessible quarry. Roman workers had hewn the
stones at a time when the building art had undergone temporary
oblivion in Great Britain. Few things are more startling in
history than the completeness with which ancient civilisations
have passed away. In what appears to have been a sun-temple
at Avebury, and in the stone circles of which that at Stonehenge
is the most important, we have evidence that building and means
of transport had existed in Britain many centuries before the
Roman invasion. Northumberland is rich in prehistoric forts
that had been erected with skill and judgment by races
inhabiting land that now is little better than desert. But there
had been a great retrogression, and in troublous times old arts had
been forgotten.

When wandering about the Wall during the World War and
observing the myriad proofs it supplied of organised government and organised labour, of intelligence and enlightenment,
it was impossible not to muse over the chance that human
progress might possibly have reached its culminating point
in the twentieth century and be followed by a Dark Age. I
did not think it would come from the victory of one side or
another, but from the break-up of nations into warring divisions.
The worst law is better than anarchy, but it is at least imaginable
that no fraction would remain united. Subdivision into groups
would go on ever growing smaller like the family. The individual
would become the unit. Then it would be " wolf to wolf's
throat." No longer would there be property, no longer education,
every generation growing more ignorant than its predecessor till
any ancient who told of a people who could navigate the air and
travel under the sea, who could chain the lightning and converse a
thousand miles apart, would be regarded as a dotard. A gloomy
vision, but not altogether fantastic ! Some such process must
have checked human progress more than once.

But the clouds have lifted and the sun is again shining.
Whatever the future may hold, the Wall affords a light on the

past. How many people have refrained from examining it, seeing little but a heap of stones here and there as the results of much excavation ? The reality will dissipate this illusion. Where the Wall has been preserved, its completeness is amazing. Where it has been practically destroyed it is strange to note to what a variety of uses the stones have been put. Here as elsewhere the imperturbable husbandman has been the greatest sinner. He has mended his roads, patched his dry stone dykes, built his farmhouse and mended his byre with stones from the Wall. Let him not be called Hun or Philistine on that account. He has only acted in the same way as those agriculturists and others (clergy included) who, further south, have built pigsties with materials torn from Tudor masonry, turned old stone coffins into cattle troughs, and laid paths through the farmyard with historical tombstones. Reverence for the past was not a striking characteristic of the eighteenth and early nineteenth centuries.

" Perhaps I am the first man who ever travelled the whole length of the Wall and probably the last who will ever attempt it," wrote William Hutton, of Birmingham, in 1801, giving an eloquent testimony to the great difficulties of travel a hundred years ago. The journey is an easy one to-day, but those who wish to obtain some idea of the Wall and cannot spare time for a complete survey may learn much by confining themselves to the portion which lies between Chesters and Great Chesters. Headquarters can be established at Hexham or the George Inn at Humshaugh for Great Chesters, and the Railway Inn at Haltwhistle for the other end. In this way they will be able to obtain a definite notion of the original fortifications, which are (1) a stone wall carried directly over the county and only deflected when it seemed advisable to make use of any natural defence already in existence, such as the crest of a hill. This wall had a ditch on its northern side. (2) An earth wall, or Vallum, south of the Wall. It was built to a great extent of the earth dug out in making the ditch. (3) Stations, castles, watchtowers and roads.

Lest he be puzzled to account for the Latin names of the camps, he who goes on a first pilgrimage should look them up in the " Notitia," of which there is a translation in the Handbook. The " Notitia " was a kind of gazette or directory compiled in the early half of the fifth century, before the Romans had evacuated

Q

Britain. Its object was to tell where the military and civil notabilities were stationed. From it we learn the nationality of the troops at each station.

When in a camp now called Housesteads many altars are found bearing the name of the first cohort of the Tungrians, a body of troops which the " Notitia " places at Borcovicus, the inference is natural that Housesteads is the Borcovicus of the Romans ; and this probability becomes a moral certainty when the stations on either side of it yield tablets inscribed with the names of the first cohort of the Batavians and the fourth cohort of the Gauls, the troops which the " Notitia " places in the stations immediately to the east and west of Borcovicus.—*The Handbook.*

The works were evidently intended for security against the population of the conquered South as well as against the wild races of the unsubdued North. Many a thorny question has arisen about them. Did the Emperor Hadrian originate and conceive this fortification as a single plan, as the Hindenburg Line, as we may assume, was prepared and constructed ? Are they all of one period ? What previous defences existed, and if so were they utilised ? Matters these for historians and archæologists to argue about for ages. Here it will be better to confine ourselves to such things as carry us back to the building of the Wall. Roman soldiers in their leisure did things similar to those of our own troops. Anyone wandering over the Wilt-shire or other Downs on which soldiers were trained will discover that, emulating the artists to whom we owe the white horses, they have drawn on the turf the badges and names of their regiments that, if they are cleaned regularly as the white horse is cleaned, may be seen with interest a thousand years hence. Roman soldiers told off for fatigue duty at the quarries in like manner wrote on the rock at times who they were and what they were doing. It gives us a sense of human continuity to learn how, in the year of our Lord 207, a squad of the second legion were on quarry work, as is duly set down in the Written Rock of the Gelt near Brampton. On the face of one of the ancient quarries in Chollerford are the words (P)ETRA FLAVI(I) CARANTINI, " the rock of Carantinus." Similar writings have been found in other quarries. Thus we realise in a little way how operations went on. We may assume the skilled work to have been done by the regular soldiers, while the hard labour was allotted to enslaved natives answering to our prisoners of war. In the

course of a visit to France during the war I was witness
of a scene that seemed to recall the very spirit of antiquity.
It was that of a very small soldier from the Far East, who with
a switch in his hand and the most insolent smile on his lips was
by gesture directing a great blonde barbarian to remove the last
microscopic bit of ordure from the road. He was obeyed
sullenly, after the captive's eye had given a rebellious flicker that

The North Tyne, Chesters.

died down at sight of the loaded rifle. War does not change
with the ages.

A most exquisite situation has been chosen for the camp at
Cilurnum, or Chesters. It was garrisoned, as inscriptions prove,
by the 2nd Ala of Asturians, and the Rev. John Hodgson said
"the Astures in exchanging the sunny valleys of Spain for the
banks of tawny Tyne might find the climate in their new situation
worse; but a lovelier spot than Cilurnum all the Astures could
not give them." Green fields, woods and hills would justify
him, even if the North Tyne did not flow past in its perfect
beauty, singing as it sang to the Roman legions. To the late
Mr. John Clayton, who owned the mansion and the estate, must
be accorded the highest credit for adding to these natural
attractions. He was a most liberal as well as enlightened

Q 2

archæologist and possessed of will-power equal to his enthusiasm. He and his collaborator, Dr. Collingwood Bruce, excavated the ruins, laid bare the famous camp, and gathered the relics which make the Museum the best of its kind in the country.

The station at Chesters is very nearly as large as that at Birdoswald in Cumberland, which the Romans called Amboglanna. Cilurnum covers an area of 5¼ acres, Amboglanna 5½, so there is only a quarter of an acre difference. Lesser stations are, like Cilurnum, rectangular in shape, but whereas they have usually only four gateways, this has six. One great portal opened to the south, one to the north, but there are two, a greater and a lesser, on the west and also on the east. The little gates would have been called posterns had they been in a Norman castle. We are reminded by the worn stones, worn by war chariots and war horses, the trample of soldiers' feet, the passing of civilian crowds, that the Roman occupation was not for a year or two but for centuries. If we date effective occupation from the defeat of Galgacus in 8 A.D., and the withdrawal from 418 A.D., the year in which according to the Saxon Chronicle the Romans collected their treasure and hid in the soil what they could not carry away, they lived with us for more than 300 years, and the Wall was held for more than two centuries. Even in that long period it is doubtful if they exercised the slightest influence on the race of Englishmen. The reasons are irresistible. First the Roman army was not Roman. That did not matter much in regard to their efficiency so long as the organisation, the discipline, and the command remained in Roman hands, but it was all-important as regards influence. Asturians, Thracians, Moors, Gauls, Frisians, could have had very little in common.

The Wall is not carried through the camp, but comes up to the eastern gateway on one side and to the corresponding western gateway on the other. To the north of the road connecting them are what appear to have been the sleeping apartments of the soldiers, and to the south is the Forum where justice was administered and business transacted. East of that is the Praetorium, the quarters of the C.O. as we should call him. It has an ingenious contrivance for heating the room by hot air. Out of the dry stones, with the aid of the altars, inscriptions, and miscellaneous remains collected in the excellent museum started by Mr. Clayton, it would be possible for the imagination to construct a living city, but though the materials are plentiful the piecing together of them would require long and patient effort. He who goes to see for himself will find plenty for his

The Roman Wall at Borcovicus.

fancy to work upon. He might devote an entire day to the extraordinary remains of a Roman bridge across the Tyne. Dr. Bruce did not exaggerate when he called it " the most remarkable feature on the whole line of the Wall." If, as is supposed, Hadrian built it he must have had the assistance of first-class engineers, and these engineers would have done credit to any period.

Borcovicus, the camp at Housesteads, occupies a situation very different from that at Cilurnum. Here the wall was carried along the desolate jagged hill-tops that rise above the only apology for a lake district that Northumberland possesses. There are many ways of reaching it. A sturdy, resolute pedestrian can do so on foot by following the line of the wall from Chesters. He would thus secure the advantage of seeing the best preserved part of the stone wall, the turf wall, and fosse, and would pass Carrawburgh, the ancient Procolitia where the Romans had a sacred well, a sort of Fons Bandŭsïae of which a goddess named Coventina was presiding genius. There is at Chesters a carving of her with an inscribed dedication by the prefect of the first cohort of Batavians, and one of her three water-nymphs.

When the well was opened out by Mr. Clayton, hidden under huge stones was an amazing and miscellaneous assortment of treasure and coins, stones, altars, vases, Roman pearls, old shoes, fibulæ, and so on. Mr. Clayton himself obtained sixteen thousand coins, four gold, the others silver and bronze, ranging from the time of Mark Antony to that of Gratian. Dr. Bruce counted 318 examples of the second brass coin of Antoninus Pius. He says :

This coin was struck in the fourth consulship of the Emperor A.D. 145 to commemorate the exploits of Lollius Urbicus in Britain, a period in which the country was reduced to its lowest state of depression. Britain personified as a disconsolate female sits upon a rock. She has no helmet upon her head, no sword or spear in her hand. Her head droops, her banner is lowered, her shield is idly cast away. The legend is Britannia.

Borcovicus occupies five acres, so that it is not much smaller than Cilurnum. The Roman masonry has stood the ravages of time wonderfully well.

The country over which the Wall passes is very wild. I cannot better give an idea of it than by quoting Mr. Abel Chapman's " Bird Life on the Border." Mr. Chapman does not write as antiquary—indeed he ignores the existence of the Wall— but as a sportsman and naturalist. He is altogether against the drawing of imaginative pictures, but is content to be very

thorough and exact. Of far more concern to him are the
habits of wild-fowl than the look of forlorn and wistful beauty
peeping out of the desolate scenery. Probably the Tungrian
conscripts who kept watch and ward on the Wall were very
much in sympathy with his point of view. Mr. Chapman says
of the loughs :

Many lying high out on the hills have scarce a vestige of covert
on their banks, not even a screen of rush or reed, nor any bush or
shrub higher than heather or bog-myrtle. Others are simply open
peat-holes, their surface not a foot below the general level of the
dead-flat bogs and moss-bogs which surround them. Some occupy
basins among the hills where the heather slopes down unbroken to
the water's edge ; the ' syke ' or gully at the outflow may, however,
enable one to approach the water at that point. Their bottoms are
usually firm—either peat or gravel, and deep to the edge. There is
seldom any extent of foreshore where fowl can sit dry, though in
some, as at St. Mary's Loch—

> " . . . A fringe of silver sand
> Marks where the water meets the land."

Where the peat-formation is exposed in section trunks and roots
of ancient oaks, pine, and other trees—up to elevations of 1,200 feet
or more—attest a period when these open moors were clad with
forest.

Mr. Chapman's remark about finding tree stems in the Lough
is very suggestive, especially when taken in connection with the
many other remains found on the land as well as under the
water in the North of England. It makes it possible that the
Wall through parts of its course ran through rough woodland,
some of mere scrub, some consisting of high trees.

A lifetime might be spent in studying the Roman remains
on the Wall, and after all it would be difficult to picture the life
of the soldiery there. In some respects the men appear to have
been very like our own—careless of danger and even death
and always merry. It would be a great mistake to fancy that
the foreign conscripts who composed the army of occupation
spent all their time in drill or mourned their exile unduly.
On the contrary, we have evidence that amusements of
various kinds were carefully planned and the merriment was
uproarious.

One of the most interesting relics on the Wall at Housesteads
is the Temple of Mithras, a little to the west of Chapel Hill.

It affords one of many evidences that the Roman soldiers had carried the worship of their favourite gòd to this wild and far distant frontier of the Empire.   Mithras is a god of eastern origin, the Sun God of Persia. It is believed that Mithras worship in Rome was started partly to counteract the teaching of the Christian faith and partly because its doctrine harmonised with the claim to absolute power put forward by the Roman Emperors.

Bardon Mill.
(Bardon Mill Station is best for Borcovicus.)

In Rome little caves had been made to imitate the secluded mountain caves in which Mithras worship was conducted in Persia and the rites were performed at night.   They included such atrocities as the offering up of human sacrifices and other repulsive barbarities.   Several altars inscribed to Mithras were found on the Roman Wall, and Mr. Kipling has " A Song to Mithras " in " Puck."   He calls it a Hymn of the 30th Legion and dates it about A.D. 350. That would be at a time when Mithras worship was declining. We quote the first two verses :

Mithras, God of the Morning, our trumpets waken the Wall !
" Rome is above the Nations, but Thou art over all ! "
Now as the names are answered and the guards are marched away,
Mithras, also a soldier, give us strength for the day !

Mithras, God of the Noontide, the heather swims in the heat,
Our helmets scorch our foreheads, our sandals burn our feet.
Now in the ungirt hour—now ere we blink and drowse,
Mithras, also a soldier, keep us true to our vows !

The Tyne, from the road between the Wall and Hexham.

CHAPTER XXII

The Moor and the mines—History of Haltwhistle—Its pele towers
and church—Two epitaphs—The old pronunciation preserved
—A Haltwhistle poet—From Cumberland to Haltwhistle—
Mumps Ha and Meg Merrilees—The Spa and Well worship—
An ancient wrong—From Birdoswald to Thirlwall and the Nine
Nicks—A Roman Wall at Walltown.

> Ha' ye heard how the Ridleys, and Thirlwalls, and a',
> Ha' set upon Albany Featherstonhaugh,
> And taken his life at the Deadmanshaugh ?
>   There was Willimoteswick
>   And Hard-riding Dick,
> And Hughie of Hawdon, and Will of the Wa'.
> SURTEES' BALLAD.

HALTWHISTLE stands so beautifully on the Tyne, here a
broad, shallow river dancing and singing over a rough bed,
with a great sweep of moors billowing round it, that not even
the squalor attendant on coal mines has destroyed its charm.
Since the pits were opened the population has increased from
fifteen hundred to three times that number. The mines do not
disfigure the landscape as much as might be imagined. In
the embrace of the huge moor they are reduced to insignificance.
Even the chimneys are inconspicuous and the smoke but wisps
of cloud, neither as black nor as large as the trail of an ocean-
going steamer. The ugliest feature of a mining locality is the
row of pit houses. During a half-century of great prosperity
the men themselves have improved immensely. I remember
when the periodic outbreak among them was a thing to be
dreaded. Literally and truly their attitude to the traveller

was: " Here's a stranger, Bill; let's 'eave a brick at 'im."
Dark and true and tender is the North, but it never has been,
probably never will be, polite. Yet a vast change for the better
has taken place in the habits of the miners. They may still
have a day out occasionally, and, if you think of the character
of their work, that is not surprising. At Haltwhistle you see
a vast number of greyhounds and lurchers, showing that the

Haltwhistle.

pitman does not neglect his ancient amusement. For all that,
he has turned into a thrifty and provident citizen, and withal
has become civil and obliging. But still he is content with
that hideous row of cottages with not a scrap of garden in front
or rear. Much may be forgiven the miners because they have
scared away the tourist. There are practically no boarding-
houses, the hotels are useful without being showy. Yet the

place has almost every attraction but the sea. It has many lovely streams near—such as Tyne, the much fished ; Irthing, noted for the quality of its trout ; the well-stocked Haltwhistle Burn, and the Tipalt. They are all available for the angler.

In the town there are two buildings of interest—the church and a pele-tower, the latter a fine example of a Border fortress, now partially inhabited by peasants and still offering a grand opportunity for anyone interested in restoring and preserving. The following account of it is from a privately printed and circulated pamphlet by the Rev. C. E. Adamson, rector of Houghton-le-Spring, under the title of "A History of the Manor and the Church of Haltwhistle " :

" The Tower of Hautwysel is first mentioned in the list of towers and castles that existed in Northumberland about the year 1416, and is probably the same as that described in 1542 as the inheritance of Sir William Musgrave and in measurable good reparation. It is (as it now stands) a plain building with a loop-holed turret built on corbels. The old roof, which was removed some twenty years ago, was formed of flags laid on heavy oaken beams and fastened thereto with sheep shank bones. The floor also consisted of flags laid on joists formed of the roughly squared trunks of oak trees. A winding stone stair-case leads to the upper part of the tower. As Haltwhistle cannot have had a resident lord during the tenure of the Musgraves, the tower was probably the official residence of the bailiffs who seem to have exercised considerable authority in the town. In 1279 Roger le Tailleur was bailiff. In 1473 Robert Stevenson, Vicar, is named as seneschal. In 1552 Nicholas Blenkinsopp was bailiff (Nicholson's Leges Marchiarum 164). John Ridley, bailiff of Haltwhistle, by his will dated 1616 bequeaths his best ox as a herryate to Lord William Howard, and another John Ridley and Nicholas Ridley held the office in 1634. (Lord William Howard's Household Book.)"

There was another pele-tower, but its remains are engulfed in the Red Lion Hotel.

In its way Mr. Adamson's monograph is a model of its kind, tracing the history of the Manor of Haltwhistle—or Hautwysel, the watch on the mount, as it was originally called—from the time when it was given with Bellister and Plainmeller by William the Lion as a dowry to his natural daughter in 1191. The Kings of Scotland were Lords Seigneur during parts of the twelfth and thirteenth centuries. It was granted by Edward I to William de Ros in 1307, and this charter was confirmed to Edward Musgrave in 1307. From him the present lord of the manor claims descent. The manor has been held among others by " Belted Will Howard," to whom it was sold by Anthony Featherstonhaugh in 1611; but in the time of his son, Sir Charles Howard, it was declared forfeit by the Commonwealth and passed through the hands of several owners before coming into possession of the " eccentric Miss Cuthbertson," who died intestate in 1836. Many tales and legends are still related about her in the neighbourhood. The Adamsons, to whom it passed as to one moiety by the bequest of the Misses Heron and as to the other by purchase, " are descended (by a chain with several female links) from the original quarter "— Sir Edward Musgrave.

The most historic building in Haltwhistle is the church. It is said that the chancel dates from the twelfth century; but it stands in the heart of the moss troopers' county, and they spared nothing they could plunder, either sacred or profane. Yet, in the words of Mr. Adamson, " considering its proximity to the Border, it is wonderful that it has come down to us with so little serious injury." For the care and thoroughness with which it has been put back to its original appearance, thanks are due to its late vicar, Canon Lowe, for nearly half a century beloved friend as well as priest to his parishioners.

In the church are several objects of interest—the gravestone of a Crusader, with beautifully flowered cross, a broken sword, a staff and wallet; a font that may have been Saxon, though evidently tampered with in the time of Elizabeth; and two epitaphs, one of which I copy for its beauty and the other for a reason to be stated.

The following is in the churchyard:

> D. O. M.
> Post Vitam brevem
> Difficilem Inutilem
> Hic
> Quiescit in Domino
> Robertus Tweddell
> De Hazlacton Monac
> in Com. Dunelm. Gen.
> Salutis 1735
> Ætatis 32.

The other is on the tombstone of John Ridley, " cousin " of the martyr :

```
        IHON            REDLE
        THAT            SUM
        TIM             DID BE
    THEN LORD OF THE WALTON
    GON IS HE OUT OF THESE VAL OF ᴹᴱˢᴱᴿᴱ
    HIS BONS LES UNDER THES STON
    WE MUST BELEVE BE GODSRSᴱ
    INTO THES WORLD GAVE HIS SOᴺ
    THEN FOR TO REDEM AL CHRESNᵀᴱ
    SO CHRIST HAES HES SOUL WOᴺ
    AL FAETHFUL PEOPLE MAY BE FAEN
    WHEN DATH COMES THAT NON CAN FLE
    THE BODE KEPT THE SOUL IN PAEN
    THROUGH CHRIST IS SET AT LEBERTE
    AMONG BLESSED COMPANE TO REMAEᴺ
    TO SLEP IN CHRIST NOWE IS HE GON
    YET STEL BELEVES TO HAVE AGAEN
    THROUGH CHRIST A IOYEFUL RESURRᴱᶜᶜᴵᴼᴺ
    AL FRENDES MAY BE GLAD TO HAER
    WHEN HES SOUL FROM PAEN DID GO
    OUT OF THES WORLD AS DOETH APPER
    IN THE YEER OF OUR LORD
            A : 1562
```

It is the mis-spelling that interests here. Although there is only one dialect in Northumberland, it is spoken with accents and other peculiarities that belong to separate localities. The Western Northumbrian is much softer and sweeter in speech than the Eastern, where most commonly voices are harsh and loud. Canon Lowe expressed the opinion that the mistakes in spelling were most likely due to the ignorance of the village mason, but I cannot agree with him. Listen to a native when he says not gate, but " gay-et " ; not faith, but " fay-eth " ; not death, but " dath " ; not here, but " hee-er " ; not remain, but " remay-en " ; not misery and liberty, but " meesery " and " leeberty," and it becomes evident that the spelling, like nearly all the other spelling of the time, was phonetic.

It follows as a normal and indeed inevitable deduction that the manner of speaking prevalent to-day was also that of the generation which saw Bishop Ridley burnt at the stake.

Whether the spelling is due to the composer or the printer, it probably renders accurately the sound of the language as spoken at the time and as it is spoken by the illiterate of to-day.

I cannot leave Haltwhistle without a little note about Ada Smith. She was born here and is buried at St. John Lee. She had lived much abroad, chiefly at Vienna, and returned to England with the hope of making a literary career. But it was not to be. She died in 1898, before attaining her twenty-second birthday, and left behind a memory of what she might have done and one or two poems instinct with love of nature and the charm of youth. I copy out one partly for the sake of her who wrote it, but still more for its delightful rendering of the very spirit of the moorland.

When she wrote it, says Mr. Garvin, who at the time wrote a very sympathetic " In Memoriam " notice for *The Academy,* " she must have been thinking all the time of Blanchland Common and its wide, cool, purple silence."

> Yonder in the heather there's a bed for sleeping,
>   Drink for one athirst, ripe blackberries to eat ;
> Yonder in the sun the merry hares go leaping,
>   And the pool is clear for travel-wearied feet.
>
> Sorely throb my feet, a-tramping London highways,
>   (Ah ! the springy moss upon a northern moor !)
> Through the endless streets, the gloomy squares and byways,
>   Homeless in the City, poor among the poor !
>
> London streets are gold—ah, give me leaves a-glinting
>   'Midst grey dykes and hedges in the autumn sun !
> London water's wine, poured out for all unstinting—
>   God ! For the little brooks that tumble as they run !
>
> Oh, my heart is fain to hear the soft wind blowing,
>   Soughing through the fir-tops up on northern fells !
> Oh, my eye's an ache to see the brown burns flowing
>   Through the peaty soil and tinkling heather-bells.

There is a very interesting walk from the western border of the county into Haltwhistle, mostly along the Wall. The Poltross Burn, as it runs into the Irthing, is the division between Northumberland and Cumberland. On the Cumbrian side is the famous or infamous hostelry Mumps Ha' or Beggars' Hotel, now much enlarged and changed since Scott described it and Meg Merrilees in " Guy Mannering." It had a very bad reputation in his time, and the Border farmers coming from fairs who stopped to refresh themselves were often waylaid by the robbers and highwaymen who were harboured there by the notorious Margaret Carrick. Those who came from Scotland had to traverse the evil-reputed and dangerous waste of Bewcastle. The background in Cumberland is the chain of mountains, the most prominent of which, Skiddaw and Saddle-back, can be seen from the wooded height above Irthing on a clear day. At Upper Denton, about one and a-half miles from Gilsland, is buried Margaret Carrick, the original of Meg Merrilees, who lived till she was a hundred. South of the railway station is the farmhouse called The Gap, where the Wall is said to have been broken down. The Wall can be seen in the Vicarage garden. There is also, to the west, a mile-castle which seems to have been very extensive. A local tradition gives it the name of the King's Stables. The Poltross had a Roman bridge near here, mentioned by Camden as " an arch over the rapid brook." Gilsland Spa has long been a noted resort, and an account is given even within recent times of the yearly pilgrimage to the chalybeate and sulphur waters as a modern survival of well-worship. " On the Sunday after old Midsummer Day, called the Head Sunday, and the Sunday after it, hundreds if not thousands used to assemble from all directions by rail when that was available, and by vehicles and on foot otherwise. From North Tynedale and the neighbourhood for many miles round these unconscious adherents of heathen rites visited the wells." In the introduction to " The Bridal of Triermain " Sir Walter Scott describes the Popping Stone said to be the scene of his own courtship and now a greatly-visited spot on the Cumberland side. The large hotel called " The Shawes " was a farm originally in the manor of Triermain. An ancient story of an ancient wrong is commemorated in the name of Gilsland. Robert de Vaux, the Norman lord, had ousted an earlier proprietor who had the Saxon name of Gilles Bueth. He naturally attempted to regain it, and was invited by the Norman to a friendly meeting where he was treacherously murdered. This tradition was corroborated in 1864 by the discovery of a Runic inscription some distance from Bewcastle Church thus translated :

" Baranr writes (these) to Gilles Bueth who was slan in truce
by Rob de Vaulx at Feterlana now Lanercosta." It is said
that Lanercost Priory [1] was built by the Norman baron in
expiation of his crime. His patronymic does not seem to
have lived on locally, but it is from Gilles that Gilsland obtains
its name, and Bewcastle commemorates Bueth, which would
be his family name. In Lanercost Priory is a fifteenth-century
brass reminding us of the old story, and it is touching enough
to remember :

> Sir Roland de Vaux that sometyme was ye Lord of Tryermayne
> Is dead, his body clad in lead, and ligs low under this stayne
> Even as we, even so was he, on earth a levand man
> Even as he, even so moun we, for all ye craft we can.

Gilles ill-used and hurried from the light of the sun might
thus have spoken had be been a philosopher.

About two miles from Gilsland in Cumberland is Birdoswald,
the largest station on the Roman Wall. It has an area of five
and a half acres. A bridge similar in character to the remains
on the North Tyne at Chollerford had evidently crossed the
Irthing. From Birdoswald there is a view of exceptional
beauty of the hill country and windings of the Irthing. From
the north of the station proceeds the ancient track called the
Maiden Way, which goes past Bewcastle into Scotland and can
still be traced.

The weakest part of the Wall lies between the Gap at Gilsland
and Thirlwall, where the northern tribes are supposed to have
first broken it down. Carvoran, the next camp, occupied three
and a-half acres and was the next station to Birdoswald. With
stones from it was built the Castle of Thirlwall, the ruins of
which stand on the steep bank above the pretty stream called
the Tipalt, into which the stones quarried by Romans and
afterwards used to build the castle are falling from the ancient
stronghold. The castle, which has been unoccupied since
the beginning of the seventeenth century, has been used to

[1] Opinions differ as to the authorship of the Chronicle of Lanercost,
1272–1346, to which the north country is indebted for a great deal
of local history. Stevenson, when he first printed the manuscript,
attributed the authorship to a Minorite friar of Carlisle, but Dr.
James Wilson, in his preface to Sir Herbert Maxwell's translation,
makes out a strong case in favour of its having been compiled in the
Augustinian Priory of Lanercost.

provide the building material for the cottages standing by the stream. The ancient family of Thirlwall probably built the castle in the fourteenth century, or they took their name from the manor. Edward I stayed at Thirlwall on one of his last vengeful visits to quiet the Borders. " A Thirlwall " was the slogan of the family, the last of whom, an heiress, married a Swinburne of Capheaton. From the castle can be seen the village of Glenwhelt, which has a very Celtic sound, and Blenkinsopp Castle, near Greenhead Station, built originally in 1339.

The plough has gone over Carvoran, which had been a very strong station built to command the valley of the Tipalt. The Stanegate, the direct Roman road, came in front of this station, the Magna of the Romans, and the Maiden Way coming up from Cumberland passed near. In the farmhouse and garden adjoining can be seen numerous memorials of the imperial race.

To follow the Wall here climb the steep hill above the Tipalt, now crossed by a bridge. Unfortunately a turret on the crags, which here start to form isolated peaks called the Nine Nicks of Thirlwall, to which we ascend, has been destroyed by quarrying operations that have spoiled the Wall in this part. The turret was only discovered in 1883, and on the north were nine courses of stone. Nowhere are the picturesque features of the basaltic Whin Sill more impressive than along the Roman Wall at the Nine Nicks. The Wall has been built along the margins of the cliffs. The Whin Sill at this point attains its maximum thickness of about 180 feet, and is loftier and more continuous and its outline grander and more broken than in any other part of the county. It is after Thirlwall and the disappearance of the basaltic heights which decline away towards Glenwhelt that the Wall became weak, although between Thirlwall and Birdoswald five camps existed at a distance of half a mile from each other. Near the pleasant little village of Greenhead one is easily traced where the Stanegate passes. The Wall, after clinging to the Nine Nicks, to which it has with great skill been adapted, now descends towards Walltown, where once was a village and a tower which belonged to John Ridley, a relative of the martyred Bishop. It adjoined the present farmhouse. A spring called The King's, or King Arthur's Well, where Paulinus is supposed to have performed one of his legendary baptisms, is near here, the convert being a Saxon

King, either Egbert or Edwin.   One strange and intimate touch
of the Roman soldier's predilections still springs here from the
unconscious bosom of earth.   In the crevices of the whinstone
rock near Walltown House, chives grow in abundance.   It is
said that this pungent, savoury herb was planted by the Roman

Featherstone Castle, near Haltwhistle.

and has persisted, as one of its flavour would persist, ever since.
All the earliest writers on the Wall have referred to its existence.
Camden says that the country-people believed that medicinal
herbs were planted all about here for the cure of wounds, and
that from Scotland those who collected simples flocked in the

R 2

beginning of the summer to gather them. The Wall here is much decayed, but it improves, and after passing Allalee farmhouse the distinctly-marked ruins of a mile-castle and the Wall may be seen. The Wall exhibits, on the north side, six or seven to nine courses of stone, although the south face is broken. It is worn away towards Cockmount Hill farmhouse, though all along this part the views are magnificent and it is but a short distance to Aesica, near Haltwhistle.

In the days of Border warfare Haltwhistle was a centre of strife, and one cannot take a walk in any direction without coming across places whose names have been made familiar by song or story. Bellister and Plenmellor are close at hand and Featherstone Castle only three miles away. It was greatly admired by so good a judge as Mr. Bates, and the name is familiar to readers of Surtees' clever imitation of a Scottish ballad which imposed upon Scott himself.

At Haltwhistle.

Ovingham.

CHAPTER XXIII

UP THE TYNE TO OVINGHAM

George Stephenson's birthplace and education—Robin with the
Beard and Prudhoe Castle—Ovingham and its church—Bywell
and its twin churches—Bewick's Tailpieces as illustrations of
old Northumbrian life—" Got over."

To go up the Tyne from Newcastle is to pass through many
miles of busy industry. Newburn, five miles up, is practically

245

a suburb and important for its steel works. Its pattern-shop was a fortified manor house. Newburn was the nearest ford to Newcastle and has been crossed by armies of Romans and Scots, and was once a considerable town, being capital of the lower Tyne before Newcastle grew to power. Here George Stephenson passed much of his youth and first learnt to work with engines. The early Norman church with the original square tower crowns the hill.

Wylam, where George Stephenson was born in 1781, is four miles higher up the Tyne. On the Hexham road, and appropriately overlooking the railway, stands the red-tiled cottage. The story of his hard childhood shows how early the forefathers of this generation expected their children to earn money. He was working when he was seven and got his education by snatches in a night school from a Scottish schoolmaster.

A little above Wylam, on a rocky steep over the Tyne, stands Prudhoe Castle. The barony of Prudhoe was given by the Conqueror to Robert de Umfraville, or "Robin with the Beard," the first of that great family and the hero of many legends. The castle was built in the twelfth century by Odinel de Umfraville, but in 1381 it passed into the possession of the Percies. Sir Ingram de Umfraville made the famous reply to Edward II at Bannockburn, who, seeing the kneeling host of Scots, when Bruce ordered prayer before battle, turned to his companion, saying triumphantly : " See ! yon men kneel to ask mercy." " You say truth, sire," answered Sir Ingram ; " they ask mercy— but not of you ! " Prudhoe Castle was an immensely strong fortress, as the ruins to-day testify, and the magnificent natural position of steep escarpment and deep ravine is similar to Norham, with a moat to complete the defence. When William the Lion's army was retreating in defeat from the unsubdued fortress of Odinel they stripped the bark from the orchard apple trees, reminding us of the more deadly damage done to the French orchards by the Germans. Gardens still grow under its walls, and part of the castle is used as a dwelling-house. But much of this magnificent castle remains to interest the antiquarian. Indeed, Mr. C. J. Bates considers that " Prudhoe, though of small dimensions, attains more nearly to the ideal of a Border Castle than does any other in Northumberland." The castle moat and garden occupy three acres.

At Cherryburn, a mile to the west, was the birthplace of Thomas

Bewick and his brother. On the opposite side of the Tyne is Ovingham, supposed to be very ancient. The name may be Saxon, the home of the Offings, or sons of Offa. The church is interesting, with a fine pre-Conquest tower belonging to the earlier Saxon building in which stones from the Roman wall have been used. Beneath the tower is the vault of the Bewick family, where " Thomas Bewick, engraver of Newcastle,"

Birthplace of George Stephenson.

is buried and here his genius unfolded. In his memoirs he says : " As soon as I filled all the blank places in my books, I had recourse at all spare times to the gravestones and the floor of the church porch with a bit of chalk to give vent to this propensity of mine of figuring whatever I had seen. At that time I had never heard of the word 'drawing' nor did I know of any other paintings besides the King's Arms in the church, and the signs in Ovingham of the Black Bull, the White Horse, the Salmon, and the Hounds and Hare." What an affecting picture of the simple boy moved by the irresistible biddings of the artist spirit. From an old family called Carr, in Ovingham, sprang another boy—" fair science frowned not on his lowly

St. Andrew's Church at Bywell.

birth "—George Stephenson, whose mother was the daughter of a dyer in the village. The late Canon Greenwell at one time held the living, and his sister, Dora Greenwell, wrote her poems in the old-fashioned and delightful parsonage.

To the north of Ovingham are the remains of Nafferton Tower, which stands to-day as the masons left it, unfinished, in the reign of John. Richard de Umfraville complained to the king that a neighbour called Philip de Ulecote was building a fortress too close to Prudhoe and he was ordered to desist. So the workmen downed tools and Philip the forester of Northumberland had to seek another home.

In a secluded corner of the Tyne, just outside the grime of the Northumbrian coalfield, are the two unique churches of the once noted village of Bywell. There is no village now. The Romans built a bridge here, the piers of which remained

The Village Cross at Bywell.

standing in the river until a few years ago, and in Saxon days St. Wilfred a church. On the site of the latter stands St. Andrew's, one of the twin churches of Bywell, with a grand pre-Conquest tower. The rest of the church is thirteenth century, much of it rebuilt. Many ancient gravestones are built into the walls of this church. It was known as the White Church, from the white canons of Blanchland to whom it belonged, and the other church, St. Peter's, as the Black, from the black Benedictine monks of Durham. The latter was built probably in the middle of the eleventh century, and in the north wall of the nave are four of its original windows. It had been much altered in the thirteenth and fourteenth centuries and has had many restorations since.

The old village cross, but not in its ancient position, is passed on the way to the castle of the Nevilles, an ancient manor of the Balliols, who received it from the Conqueror. The castle, which is really only a gate-tower, was built in the fifteenth century. It is three-storied and very picturesque, clothed in ivy, with four turrets. The Nevilles forfeited the estate to the Crown. The last of them was Charles, Earl of Westmorland, who took part in the abortive " Rising of the North " in 1568.

To return to Bewick, the most considerable artist Northumberland has produced. His father was a small farmer who rented a land-sale colliery, that is, one where the coals were sold to people in the neighbourhood. The story of his life does not concern us much here, but no stranger could possibly obtain a better insight into old Northumberland—that is to say, Northumberland of the eighteenth century—than can be had through the famous tailpieces of which the best are found in the two volumes of " British Birds." As an artist, Bewick was self-educated. His earliest exercises in drawing were made on the margins of books, the flagstones and hearths of his home, and his first studies of pictures, according to the delightful memoir which Austin Dobson wrote for the " National Dictionary of Biography," were " the inn signs and the rude knife-cut prints then to be found in every farm or cottage, records of victories by sea and land, portraits of persons famous or notorious,

> ballads, pasted on the wall,
> Of Chevy Chase and English Moll,
> Fair Rosamond, and Robin Hood,
> The little Children in the Wood.

Then, by the kindness of a friend, after a probation of pen and ink and blackberry-juice, he passed to a paint brush and colours, and began to copy the animal life about him."

With Ruskin's notes available it would be superfluous to dwell on the artistry of the tailpieces, but many of minor importance from Ruskin's point of view are the most interesting to true Northumbrians. A few examples may be cited to show how one of the most observant of artists caught the country life of his time. Most of the habits and customs have faded away, but the wanderer in Northumberland may now and again come across remnants and indications of manners as they were in the time of the great engraver and as they had been for centuries before his time. After the railways were built it was never the same in rural life.

Perhaps the most amusing of the cuts is the one placed before the preface to the second volume of " British Birds." It shows the interior of an old-fashioned Northumbrian cottage. The inmate is obviously one of those referred to by Touchstone when he declared it was meat and drink for him to meet a clown. His hat hangs on a chair and discloses a head bald at the top with grey " haffets." His lanky, unintelligent face is raised upward with closed eyes. His mouth is open, showing that time has made havoc with his teeth, and his hands are raised above his full porridge platter. In a word, he is " asking a blessing." As he thanks the Deity for the good things provided, a tabby cat with upturned tail is helping himself liberally to his supper. The wooden spoon, the little bowl for the milk, the roughly made table, the print on the wall, are all typical of an old cottage interior. At times Bewick's humour was grimly ironical, as in the tailpiece following the chapter on the goose. In it four youths are seen mounted each on a tombstone as though they were cavalrymen. One is blowing a horn, each of the others carrying a sword, and all are got up to look as military as possible. A skull and crossbones on a fallen tombstone speak of the grave, while the smiling vicarage and the rookery beside it suggest a life that is unchanging.

The touch of Rabelais is to be seen in the picture of two anglers, the elder of whom is carefully extracting gentles from the body of a dead dog while the younger holds his nose. But that is a mild example of country humour a hundred years ago.

Interesting as recalling the past is the picture of a very spare man holding on to the tail of a lean cow, which he has evidently driven into the river to escape the tollbar situated, as was often the case, on the bridge above. Innumerable stories are still bandied about amongst ancient rustics of the various ways in which the toll-keeper could be cheated. Perhaps the most remarkable was that of a Berwick character called " Jimmy Strength," who used to lift his donkey bodily over the gate. But swimming behind the cow was more common.

The drawing of a man clinging to the branch of a tree, which has been evidently broken by his weight, and being precipitated

into the foaming river is wit very characteristic of the rude
forefathers of the hamlet.

Bewick was never tired of drawing the wayfaring or gangrel
folk who passed along the highways and byways of his day.
There was the packman carrying what Ruskin, commenting on
these tailpieces, calls simply "a big box." It was really a pack
such as that commemorated in the story of the Long Pack, a
favourite chapbook of the nineteenth century. The packman in
some instances carried webs of cloth, in others only " fine knacks
for ladies " ; sometimes he was a " clocky " dealing in clocks and
watches. I remember one, who must have been probably nearly
the last of his race, who tramped the country districts in the
snuff-coloured, brass-buttoned clothes of a past generation.
He used to recommend to the rustics his spectacles as "not gold,
marm, but equally as good." Over and over again figures
of his type appear in the tailpieces. The terror of the gaunbody
was the dog, and Bewick evidently knew well the dodges to
overcome that enemy, getting him to take hold of a stick, or
wrapping a cloak round his arm through which the animal could
not bite.

There was also the beggar, or gaberlunzie man. He was
familiar to people who lived at such a homestead as is figured
before the introduction to the first volume of " British Birds."
It is a farmstead of a kind that has almost become obsolete.
The farmhouse is a thatched cottage. In a stackyard are two
well-thatched ricks. There are a stable, outbuildings, dovecot,
a man is carrying a full sack on his back, turkeys and chickens
are picking up what they can, and over the house a string of
birds is passing in flight.

The moor had a fascination for Bewick, but it was the terror
of it that seized his imagination. Look at the picture
above the table of contents in the second volume. In the
middle of a storm of wind and rain an old and fearful traveller
sits on a packhorse, a full basket on his arm and creels on
the animal. It is pouring with rain and blowing as well. His
hat has just blown off and he is distracted with alarm and
anxiety as he strains to read the tottering fingerpost in the failing
light. He hates the moor. In the tailpiece on p. 5, vol. 1,
there are again a blinding storm, a horse and his rider, the latter
probably a farmer. There is fear alike in the thrown-back ears
of the nag and the averted face of the man. They have passed

a fingerpost and are nearing a gallows with its burden. You can almost hear the chains creak in the storm. How common it was for the traveller to pass a body dangling from a gallows may be judged from the frequent recurrence of such place-names as Gallows Knowe, Gallows Hill, and even Gallows Close. A gallows on a wild moorland road is shown on p. 71, vol. 1, and a convict being driven to one on p. 50, vol. 2.

In a moor picture a man is following a packhorse laden with sacks and holding his hat on against the tempest while he is approaching another dimly-seen little fingerpost. The sacks will serve as a reminder that up to recent times the bridle path, so called because it was used by packhorses, was the only approach to the mills in that land of streams wherein Bewick was accustomed to wander. You can see many ruined mills on the streams. In their day each had its " poker " or man who delivered the " pokes " or sacks of flour, whitey-grey figures that might have come out of Chaucer.

Dismal is the picture of two travellers, apparently gypsies, followed by a dog wending their way across a moor in the usual storm, the woman carrying a bundle in her shawl which may be a baby, and the man with a tinker's outfit. It will remind lovers of Thomas Hardy of that famous journey over Exmoor by a similar set of characters. Shops and commercial travellers have been the undoing of gangrel or gaun folk such as muggers, pedlars, basket-makers, and the like.

A wonderful feeling of desolation is conveyed by the hilly moor on p. 231, vol. 2. The tree, dwarfed by the wind and standing as if its back were turned to it, the little dog, the man holding on to his hat, and the barren hillocky land give expression to the forbidding character of the moor.

There are other less dismal changes chronicled by Bewick's pencil, such as Carlin Sunday or Shrove Tuesday in the olden time. The Sundays in Lent used to be commemorated by a rhyme known throughout the British Isles :

> Tid, mid, misera,
> Carlin, palm, and pace egg day.

Just as pancakes form the appropriate dish for Shrove Tuesday, salt fish for Good Friday, dyed eggs for Easter, so peas, fried and very peppery, formed the right meal for Carlin Sunday. These were part of the pretty observances that saved the country from

dullness in the olden time. Like many other customs, they have
fled before the steam engine. Other changes are incidental to
the development of the soil. Everyone who knows the old
history of Northumberland is aware of the vast number
of bogs, mosses and mires which only the moss-troopers
could traverse in safety. In the time of Bewick they
still existed to such an extent that the booming of the bittern
was one of the common country sounds. Since then the drainer
has been busy, and what before was bog is now in many cases
dry land, attracting new birds and growing new flowers. It had
a curious effect on sport, and nearly every Northumbrian is a
bit of a sportsman. The use of stilts appears to have been very
common in Bewick's time and indeed remained so long after he
had passed away. He shows us men walking on stilts in the
water, and sportsmen evidently after duck or other water birds,
the gun strapped to the shoulder, the little dog swimming after
his master, and the latter needing, as it seems to modern eyes,
all his dexterity to be able to cross the flooded country on
these artificial limbs.

Bewick had evidently a boyish sympathy for illicit sport.
In what Ruskin called " the most splendid " of these pictures
a poacher with his gun is following the tracks of hares and
rabbits on the snow. Fish-spearing appears to have been not
unlawful, as the four-toed leister frequently occurs in these
pictures, sometimes lying beside the fish that had been killed,
sometimes carried by a burly peasant through the water in which
he is wading. Bewick delighted also in picturing the various
troubles that lay in wait for the fisherman. His line gets hanked
just after he has hooked a fish ; while he is running a big one an
angry bull makes its appearance, so that the unfortunate angler
is between the devil and the deep sea.

This is all part of the joyous side of the engraver. He is in
a different mood when portraying the wayfaring beggars,
wanderers, and wastrels of the old time. The number of one-
legged or otherwise disabled men is extraordinary. So is the
number of blind men who are under the guidance of a little
dog, and he takes strange delight in showing these men in
most perilous circumstances. The little dog becomes excited
by an angry bull just at the time when he should be carefully
leading his master over a narrow plank bridge. We see the water
bubbling below and expect the itinerant to fall in at any moment.

Old age he depicts with curious vividness, as in that hovel with its most wretched inhabitant over which he has painted the inscription : " If Youth but knew what age would crave, every penny it would save."   In another he shows a tomb of which the inscription conveys the philosophy of the rustic in the briefest possible words. The inscription is : " Good times, and bad times, and all time got over." The phrase " got over " gives the very essence of the old Northumbrian rustic's outlook on life.   The

The Tyne at Bywell.

pictures of house and homestead, which form a large part of the tailpieces, go far to explain the hardness of country life a hundred years ago. Hedworth Williamson, with " A Northern Headstone " for a text, put it all into a little poem.

A NORTHERN HEADSTONE

Strong with its stunted tower, gray in the driving shower,
  Stands the old Church with the moors for a setting.
Under this turfy heap my old friend sleeps his sleep,
  Lichen and sea wind, the headstone are fretting.

What did he with his life ? ·Tended an ailing wife,
  Buttressed the bridge and rebuilt the byre,
Drained the five acre field, doubled the yearly yield,
  Tiled the west gable-end after the fire.

Drought in the early spring, rain in the harvesting,
  Even a good season's niggardly bounty
All his life long he knew, yet oats like his were few,
  And his swedes famous, on this side the county.

Now his day's work is done, night begun, resting won,
  He lies so quietly under the clover,
Heeds not the rain and wind, this world well left behind,
  Good times, and bad times, and all time got over.

CHAPTER XXIV

HEXHAM

Hexham the most beautiful Northumbrian Town—Its Saxon church—Scottish raids and the Abbey—Historical objects in the Abbey—The Fridstool and sanctuary—The Night Stair—A standard-bearer's headstone—The crypt and a famous Roman inscription—Modern Hexham and its poet.

HEXHAM is the most beautiful and one of the oldest of Northumbrian towns. Its situation bears some resemblance to that of Melrose. The Tyne, broad and rippling, flows past the one just as the Tweed flows past the other. The appearance of the place at a first glance impresses on one the feeling of a sheltered land and a fertile soil. Trees of every kind grow freely and happily in the town and fine plantations surround it. Although raised considerably above the banks of the river, Hexham reminds one of a cradle. Cultivated land swelling on every side gently gives place to brown upland pasture and heather. The situation seems to have recommended itself to each successive race that inhabited Britain. Neolithic and Roman remains have been discovered all round it. Hexham does not seem to have been at any time a Roman station. But that was probably because Corbridge, the Roman Corstopitum, in Roman times the most important town north of Eboracum, lies within three miles of it. No Roman name has been found for Hexham. Bede calls it Hagustald, and Bates made a shrewd guess when he said that originally it was in all likelihood " a petty State that some forgotten Hagustald had probably conquered from the Britons." Its ascertained history begins in the seventh century, when Wilfrid chose it for the site of his

magnificent church. The town and land had been given him
by Queen Etheldrida so that he might build a monastery and
make it an ecclesiastical centre. Etheldrida may have proposed
to retire to it herself. She was a devout woman who after being
twice married, first to Tunbert, a Chief of the South Gervii,
and afterwards to Ecgfrid, ultimately retired to lead a religious
life at Ely.

Wilfrid was the first of a type of churchman soon to become
numerous and powerful. He had been educated at Lindisfarne,
and magnificent as his ideas became in many respects, he retained
to the last the simple, frugal habits which distinguished Aidan
and his successors. But once in early life and twice subsequently he made a journey to Rome and brought back with
him a taste for the noble ecclesiastical buildings that had begun
to arise in Italy. He was a man of great ambition, whose love
of power brought him into conflict with the highest dignitaries
of Church and State. He built the original church at Hexham,
but was not its first bishop owing to his being out of favour.
There were twelve bishops altogether, of which one, St. Cuthbert,
never assumed office, preferring Lindisfarne. Among the
others were many whose names became familiar—Eata, John
(who was later to attain to fame as John of Beverley), Wilfrid
himself, Acca, Frithbert, Alchmund, Tilbert, Ethelbert, Eadred,
Eanbert, and Tidfrith. In " The Chronicle of Lanercost "
there is a reference to the Abbey as having been built by " that
illustrious bishop of the Lord, St. Wilfrid," and having of old
several shrines enclosing relics of the holy fathers. The chronicler
proceeds to say " that very church carved with Roman work
was dedicated by the ministry of St. Wilfrid to the honour of
Saint Andrew, the meekest of the apostles and the spiritual
patron of the Scots." In building the church the workmen
had a quarry close at hand in Corstopitum, the Roman town,
now Corbridge. In Saxon times it was easier to take the stones
from some existing and perhaps ruinous building near at hand
than to quarry them at a distance. Of the many proofs that
the stones were brought from Corstopitum it is difficult to select
the most interesting. One or two may be mentioned, however.
The first is that in doing so a common custom was followed.
Hodges and Gibson give the following list of churches which
contain large quantities of Roman worked stones: Alwinton,
Gosforth, Heddon-on-the-Wall, Haydon, Chollerton, Warden,

Newbrough, Bywell, Corbridge, Ovingham, Lanchester, Ebchester, Escomb, and the Abbeys of Jedburgh and Lanercost. In 1887 three Roman stones were discovered in the bed of the Tyne at a point known as an ancient ford. One was the upper half of a very large altar which had evidently been cut in two for convenience in transport. It was obvious from their water-worn surfaces that they had been submerged for many centuries. The conclusion is drawn that they constituted a cartload on its

Hexham Abbey.

way to St. Wilfrid's buildings. It had been overturned in the ford and left there, as the labour of recovering and reloading would have been greater than that of going back for another load. The nature of the stone shows it to have come from quarries on the north bank of the Tyne nearer to Corbridge than Hexham. Then there are the sculptured stones actually found in the abbey ruins, of which something must be said hereafter.

Hexham had a very troubled history, the early portion of which culminated in 875, when the Danes, under Haldane,

S 2

landed and pillaged and destroyed Hexham along with many other churches. The church was not reconstituted until 1113, when it was made into a priory of the Austin Canons. The buildings were never completed because of the Scottish raids which culminated towards the end of the thirteenth century. As we have already seen, very troublous times occurred in the north after the Norman Conquest, and Hexham, close to the Border, was for centuries subjected to the incursions of the Scots. A very vivid account of these raids is given by the chronicler of Lanercost, who writes with an intense hatred of the Scot that was no doubt reciprocated. On Friday of Passion Week, 1297, a detachment of the Scottish army made an incursion into England, burning and slaying among the country villages as far as the monastery of Carham. In April of the same year a band of young knights and fighting men forced their way through Redesdale under the leadership of the Earl of Buchan. The Lanercost chronicler says :

In this raid they surpassed in cruelty all the fury of the heathen ; when they could not catch the strong and young people who took flight, they imbrued their arms, hitherto unfleshed, with the blood of infirm people, old women, women in child-bed, and even children two or three years old, proving themselves apt scholars in atrocity, in so much so that they raised aloft little span-long children pierced on pikes, to expire thus and fly away to the heavens. They burnt consecrated churches ; both in the sanctuary and elsewhere they violated women dedicated to God, as well as married women and girls, either murdering them or robbing them after gratifying their lust. Also they herded together a crowd of little scholars in the schools of Hexham, and, having blocked the doors, set fire to that pile (so) fair (in the sight) of God. Three monasteries of holy collegiates were destroyed by them—Lanercost, of the Canons Regular ; and Hexham of the same order, and (that) of the nuns of Lambley ; of all these the devastation can by no means be attributed to the valour of warriors, but to the dastardly combat of thieves, who attacked a weaker community where they would not be likely to meet with any resistance. (" The Chronicle of Lanercost," Sir Herbert Maxwell's translation.)

The attack on the church was described as follows :

And although both the dignity of the saints and respect for the pious friars ought to have been a defence against the irreverent, yet these madmen aforesaid neither had any regard for these things nor felt any dread of all-seeing God, but with barbarous ferocity committed the consecrated buildings to the flames, plundering the church property stored therein, even violating the women in that very place and afterwards butchering them, sparing neither age, rank nor sex. At last they reached such a pitch of iniquity as to fling contemptuously into the flames the relics of the saints preserved in shrines, tearing off them the gold or silver plates and gems. Also, roaring with laughter, they cut the head off the image of St. Andrew, a conspicuous figure, declaring he must leave that place and return to his own soil to be trodden under foot.

Hexham never fully recovered from these misfortunes. The priory and convent were impoverished, though they still retained possession of the church at Hexham and the land belonging to it until the dissolution of the monasteries. A number of them rebelled and took part in the Pilgrimage of Grace, but want of combination ruined their chance of success and Henry VIII took stern measures with them. He ordered Norfolk " without pity or circumstance " to see that " all the monkes and chanons, that be in anywise faultie, *to be tyed uppe, without further delaye or ceremony, to the terrible example of others ;* wherein we thinke you shall doo unto us highe service."

In 1571 Sir J. Forster, later Warden of the Middle Marches, purchased the manor of Hexham from the Crown, to which it had been sold by the Archbishop of York, and it subsequently devolved on his son-in-law, Sir John Fenwick, who was killed in the battle of Marston Moor. The other Sir John Fenwick, who was beheaded for high treason in 1697, had previously sold the manor to Sir William Blackett. The present owner of the property is Viscount Allendale.

The abbey church has been beautifully restored now and claims to be the finest Early English church in Great Britain.

The feature most interesting to a visitor is the unequalled number of historical objects that have been preserved from early times. Some of these stir the imagination to an extraordinary degree. First in romantic interest one would place the Fridstool, or Seat of Peace. Wilfrid brought it from Italy and it is probably of Pagan origin. Here, it marks the centre of the sanctuary. Wilfrid obtained the privilege of sanctuary for the church. Its extent was a mile all round the building, and the limits were marked by stone crosses, the names of some of which still remain, as Maiden's Cross in the west, White Cross Field in the east, and Lady Cross Bank on the north bank of the river. There is a room called the Sanctuary Chamber. It is over the internal porch at the east end of the slype and seems to have been used by him who watched for those who fled from the avenger of blood.

The Night Stair is another prominent though not peculiar feature of the abbey. Of old we can fancy the cowled monks ascending it to their dormitory. Nowadays the original steps have been replaced in position and the effect is very remarkable when the red-clad choir go up or down. It seems to recall in a very striking way the pomp and ceremony of the medieval church.

Of the Roman stones two stand out beyond all the others. One is the gravestone of a Roman soldier, of the rank of standard-bearer, who was killed at the age of twenty-five and buried at Corstopitum. I cannot do better than quote the description of it by Hodges and Gibson.

" It is a stock design used largely all over the Roman Empire, and represents a mounted soldier riding over a prostrate barbarian. In this instance the details of the figures are of great interest. The soldier is well armed, he wears a helmet with high crest and plume, and round his neck is a torque, which indicates his high rank. In his right hand he carries the standard which displays the sun god in a circle. The long sword is sheathed, and no other weapon is seen. The horse is amply harnessed, furnished with martingales, covered with a square-cut saddle-cloth, and shod. The barbarian is naked, and carries a large oval shield by a strap with his left arm, while his right hand grasps a short leaf-shaped sword of strikingly different form to that worn by his conqueror. Below the sculpture is a sunk panel with ansated ends, in which is the inscription :

> DIS. MANIBVS. FLAVINVS
> EQ. ALAE. PETR. SIGNIFER
> TFR. CANDIDI. AN. XXV
> STIP. VII. H. S.

> " To the gods the shades Flavinus
> standard-bearer of the cavalry of Petriana
> of the white troop twenty-five years of age
> and seven years' service is laid here."

Of almost greater interest is a stone found in the crypt which in itself constitutes a most interesting feature of the abbey. The crypt of an early church might serve two purposes. This one has served as a burial place and also as a place of worship where the sacred relics of saints were exhibited and adored.

One of the many interesting features of the Hexham crypt is that it was built of Roman stones, one of them of great historical importance. The original stone was broken in two and for long the inscription was curtailed. Even now it is deficient, but as far as it remains it reads :

> IMP . CAES . L SEP . SEVERVS . PI
> PERTINAX . ET . IMP . CAES M .
> AVR . ANTONINVS . PIVS . AVG
> VSTI . ET . PVB . SEPTIM
> CAES . COHORTES . · · · M
> VEXILLATION . M
> FECERVNT . SVB

This may be expanded into :

> Imp(erator) Caes(ar) L. Sep(timius) Severus Pi(us)
> Pertinax et imp(erator) Caesar M. Aur(elius) Antoninus
> Pius, Augusti et Publius Septimius Geta Caesar
> (erased), Cohortes M. Vexillation fecerunt sub
> (a general's name lost)

or :

> The Emperor Lucius Septimius Severus Pius Pertinax
> and his sons the Emperor Marcus Aurelius Antoninus Pius
> Augustus and Publius Septimius Geta Caesar (reigning)
> the cohorts and detachments made this under the
> command of . . . .

Nothing could more strikingly illustrate the organised power of the Roman Empire. After the Emperor Geta was murdered by his brother an edict was issued from Rome commanding that wherever the two names appeared in combination that of Geta was to be erased. This has been done on the stone at Hexham, but not so effectually as to make it impossible to read the name. There have been found only two other instances of the survival of this inscription. One was discovered at Cairo and another in Rome. The reason why many inscriptions have been preserved on the stones of the crypt is that the Saxon builders always put the lettering outside so that it might be a key to a plaster that they used. When the crypt was dried and ventilated by modern methods this plaster fell off and the inscription became readable. In the early destruction of the abbey the crypt appears to have been missed altogether, and it was only discovered accidentally in the eighteenth century. Fairless contributed the first modern account of it to the "Archæological Journal," in the course of which he said: "There have been three approaches to this solemn and drear retreat one of them at present reaching nearly into the body of the church : another to the south leading to the cloisters : the third rising into the nave."

It is tempting to go on describing the rude pictures of which the Dance of Death is the most arresting, the old almsbox and a thousand other things that are calculated to beguile the antiquarian into spending the sunniest hours within the building. But enough has been said to whet an appetite that can only be properly gratified by a personal visit to the beautiful abbey which is the pride and glory of Hexham.

The Hexham of to-day is a country town with an air of peace and content. "Formerly ample and magnificent as the vestiges of antiquity testify," wrote Prior Richard in the twelfth century. Something of that ancient state it has regained. The reconstructed abbey stands beautifully in the centre of a town of well-built houses and shady gardens ; down below, the Tyne gurgles over a broad shallow channel causing a thousand little whirls and eddies.

In its tranquil security the terrible adventures of its past seem far away, even though antiquity has left many remembrances in the shape of old houses, the most interesting and important being The Moot Hall and the Manor office. The country people who bring their wares to the Market, with its picturesque roof supported on pillars, and recommend them in the broadest Northumbrian, probably differ little externally from those who timidly looked on when the Duke of Somerset was beheaded here after the battle of Hexham. The raiding Scot has settled down into a friendly neighbour. In the Seal, the Abbey Grounds, and Tyne Green there is provided an abundance of open spaces where age can talk and youth play. Hexham is the birthplace of the well-known poet, Wilfrid Wilson Gibson, the son of a distinguished citizen and one of a clever family which includes the lady who is best known by her maiden name, Elizabeth Gibson. As the poet of Northumberland, Gibson is at his best in the volumes " Whin," " Stonefolds,"

and " Borderlands." The lines at the opening of " Stonefolds "
give a faithful, vivid picture of moor and fell :

> The ragged heather-ridge is black
>   Against the sunset's frosty rose ;
> With rustling breath, down syke and slack,
>   The icy, eager north-wind blows.
>
> It shivers through my hair, and flicks
> The blood into my tingling cheek.

The Market Place, Hexham.

There are in " Whin " many thumb-nail sketches that are
in literature what Bewick's tailpieces are in drawing. Here are
a few of them picked at random :

> Just to see the rain
> Sweeping over Yeavering Bell
> Once again.

Soldier, what do you see
Lying so cold and still ?
Fallowfield Fell at night
And the stars above the hill.

The heather's black on Hareshaw
When Redesdale's lying white ;
When grass is green in Redesdale
Dark Hareshaw blossoms bright.

I came by Raw from Hungry Law,
When who should pass me by
But Pedlar Jack, with a pack on his back
And a patch across his eye.

Thirlwall is the subject of the following :

In the last gleam of winter sun
A hundred starlings scream and screel
Among the ragged firs that stand
About the ruined Pele.

But Mr. Gibson is much more than a local poet, as is shown
by such a piece as that called " Blind " :

Blow, blow, O wind, the clouds aside
That I may see the stars !
In heaven glimmers far and wide
The burnished shield of Mars ;
And Jupiter and Venus ride
The night in glittering cars !

Blow, blow, O wind, the clouds aside
That I may see the stars !
Nay ! God has flung his darkness wide
And set the unyielding bars ;
And day and night, unheeded, ride
The world in glittering cars !

CHAPTER XXV

HEXHAM AND ITS NEIGHBOURHOOD

The old bridge at Linnels—The Devil's Water—The defeat of the
Lancastrians and Queen Margaret's adventure—One of the
most remote and beautiful moorland villages—Foundation and
history of Blanchland—Corbridge, an ancient capital of
Northumbria and a famous Roman town—A fortified mansion
of the fourteenth century—Dilston Castle, the home of the
Radcliffes—The story of Lord Derwentwater and his fate—
Grey of Dilston.

THE Battle of Hexham fought on Hexham Levels on May 8th,
1464, may be said to have ended the Wars of the Roses. The
Lancastrians received a blow from which there was no recovery.
Whether there was only one battle of Hexham or two battles
in successive years is open to doubt. One was recorded, but as
the inquest on the death of the Duke of Somerset is signed
April 3rd, 1463, and he was executed immediately after the battle
fought on May 4th, 1464, Mr. Crawford Hodgson suggests
that the clerk may " have confused the date of two battles
fought about the same date near the same place."
It is an easy walk from Hexham to Hexham Levels by
Hackwood, Beacon Grange, and Sunnyside, close to Linnels
Bridge and Mill. The bridge carries an inscription :

> God Presarve Wmfoira Evengton,
> Belldete This Brege Of Lyme And stone,
> 1581

The date 1581 is borne out by the character of the mouldings,
but the bridge of that date appears to have been superseded by

another built in 1698, or after Benedict Errington and John
Heron, owners of the Linnels, "were presented by the Grand
Jury for having suffered the Linnels Bridge to go out of repair,
it having been at first built by the owner of the Linnels."
To-day it is part of a fine bit of scenery. The Devil's Water is a
very rough water and comes jumping and foaming over its bed
of rock, above which the trees on either side almost meet.
In days not very old the mill was a haunt of doubtful characters,
but all was changed after the property was sold by Sir John
Haggerston. A beautiful residence has been built almost on the
edge of the noisy stream, whose waters are now partially employed in the ditches and channels of a very modern water
garden, and though the ancient mill is retained it is only as a
curiosity. One cannot help envying the owner of such an
ideal home, near the road yet hidden from it, sheltered by the
high bank and the trees, and always within hearing of the madly
gay little river.

At a short distance up stream are the levels, or haughs, where
the battle was fought. It was a very bloody encounter. Lord
Montacute and his followers were in an overpowering majority
and still flushed with their victory at Hedgeley Moor. The
Lancastrians fought with their backs to the stream and lost
heavily in consequence.

It was here that Queen Margaret met with the most romantic
of her adventures. With her son she managed to escape from
the field of battle, but only to get lost in a thick wood, Dipton
or Deepdene, which even to-day puts one in mind of a stronghold
of robbers such as abounded in the fifteenth century. It is a
huge ravine, the banks of which fall precipitously to the West
Dipton burn which flows between them on its way to join the
Devil's Water. Here the unhappy queen was held up by one
of a band of robbers and she was again confronted with the fate
from which she had apparently escaped. Much difference of
opinion as to the truth of the story has been expressed, but one
feels inclined to share the view put forward in the "History of
Northumberland," where the story is continued as follows :

The situation was a critical one, but it was saved by the courage
and presence of mind of Queen Margaret. Calling the man to her,
she told him he had been born in a fortunate hour. A chance was
given to him of redeeming by a single act a life of vice and crime.
The son of his king was at his feet for him to save. The unhappy

queen besought him to protect his prince and endeavour to convey him to a place of safety. Overcome by Margaret's entreaties and prayers, the bandit agreed to become the protector of the fugitives, swore he would suffer a thousand torments ere he would abandon the prince, implored the queen's pardon for his misdeeds, and vowed he would devote the remainder of his life to acts of mercy. Convinced of his fidelity, the queen left her son in the hands of the robber while she went in search of her husband. The cave on the West Dipton burn is said to be the place where Margaret and Prince Edward were temporarily lodged by their protector. It is 31 feet long and 14 feet broad, but scarcely high enough to allow of a person standing upright. In the middle is a massive pillar of rude masonry which is said to mark the line of a wall which formerly divided the cave into two parts. The chief authority is Chastellain, who says that he had it from the queen herself, and gives a very circumstantial account of the affair. In the face of such testimony it is difficult to question the substantial truth of the incident.

In the wild and overgrown woods it is no easy matter to find the cave amid the rank undergrowth, but there is on the local map the Queen's letch—the place where her horse slipped—and the cave is near by and may be found by noticing the trodden path leading to it. The Dene is the most remarkable, and in some ways the most beautiful, in the county, but good climbing legs are needed for its full enjoyment.

Far in the south of the county, inaccessible by rail and seemingly entirely remote from all modern industry and bustle, yet within ten miles of the blast furnaces and unsightly chimneys of Consett in Durham, lies Blanchland. Although twelve miles from Hexham, it is easily reached by driving, the road going by Slaley and Bolbeck Common and Blanchland Moor. No way is better calculated to give an idea of the high fells of Northumberland. In the deep valley of the infant Derwent Blanchland's grey walls, with their dim romance of human devotion and art, are circled by the changeless moors. In the centuries since first the white-robed monks travelled the lonely fells and founded the abbey, no other civilising influence has laid its hand on the miles and miles of solitude which encompass Blanchland now as in the twelfth century. Its exquisite name is supposed to spring from the white habits of the canons. Three other contemporary religious houses were similarly named, Blanche Land near Cherbourg, Blanca Lande in Guernsey, and Alba Landa, or Whitland, in Carmarthenshire. Walter de Bolbeck founded the abbey for the Premonstratensian canons.

A seal of the abbey is preserved at Durham.   The distant Abbot of Premontré was the head of the order and visited the house from time to time.   Records of his visitations are preserved. Its seclusion did not protect it from the Scottish raiders, and the disorganisation due to that was possibly the cause why in 1343 Blanchland had " fallen in temporals and spirituals and was in much need of reform."   Edward III, in 1327, in pursuit of the elusive Scots, arrived at Blanchland, which had been recently burnt by the raiders.

Little is known of the history of the abbey, and at the dissolution of the monasteries it was sold.   In time it came to Nicholas Forster of Bamburgh and thence to Lord Crewe, and now belongs to the trustees of the famous charity founded by h'm.   The chancel of the abbey church, the north transept, and the noble tower now form the parish church.   In some of the windows are fragments of medieval painted glass depicting the canons in their white robes.   On the floor of the transept are some interesting grave covers, one of an abbot with a crozier and chalice on either side of a cross ;   another with a bugle, sword and arrows ;   another with a cross above five steps and the letters I H C.   In the transept aisle is the most striking of the memorial stones, a blue slab with a sword, bow and arrow, and the name of the hunter, Robt. of Egylston, probably the abbey's forester.   In the churchyard is an ancient cross.   A portion of the conventual buildings on the west side of the cloister garth, dating from the thirteenth century, is now the " Lord Crewe Arms."   The gatehouse, which makes such an impressive entrance to the village square, is possibly fifteenth-century, and also the house on the west of it.

Where two streams unite to form the Derwent, a mile above Blanchland, in lovely scenery, is a high cliff, imposing and picturesque, called Gibraltar Rock.

Corbridge, about three miles from Hexham in the opposite direction to Blanchland, has an altogether different interest. Excavations   were   begun   at   Corstopitum,   a   Roman town   rather   than   a   military   station,   in   1906   and   are still   going   on,   with   results   of   the   highest   importance. This ancient capital of Northumbria is entered on the south side by a bridge of seven arches built in 1674, from which a splendid view is obtained.   In the corner of the church-yard is a pele tower built in the fourteenth century and the residence of the early vicars and the best example of the fortified vicarage peculiar to Northumbria. The large and beautiful church has a Saxon porch, and with the exception of Hexham is the earliest ecclesiastical building in Northumberland. It is largely built of stones from the Roman town. The arch into the nave is supposed to have been transferred from a Roman gateway.

From Corbridge there is a delightful walk through the fields to Aydon Castle, a fortified mansion of the fourteenth century standing in a fine position on the bank above the dene through which the Cor burn runs, looking over the valley of the Tyne with Hexham Abbey in the distance. It is now used as a farmhouse, and besides its picturesque situation has many beautiful features. The stables remain to show the turbulent times of their erection, for they are both built and roofed with stone, and with stone mangers to protect the dumb animals from the fires the Scots invaders kindled on their red road through North England. Several carved windows remain, and in the interior are beautiful early fourteenth-century fireplaces.

A mile from Corbridge are the ruins of Dilston Castle, once the home of the Radcliffes. Romantic and pathetic are the dismantled walls from which, with foreboding in his heart, the last Earl rode forth in 1715.

> O Derwentwater's a bonnie lord
> And golden is his hair.

In the annals of Northumberland there is no more touching story than that of his short and noble life. His doom was written at his birth. His mother, Lady Mary Tudor, was a natural daughter of Charles II, and her married life with the Earl of Derwentwater was so unhappy that they separated. Her eldest son James was brought up at the exiled Court of St. Germains, so that both his blood and association with the young Pretender ensured his sympathy with the Stuart cause. When he was twenty-one he came home to the ancestral seat at Dilston, and taking up his duties as the landlord of a great estate became generally beloved by the north country people, who succumbed to his attractive appearance and charming, generous personality. The portraits existing to-day at Thorndon, where his body was at last buried, testify to his good looks. Although a strong adherent of the Church of Rome, his benevolence extended as much to Protestant as Papist. The ballads relating his fate point to the love he had inspired during the few years he lived on his patrimony. His marriage to Anna, daughter of Sir John Webb, whom he had met whilst she was being educated in a convent in Paris, helped to confirm his attachment to the Stuarts. When he hung back from the rising, she rallied him. He foresaw the failure.

> Farewell, farewell, my lady dear,
> Ill, ill thou counsell'dst me,
> I never more may see the babe
> That smiles upon thy knee.

The " wee German lairdie " who reigned in England was adamant to all the unfortunate Jacobites who, after surrendering, were at his mercy. They consisted of seventy-five gentlemen of Northumberland and about one hundred and forty-three of Scotland, with just over a thousand of humbler followers. George need not have shown such a lack of clemency. They were hardly to be feared, in a stable realm, who were merely the dupes of a romantic and pious dream. Some died from cruel treatment, some were executed, some transported. Every effort was made to save the Earl's life. The Countess knelt at George's feet, many noble ladies petitioned him, the Earl at his trial pleaded his youth, and his submission, and that of his adherents. The judges, his peers, were anxious to show mercy, but George was implacable. The last Earl of Derwentwater was executed on February 24th, 1716, on Tower Hill. That night, over Dilston's melancholy tower, the red fingers of the Aurora Borealis shot across the sky, and the watching peasantry saw in it the portent of the passing of their beloved lord. Since then they have called them, not the Northern, but Lord Derwentwater's lights. His body was brought to the family vault at Dilston. In 1805 the coffin was opened to see if the head had been buried with the embalmed body, and the Earl was lying, still young, with his severed head and its light brown hair still perfect. Unfortunately, the vault was not closed properly, and people in the neighbourhood visiting it, a blacksmith actually pulled out several teeth and sold them. After that, all the family coffins were removed, and with them the body of the last Earl, to Thorndon in Essex, where his descendant, Lord Petre, lives.

After the confiscation of the estates they came into the possession of Greenwich Hospital, and the castle was allowed to go to ruin, vagrants occupying the Radcliffes' lordly halls, and the furniture, through lax management, found its way into many houses in the district. The mansion of the Radcliffes was destroyed in 1768, and the tower now to be seen is part of the ancient castle built by the Dyvelstons in the fourteenth century. Their name was originally D'Eivill, and the effigy of a knight of the family lies in Hexham Abbey, clad in armour. Dilston and Devil's Water are derived from the name of the first barons.

Near the ruins stands a little chapel among the trees, beneath which was the vault of the Radcliffe family, and where they lay for so many years till curious sightseers made their removal necessary. Not far from the tower stands the pleasant house built by the noted agriculturist, John Grey, a fine type of the Northumbrian gentleman, and the father of that new crusader, Josephine Butler. Grey was appointed in 1833 to take charge of the Greenwich estates, and he cleared away from the castle the unsightly *débris* of years of neglect. Later removals disclosed the foundations of the old castle of the D'Eivilles. Below the ivy-clad ruins, which stand on a steep bank, runs the lovely, flashing Devil's Water, sometimes flowing quietly past green haughs or dancing over the flat rocks between precipitous wooded banks. The walk up the Devil's Water is of entrancing beauty and solitude, past wild, wooded slopes, with deep pools in the shade below. Nearer Hexham is the romantic reach of the river, flowing between lofty cliffs called Swallowship. And all the scenery is reminiscent of Derwentwater's romantic figure and his " Farewell."

> Farewell to pleasant Dilston Hall,
> My father's ancient seat ;
> A stranger now must call thee his,
> Which gars my heart to greet.
>
> Albeit that here in London town
> It is my fate to die ;
> O carry me to Northumberland,
> In my father's grave to lie.
> There chant my solemn requiem
> In Hexham's holy towers ;
> And let six maids of fair Tynedale
> Scatter my grave with flowers.

T

CHAPTER XXVI

REDESDALE AND ITS BALLADS

The Middle Marches—"The deadly feud"—The life of a moss-
trooper—A famous Reed and how he died—Border manners
reflected in the ballad—The raid of the Reidswire—Wardens
of the Marches in the sixteenth century—A dispute and how it
ended—Jedburgh to the Reidswire.

To follow the North Tyne towards its source is to enter the
region which composed the Middle Marches. It includes North
Tynedale and Redesdale and differs materially in character
from the Eastern and Western Marches. The Eastern Marches
embraced that level Gate to and from Scotland which extended
from the Cheviots to the sea and also the Forest of Cheviot.
It provided the stage whereon were fought the great battles
that date from Malcolm Canmore to the Union, and is studded
with great Castles or their ruins. The Western Marches performed the same function for the entrance by Carlisle. "Warkworth and Naworth and merry Carlisle" existed to withstand
invasion, but in "the land Debateable" each was for himself,
and thieves of Redesdale and Tynedale foraged or fought among
themselves or with thieves of Liddesdale. In it the king's writ
did not run, and the typical inhabitant was that Robson who was
described as a good and honest man "saving a little shyfting for
his living." Instead of justice they had "the deadly feud."
They were bound together in clans and families and woe to him
who brought one of them under the punishment of the law.
He was a marked man henceforth and the odds were strongly
against his escaping the vengeance of the dead man's
kindred. Surprise has been expressed that some of their deeds
have been commemorated in ballad poetry which is unequalled the world over, but their adventurous lives could
not fail to produce that emotion of which the best poetry
is compact. Work they reduced to a minimum, but they

were adepts at traversing their wild country at all times and seasons secretly and swiftly. Lesly, Bishop of Ross, has described them in words that enable one to picture the whole raid. The raider lay close all day and sallied out at night, making for his quarry by unfrequented byways and many intricate windings to the place he meant to raid. Having secured his booty, he started for home " through blind ways and fetching many a compass," in order to baffle pursuit. He still was not free from apprehension, which became agony when a distant baying announced that bloodhounds were on his track. Not always could he enjoy the good fortune of Deloraine, who

> By sudden leaps and desperate bounds
> Had baffled Percy's best bloodhounds.

If taken red-handed, then short was his shrift and unavailing his persuasiveness and plausibility or the appeal to mercy. Risking death and often inflicting it, running into great perils and under constant pressure alike of bodily pain and anxiety, his primitive fears and passions were expressed in keen, hard words that had a force beyond attainment in the study.

The best example that has come down to us to illustrate the ancient manners of Redesdale is that called " The Death of Parcy Reed." He belonged to the family of Troughend, a strong tower of which the massive foundations can yet be traced at a short distance from Troughend Hall. In Redesdale the Reeds ranked with the Hedleys, Fletchers and Spoors as next to the Halls, the most powerful family corresponding to the Robsons and Milbournes of North Tynedale. He appears to have been a typical Borderer of his day, a great hunter and fighter, rude of speech and contemptuous of religion and restraint. He was appointed Keeper of Redesdale and discharged the duties of that office with a fearless vigour that brought him into collision with some of his powerful neighbours. He dared even to administer justice to one of a band of moss-troopers named Crosier, and the ballad is the story of their revenge with the Halls as accomplices.

> Now Parcy Reed has Crosier ta'en,
> He has delivered him to the law ;
> But Crosier says he'll do waur than that,
> He'll make the tower o' Troughend fa'.

Parcy, unwitting that he has made them enemies, goes hunting with the " three fause Ha's o' Girsonfield " :

> They hunted high, they hunted low,
>   By heathery hill and birken shaw ;
> They raised a buck on Rooken Edge,
>   And blew the mort at fair Ealylawe.

At Batinghope, a high and lonely glen under the shadow of Carter, when the sun was sinking low

> Says Parcy then, " Ca' off the dogs,
> We'll bait our steeds and homeward go."

They alighted " atween the brown and benty ground " to do so, and the mighty hunter no sooner was stretched on the sward than " Parcy Reed was sleeping sound." Now the traitors had their chance :

> They've stown the bridle off his steed,
>   And they've put water in his lang gun ;
> They've fixed his sword within the sheath
>   That out again it winna come.

This being accomplished they give the alarm and awaken him by the cry that " the five Crosiers are coming owre the Hinginstane." The stout Parcy laughs at the odds ; if they will engage three he will deal with two and make them either fight or flee. But they refuse :

> " We mayna stand, we canna stand,
>   We dairrna stand alang wi' thee ;
> The Crosiers haud thee at a feud,
>   And they wad kill baith thee and we."

In vain he beseeches them individually, and he had scarcely time to cross himself " a prayer he hadna time to say," till the Crosiers keen were upon him

> All riding graithed and in array,

He felled the foremost to the ground with " his fankit sword," but the others swarmed in and overcame him. After many wounds

> They hacked off his hands and feet
> And left him lying on the lee.

Then after a few words of savage exultation they rode off in the direction of Liddesdale and

> It was the hour o' gloaming grey,
>   When herds come in frae fauld and pen ;
> A herd he saw a huntsman lie,
>   Says he, " Can this be Laird Troughen ? "

The ballad-maker had no thought of happy endings, and the ballad ends with the last words of the dying man.

It is a horrible story only redeemed by the restrained strength and beauty of the ballad. The incident narrated does not stand out as exceptional. It could be paralleled by similar occurrences in various countries at an early stage of their civilisation. Compare it, for instance, with the terrible scene in " The Horse Thieves," by the Russian novelist, Kuprin, where Buzega, the German, chops off the fingers of Kozel with a hatchet. Here is nothing but unrelieved horror, a sensational crime as compared with a tragedy of life and death.

The " Raid of the Reidswire " is another ballad which gives a striking account of the customs of Tynedale and Redesdale. It is notable, too, as commemorating the last Border dispute previous to the Union. The Reidswire is so close to the boundary that the water falls on one side into England, that is the valley of the Reed, and the other into Scotland. Sir Walter Scott's account of the fray may be found in "The Minstrelsy of the Scottish Border " and is substantially correct. The dispute arose at a meeting held by the Wardens of the Marches upon the 7th of June, 1575. The object of such meetings was to clear up grievances on either side and for the settlement of disputes. Sir John Carmichael was the Scottish Warden and Sir John Forster the Warden of the English Middle March. In the course of proceedings a true bill was found against a notorious English Freebooter named Farnstein. Forster claimed that he was a fugitive from justice, whereupon Carmichael, taking this as a pretext to avoid payment, shouted out, " Play Fair." Forster retorted with some insulting expressions regarding Carmichael's Family. His retinue, chiefly men of Redesdale and Tynedale, discharged a flight of arrows among the Scots, and the battle was begun. The ballad begins by describing the tryst and its object and gives a list of those who were present, men of Liddesdale led by Elliots, others from Teviot,

Rule Water and Hawick Town. Turnbulls and Rutherfords were present from Jedburgh. On the English side were Sir John Forster, George Heron of Chipchase, and the various Northumbrian dales were represented. The meeting began with merriment, and all went well till the Clerk sat down to call the rules. Dandue Hob and Jock were called to settle for the kine and ewes they had stolen. Then the Scots saw " five hundred Fennicks in a flock " come marching over the hills. But the Scottish ballad-maker says they feared no ill :

> Some gaed to drink and some stude still
> And some to cards and dice them sped
> Till on ane Farnstein they fyled a bill
> And he was fugitive and fled.

Then began the dispute between Carmichael and Forster which caused the Tynedale men to let off a flight of arrows.

> Then was there nought but bow and speir
> And every man pulled out a brand ;
> '' A Schafton and a Fenwick " thare :
> Gude Symington was slain frae hand.

Slogans were shouted, " Fy, Tindaill to it," " Jedburgh's here." The Englishmen, as was still their custom, used the long bow, but the Scotsmen firearms, and they got the better of the conflict. Among those who distinguished themselves most were, George Douglas of Bean Jeddart, Rutherford of Hundlie, Sir Andrew Turnbull of Bedrule upon Rule Water and others whose names were celebrated in the ballad. Sir George Heron, the Keeper of Tynedale and Redesdale, with five other gentlemen of rank, were slain and Fenwick of Wallington severely wounded. The prisoners were taken to Dalkeith, but the Regent Morton, who was looking forward to what might happen after the death of Elizabeth, treated them well and eventually sent them home.

There are many ways of crossing the Border into Northumberland. Over the Tweed at Berwick is perhaps the most historic, and many a tumbling burn and lonely moor on the west side unite the mountains of Cumberland to the softer hill country between our eastern and our western seas. But to know the harsh entrance to Northumberland, familiar yet dreaded, that the Lowland moss-troopers out of Roxburgh rode, there is no way equal to the rough road over the hills by Jedburgh and Carter

Fell. Over these high moors the track runs many a brown mile
in unsurpassable solitude, where only the flash of the peewit's
wing and his startled cry break the loneliness.

Untravelled as it is to-day, except by those who love walking
far from the dust of the highway, yet it is near the Debateable
Land and we do not walk unaccompanied, for fierce altercation
and Border cries come down with the wind from Peel Fell and
Carter Fell. Along the bridle-path men from Liddesdale
galloped hot to the tryst at Reidswire which ended so fatally
after beginning " meek eneugh."

Last night a wind from Lammermoor came roaring up the glen
With the tramp of trooping horses and the laugh of reckless men,
And struck a mailed hand on the gate and cried in rebel glee,
" Come forth ! Come forth, my Borderer, and ride the March
    with me ! "

I said, " Oh ! Wind of Lammermoor, the night's too dark to ride
And all the men that fill the glen are ghosts of men that died !
The floods are down in Bowmont Burn, the moss is fetlock-deep.
Go back, wild Wind of Lammermoor, to Lauderdale—and sleep ! "

Out spoke the Wind of Lammermoor, " We know the road right
    well,
The road that runs by Kale and Jed across the Carter Fell.
There is no man of all the men in this grey troop of mine
But blind might ride the Borderside from Teviothead to Tyne ! "

The horses fretted on their bits and pawed the flints to fire,
The riders swung them to the South full-faced to their desire ;
" Come ! " said the Wind from Lammermoor, and spoke full
    scornfully,
" Have ye no pride to mount and ride your fathers' road with
    me ? "

A roan horse to the gate they led, foam-flecked and travelled far ;
A snorting roan that tossed his head and flashed his forehead star ;
There came a sound of clashing steel and hoof-tramp up the
    glen. . . .
. . . And two by two we cantered through, a troop of ghostly men !

    *   *   *   *   *   *   *

I know not if the farms we fired are burned to ashes yet !
I know not if the stirks grew tired before the stars were set !
I only know that late last night when Northern winds blew free,
A troop of men rode up the glen and brought a horse for me !

The road falls abruptly from the moor to the edge of the high bank above the dashing Kielder, into which the unwary cyclist, should one essay the rugged road, might easily fall. But almost as unexpected as that is the termination of solitude in the little railway station with a single cottage adjoining, where a scared child sees the coming of a stranger and fades away beyond recall. Three trains a day and very few passengers make the human face strange and possibly unpleasant.

The Stepping Stones.

CHAPTER XXVII

Andrew Lang's account of Otterburn—Confused ballad accounts—
The Elizabethan ballad and the Sir Walter touch—Froissart's
account—The battle—The death of Douglas and capture of
Hotspur—Foeman's courtesy—An enchanting village : its
Green, with bull-ring, cockpit and pinfold—Badger-baiting and
ratting in the last century—The Moat Hills from primitive
man to Roman and Saxon—The old church and its memorials—
A fortified rectory—Its connection with the Umfravilles—
Winter's gibbet.

CLOSE to the point at which the pretty Otter burn joins the
Rede is Otterburn. Little needs adding to the account of
Otterburn in Mr. Andrew Lang's posthumous " Highways and
Byways of the Border." Though the work had to be completed
by other hands, this bears obvious evidence of his personality.
In it he had a theme after his own heart, a great and chivalrous
fight described from contemporary evidence by Froissart and
enshrined in ballad poetry. But I think much is to be said in
favour of the opinion of Cadwallader Bates that the ballad
accounts were considerably mixed. It was an era crammed with
hard fighting, and incidents of various battles became hopelessly
intertwined. Even the version quoted by Mr. Lang from " The
Minstrelsy of the Scottish Border " does not impress one with
its accuracy. We know that Sir Walter was but too eager to
welcome a new ballad. He accepted the vamp of Surtees,
though a colder critic might easily have detected the imposture.

> I canna tell a' I canna tell a'
> Some gat a skelp and some gat a claw
> But they garred the Featherstones haud their jaw
>   Nicol and Aleck and a'.

Its vivacity has not the ring of old. Both vivacity and lilt are far removed from the rugged simplicity of the true ballad. Equally open to criticism is the version of Otterburn quoted approvingly by Mr. Lang. It is claimed to be of Elizabethan origin, but as printed it was pieced together by Sir Walter Scott from the recitation of two old persons living in the vale of Ettrick. The Sir Walter touch is very apparent.

The account given by Froissart is more to be trusted. He collected information from participants in the fight and wrote a clear and intelligible story. The minstrels had many doughty deeds to celebrate in the stormy fourteenth century, and probably as the original ballads were passed on by word of mouth, incidents from one fray got interlarded with incidents from another. On the other hand, there are passages in the more modern version which bear traces of having been inserted by the greatest romantic novelist in our literature. A few discrepancies will be noticed in our summary.

Otterburn was not one of the great battles of history, but a typical Border fray in which the qualities developed during generations of hard fighting are vividly illustrated—the keen rivalry between the houses of Douglas and Percy, the valour equally of Scots and English, the chivalry and courtesy of the fighters and so on.

The scene opens with a skirmish before the walls of Newcastle, in which Douglas captured Hotspur's pennon and vowed he would display it on the highest tower of his Castle of Dalkieth. " By God you shall not carry it out of Northumberland," swore Percy. They trysted to meet at Otterburn in the high wild Cheviot country thirty miles from Newcastle. Percy would have followed Douglas at once had not wiser counsel prevailed. Experienced chiefs pointed out that the Scottish force was probably but the advance guard of an army which they could not hope to attack successfully with the small force at their disposal ; better to lose a pennon than a battle which would leave the country defenceless, urged the cautious veterans. But a day or two later armed Scots rode in with the news that Douglas had not more than three thousand men with him and had captured Pontland Tower and taken Sir Raymond de Laval in his castle. Percy joyfully gave the order " To horse ! To horse ! " and led his followers at once on the enemy's track.

The young Earl Douglas, a brave and wary soldier, had taken precautions against a surprise by night.

After a long march the English must have lost their freshness when they arrived at the Scottish camp late on a moonlight night in August. Yet at first it looked as if they would carry the camp by a *coup de main*. Some of the Scots were at supper, others had retired to sleep after their fruitless attacks on Otterburn Tower, when to shouts of " Percy ! Percy ! " the attack was begun. Douglas, however, had arranged his men so that the servants' quarters, which he had strengthened with men-at-arms, would be entered first. They were placed at the entrance of the marsh on the road to Newcastle. Douglas had a plan carefully prepared beforehand. While the lords were arming, a body of infantry was despatched to help the servants to make a fight and cause delay. It is obvious that there could have been little opening for the bowmen. Froissart expressly says the night was advanced and what light there was came from the moon. Some of the lines in " Chevy Chace " were probably taken from some minstrel's version of the Battle of Homildon Hill. For example, the following lines apply directly to the later battle :

> The Englishmen had their bows bent
> Their hearts were good enow.
> The first of arrows that they shot off
> Seven score spearmen they slew.
>
> Yet bides Earl Douglas upon the bent,
> A captain good enow
> And that was seen verament
> For he wrought them both woe and wouhe.

This fits in exactly with what we know of Homildon ; but at Otterburn, while Percy was hacking his way through the medley of armed servitors and trained soldiers, the Scots were marching round the mountain side to fall on the English flank unexpectedly. But it was a day of no flinching. The English, though taken by surprise, met the attack in good order and the battle now raged. " Great was the pushing of lances and many men were struck down at the first onset." It was an encounter of heroes. Douglas, with the ardour of youth, ordered his banner to advance to the shout of " Douglas ! Douglas ! " The two Percies, Harry and Ralph, equally hot, rushed to answer the challenge with the counter-cry, " Percy ! Percy ! "

At first the English prevailed and the Scots were pushed back, so that the battle would have gone in their favour but for the exceptional gallantry of Sir Patrick Hepburne and his son, who rallied their followers and fought like the heroes they were to defend the banner of Douglas. In fact, both armies earned the high tribute paid them by Froissart. " It was the hardest and most obstinate battle ever fought, for the English and Scots are excellent men-at-arms." With both hands Douglas seized his battle-axe and dashed into the middle of his enemies, dealing mighty blows to right and left till three spears struck him at once—his shoulder was pierced by one, his stomach by another and a third entered his thigh. He was borne to the ground fighting desperately, but never rose again. Fortunately for the Scots the English did not know the leader had fallen. Douglas received another and this time a mortal blow from a battle-axe, but, when found and recognised, continued with his last breath to direct the fight. His was a soldier's death and Froissart's account of it needed none of the embroidery—fine though that embroidery is—which is found in the later ballads. " I dreamed a dead man won a fight and that dead man was I " is evidently a ballad-maker's addition. So is the command, " Bury me by the bracken bush and say a kindly Scot lies here."

The capture of Ralph Percy, " so weakened by loss of blood that he could scarcely utter his own name," and the vivid detail that Sir John Maxwell, to whom he yielded, asked who he was, for he knew him not, is in keeping with other events of the great fray. Even to-day the feeling of regret is fresh when we read of the tired-out Hotspur fighting long and valiantly with Sir Hugh Montgomery and being compelled to give in at last.

No other battle has so frequently been described in prose and verse, and there is no need here to go into the details so fully given by Froissart. But one of them at least leaves a pleasant savour behind it. This was the capture after a long struggle of Sir Matthew Redman, the Governor of Berwick, by Sir James Lindsay and the promise given and accepted that if allowed to go for fifteen days to Newcastle he would thereafter " come to you in any part of Scotland you may appoint." Before the period had expired, Sir James Lindsay was himself a prisoner in Newcastle, having been taken by the forces under the Bishop of

Durham. " I believe," he said ruefully, when he had met Redman and recounted his ill-luck, " there will be no need of your coming to Edinburgh to obtain your ransom, for we may finish the business here if my master consent to it." " We shall soon agree to that," replied Redman, " but you must come and dine with me. . . ." " I accept your invitation," answered Lindsay. In such manner did these two sup in each other's company.*

* There is a marked difference between the poets and the historians as to who it was who really was responsible for the Scottish success. Douglas in the ballad is made to say :

"Last night I dreamt a weary dream beyond the Isle of Skye,
I saw a dead man win a fight and that dead man was I."

But the facts are that he rushed out impetuously with his battle-axe before seeing that his armour was secure, and was borne to the ground by three lances at a very early stage of the battle. That his last words should have been an order to raise the Douglas banner and avenge his death was very natural to so brave a soldier. Captain George S. C. Swinton, pursuivant to the Scottish marches, in the " Scottish Historical Review," July, 1919, makes out a case to show that victory was due to " the stalwart stepfather " of the Douglas. In these days many a stricken field was decided by the valour of a great fighter, and that this description applies to Sir John Swinton of that Ilk, who was to fall years after at Homildon, there is no denying. Earl William Douglas died in 1384 and Swinton married his widow in 1387. She was Margaret of Mar, and her husband, the Lord of Swinton, was thereby entitled to the designation Lord of Mar. Froissart, imperfectly acquainted with our language, in various passages confuses the words " Mar " and " March."

The old ballad has it that Swinton commanded one of the three forces :

" Swynton fayre fylde upon your pryde
To battel make you bowen
Syr Davy Scotte, Syr Walter Stewarde,
Syr Jhon of Agurstone."

Douglas and Swinton in 1388 rode to Melrose, where the charter confirming the Church of Cavers to the Abbey bears Swinton's name, Douglas calling him " carissimo patre nostro." Then they rode on to the celebrated fray.

Captain Swinton prints an extract dated 5th December, 1389, from one of the Drumlanrig Charters which begins : " Johne of Swyntoun, Lord of Mar and Margaret his spous Countess of Douglas and Mar," which explains how Froissart may have been led to refer to Swinton by the designation Mar or March.

In the ancient chronicle there is a passage telling how the born

Nowhere are the characteristics of old Northumberland more clearly revealed than in the remote and now shrunken village of Elsdon, which nestles in a pretty valley a few miles from Otterburn. Its probable connection with the battle arose from the discovery, when the church was renovated, of more than a thousand skulls, described by the late Professor Veitch as being of " lads in their 'teens, and of middle-aged men, but none of old men or women." That they may have been the remains of those slain is at least possible. A similar discovery of what appears to have been a common grave at Southdean on the Scottish side may be explained on the supposition that the Scots carried as many of their dead as they could to the nearest consecrated burial-place over the Border.

The village is built round a green where the people of a comparatively recent date used to enjoy the sports considered unsuitable to a more refined age. Here is a stone for the ring used in bull-baiting and also the cockpit. No trace is left of the equally cruel badger-baiting, but this required no permanent fixture, as the gameness of a dog was tested either by setting him to draw the brock from under a heap of faggots or out of a long box soaped inside to make it slippery. Up to the second quarter of the nineteenth century nearly every inn had its rat-pit. A common form of bet was that a dog should kill its own weight in rats in as many minutes as it weighed pounds. For this purpose a black and tan terrier was bred so small that it could pass through the rough circle formed by joining the thumbs and outstretched fingers of a man's two hands.

There is a village pound, too, which can scarcely be yet called a relic as there are many pounds on English commons still extant, though few in Northumberland. Bull-baiting and cock-fighting are of yesterday, but Elsdon has in the Mote Hills a heritage that takes us back through many civilisations. Originally it was perhaps only a heap of detritus formed by the hill-stream which, though in summer but a slender burn, is, like other mountain waters, subject to raging floods in winter. Neolithic man perhaps took advantage of the accumulations and added to them for purposes of defence. They may have begun that hollowing-out of the road by which the height of the rampart

fighter broke in at a moment when things were not going too well for Scotland, and the passage is confirmed by the other early chronicles.

was increased. Following them came the Roman, whose military eye did not fail to notice how suitable the mounds were for the purpose. Saxons, when their time came, brought over their own ideas and saw in them the Mote Hills ready made. They were Law Courts and places for deliberation.

In the old church built on the foundation of one still older a great deal of local history may be traced. There is the tablet of the Reeds, " the ancient family of Troughend for about 800 years," and the one to the memory of Mrs. Anne Elizabeth Grose, daughter of the antiquary, Capt. Grose, immortalised by Burns.

A chield's among ye takin' notes and faith he'll print it.

There are beautiful fourteenth-century windows and Roman stones, well-preserved sedilia and many other relics and memorials.

Elsdon Rectory is also Elsdon Castle. It was a tower in the possession of the rector as far back as 1415. The arms of the Umfravilles were probably placed there in 1436 in the time of Sir Robert Umfraville. He was better known as Robin-Mend-the-Market, from the success of his raids into Scotland. According to Mr Howard Pease he possessed the Manor of Otterburn and he was Warden of the Middle Marches. When he died, in 1436, he was interred before the altar of St. Mary Magdalene in Newminster Abbey. After the Conquest, Tynedale and Redesdale were bestowed on Robin-with-the-Beard, that is to say, " Robert de Umfraville, Knight, lord of Tours and Vian, to hold by defending that part of the country forever from wolves and enemies with the sword which King William had by his side when he entered Northumberland." Gilbert Umfraville, known as " the Guardian and Chief Flower of the North," in 1226 married the Countess of Angus and brought the Earldom of Angus into his family for at least two generations.

Some three miles east of Elsdon is the Steng Cross, near which on high ground the body of William Winter dangled in chains till it fell to pieces and had to be put into a sack. He was executed at Newcastle with his female accomplices for the murder of an old woman at Haws Pele, and his body was exposed near the scene of his crime. It is believed to be the last occasion on which that practice was carried out. Many superstitions linger still about the gibbet, one of them being the rustic belief that toothache might be cured by rubbing the teeth against a chip cloven from it.

Though dreary enough in winter, no village could be more enchanting than Elsdon in summer, set among its hills of green grass or purple heather with a pretty brook running past and all the charm of an old and pleasant world hanging about its houses.

The Black Gate, Newcastle.

Haughton Castle.

CHAPTER XXVIII

A LITTLE JOURNEY INTO NORTH TYNEDALE

The tower house of Haughton—Pity Me, and the origin of the name—The finest example of Jacobean architecture in Northumberland—Simonburn and its poet—The capital of Tynedale—A walk along the North Tyne from Bellingham— The moss-troopers' spur—" Tarret Burn and Tarset Burn, Yet ! yet ! yet ! "—Catcleugh and Sundaysight.

BELLINGHAM is the best centre from which to explore North Tynedale, but between it and Hexham there are several places worthy of attention.

Above Chollerford is the pleasant little village of Humshaugh, standing amid trees. A path through the fields leads to Haughton Castle. It was probably built by William de Swynburn in the thirteenth century. Afterwards for several centuries it belonged to the Widdringtons. In 1542 the Liddesdale ravagers " broke " Haughton Castle, scaling it with ladders, but it was then dilapidated and remained so for two hundred years. In the middle of the eighteenth century it was repaired, and again in the nineteenth, by different owners. It is beautifully situated, this " tower-house," of which there is only another so described, viz. Langley Castle. A similar stronghold, Widdrington Tower, " mother of many a famous son," was ruthlessly levelled in the eighteenth century. Standing amid pines and firs, it looks down on a lovely stretch of the North Tyne. Haughton is very strong, the grey walls being from eight to eleven feet thick, crowned by five square turrets. Four newel staircases lead to the roof. The interior is modernised and contains two ancient oak chimney-pieces from the Sandhill at Newcastle. A beautiful view of the Castle is to be had from the ferry which crosses the Tyne to Barrasford. Here a large barrow was opened above the burn, and until lately there stood a solitary monolith supposed to have belonged to a group of standing stones. To the east of Gunnerton Village are Gunnerton Crags, the highest, 576 feet, formed by an outcrop of the great Whin Sill, very picturesque, where many camps can be traced of great strength, showing the presence of a considerable population.

A little hamlet to the north is called Pity Me. The name may be derived from the British Beddan Maes, field of graves. If so, the transformation of the name has been singularly appropriate if it was only based on sound. Two miles further on up the river is the great Castle of Chipcase, grandly situated in a park where " bonnier shine the braes of Tyne " than in almost any other part of its lovely valley. The name is derived from the Anglo-Saxon *chepan*, to buy and sell (hence the Cheapsides and Chippings) and *chasse*, a hunting-ground. It is strange that the vanished village here had been important enough to be a market, " the market in the chase." The tower was probably built in the fourteenth century, when the manor came into the possession of the Herons of Ford Castle, and they added to the Keep the picturesque manor house in 1621. It has been considered the finest example of Jacobean architecture in Northumberland. Cuthbert Heron's initials and the date appear above the south entrance. The description given of the ancient tower and its unique features by the Reverend C. Hartshorne fifty years ago is the best that can be quoted. " The pele, properly so called,

is a massive and lofty building, as large as some Norman Keeps.
It has an enriched appearance given to it by its double notched
corbelling round the summit, which further serves the purpose
of machiolation.   The round bartisans in the angles add to its
beauty, and are set in with considerable skill.   The stone roof
and the provisions for carrying off the water deserve careful
examination.   Over the low winding entrance doorway on the
basement are the remains of the original portcullis, the like of
which the most experienced archæologist will in vain seek for
elsewhere."   The grooves are still visible and the framework of
the wooden portcullis, which was lifted " by the leverage of a
wooden bar above the entrance and let down in the same manner."
On the ground floor was the vaulted room where the cattle were
placed in time of danger, and the well.   Above it was the
guardroom, and the third story would be the family house place.
In the thickness of the wall in the second story is a mural recess
which seemed to have been an oratory, possibly used by Catholics
in time of persecution.

Let us not miss Simonburn, to-day another Auburn with its
old-fashioned cottages set round a village green, its old Parish
Church, its holy well and treasured bits of ancient cross and
masonry.   What stranger seeing for the first time its rustic
charm could fancy that was one of the places where as late as
the middle of the eighteenth century the King's Writ did not
run !   All its rude lawlessness has passed away to be remembered
no more by the simple agricultural folk who now inhabit it.
Yet it is no wonder that the place has literary associations—at
any time it must have attracted the musing eye.   Here Wallis,
who wrote the " History and Description of Northumberland,"
published in 1769, was curate.   It also brought forth a poet,
George Pickering, born in 1758.   Burns wrote to his friend,
Thomson, that he would have given ten pounds to be the author
of " Donocht Head."   It is well worthy of the compliment, a
little masterpiece in the style Burns made his own :

> Keen blaws the wind o'er Donocht Head,
> The snaw drives snelly through the dale,
> The Gaber-lunzie tirls my sneck,
> And shivering tells his waefu' tale—
> " Cauld is the night, O let me in,
> And dinna let your minstrel fa' !
> And dinna let his winding-sheet
> Be naething but a wreath o' snaw.

" Full ninety winters hae I seen,
And piped where gor-cocks whirring flew ;
And mony a day, ye've danced, I ween,
To lilts from which my drone I blew."
My Eppie waked, and soon she cried,
" Get up, gudeman, and let him in ;
For weel ye ken the winter night
Was short when he began his din."

My Eppie's voice, oh wow ! it's sweet,
E'en though she bans and scaulds a wee ;
But when it's tuned to sorrow's tale,
Oh, haith, it's doubly dear to me.
" Come in, auld carl ; I'se steer my fire ;
I'll mak' it bleeze a bonnie flame ;
Your bluid is thin, ye've tint the gate ;
Ye shouldna stray sae far frae hame."

" Nae hame hae I," the minstrel said :
" Sad party strife o'erturned my ha' ;
And, weeping, at the eve of life,
I wander thro' a wreath o' snaw."

" It appeared first," wrote Burns in 1794, in the " *Edinburgh Herald* and came to the editor with the Newcastle postmark on it." Mr. Robinson, in his " Thomas Bewick, his Life and Times," tells that when he was visiting Miss Isabella Bewick, the daughter of the artist, who was then in her 94th year and within a month of her death, she recited this poem with much feeling. The unfortunate author died insane at Kibblesworth, at the house of his sister.

There is a well-known passage in Burns that makes one think he would have liked the scenery round Simonburn as much as he liked the poem.

The Muse nae poet ever fand her,
Till by himsel' he learned to wander
Adown some trottin' burns' meander
          An' no think lang.

This is the very land of burns or sikes, *anglicé* brooks or running streams, with all their charming incidents, of dell and dene, cascade and stepping-stones, pool and shallow. But to find them in their charm you must break away from the beaten track and take the luck of the by-path.

Wark on Tyne, which must not be confused with Wark-on-Tweed, was of old the capital of North Tyne. Like Elsdon, it has a mote hill, which points to its antiquity. Some idea of its ancient importance may be gleaned from the record of legal proceedings here in the time of Alexander III, when the Scots had it, and in 1293 when it was again English. They are preserved in the Record office.

Bellingham is pronounced " Bellinjam," although no reason can be given for this except local custom, and was so written in early documents. In similar place-names the pronunciation is sometimes hard and sometimes soft. It is a rugged and homely village with an air of sport always hanging round it. Situated as it is on the very outskirts of England and subject to the raids of the Redesdale men and others, the inhabitants of old could not afford to spend their wealth in erecting buildings that at any time might be levelled with the ground. The situation is wild and picturesque. Nowhere is the northern Tyne more beautiful than as it flows past this stone-built village to receive, a little further on, the beautiful tributary, the Reed at Reedsmouth, which during the war was used as the station for Bellingham. It has a church built nearly at the end of the eleventh century and dedicated to St. Cuthbert, with a fine stone roof, an obvious protection against the incendiary proclivities of the marauding Scot. Around it cultivated fields pass into billowing moorland, and Bellingham derives its attraction far more from nature than from antiquity. I remember it on a day in early autumn when the heather was already withered and dark-coloured and the tree leaves were prematurely assuming the tint of decay. Nevertheless even the pelting rain could not destroy the wild charm. The walk began by three miles along a road that runs very nearly parallel with the Tyne and so close that the murmur of the river over its stony bed was a constant accompaniment to the swishing wind. The country is that of the Charltons, a famous North Country family conspicuous in the days of border warfare. At Hesleyside, a house on the west bank of the river which used to be their chief seat, the spur is preserved which the mistress used to present at breakfast in a covered dish when the state of the larder was such as to call upon the men to ride and foray for provisions. A little further on stands Charlton, on the opposite side, and the first halt occurs at Lane-head. At four cross roads, near a little chapel standing on an ascent, a historic landscape is spread before the eye. In front the course of the Tyne is seen as it wends its way from the Dead Water, so called because the eye cannot discern in which way it runs, to receive the Kielder Burn and then flow down the valley. At the left-hand side, at the foot of the hill, a green mound and some good stone-work mark the place where Tarset Castle stood. It was not a fortress of great historical importance, but is interesting as belonging in his day to that Red Comyn slain by Robert Bruce in the church of the Minor Friars at Dumfries. A little further in the same direction brings one to Falstone, but to-day we prefer to follow the road which the signpost indicates as one mile to Greenhaugh and four miles to High Green, so that we may get on to the Tarset Burn in about two miles. Tarret Burn and Tarset Burn meet just above the bridge. Inhabitants of this district used to be among the most barbarous of the Borderers, and at fairs and other meetings as late as the middle of the nineteenth century not unfrequently raised the slogan which had resounded in many a border foray, " Tarret Burn and Tarset Burn, Yet ! Yet ! Yet ! " But there is little left to-day that reminds the visitor of these wild deeds. The burn is famous now for the two linns over which the water comes tumbling. We all remember Burns's reference to the brook " whiles loupin' ower a linn." A little touch of the old lawlessness comes out on the part of the simple countryman of whom one makes some inquiry about the direction. There are two linns, and he is mostly interested in the upper one, because just at this season of the year, namely, the end of September, the salmon can be seen making their way up. There is a twinkle in his eye as he suggests that it is a fine sight, and a leading question or two brings out the fact that the deadly poaching instrument, the cleek, is not unknown in these solitudes. On one occasion, in fact, he took forty-five large salmon from this burn, and during the war the rations appear to have been very materially supplemented in the district by the free use of the leister and the cleek during the absence of the usual custodians of the water. The Northumbrian rustic is nothing if not reasonable and argumentative, and he pointed out that the first salmon that go up these burns are fair game. The floods which enable the earlier fish to ascend do not last long, and in the end the fish are marooned in pools where in default of capture by human beings they become easy victims of the otter. So he salves his conscience with the belief that there is very little

chance of the supply being increased by this premature attempt
to reach the breeding-places.

Later on, the volume of water is permanently increased and
the poacher's opportunity gone. Our rustic described the

Chipchase Castle.

change tersely and graphically in his own language when he
said there was " not watter enough in summer to wet your feet,
but in winter you couldn't drive a horse and cairt through
the burn." It was enough for us, however, to eat a cold lunch

on the rocks within reach of the spray from the waterfall and then to wander upward toward the source. No one could have wished for greater silence and solitude. On each side is the characteristic Northumbrian moor, never as flat as the fen land and never rising into the rocky and precipitous hills which one would expect to find in the grander scenery of Scotland. Leaving the bank of the stream, I climbed up a brae on the right-hand side to get the bearings of the place and saw two farmhouses almost on the side of Lordship Law which form the turning point of the walk. To reach them it was necessary to cross the Catcleugh, a spot well known to the fox-hunter in this wild country. " Cleugh " is a very common word in these regions, and over the whole of the north, as may be seen from its entry into so many place-names, such as Goudscleugh, Buccleugh, Wolfcleugh, and so on. This one is called Catcleugh, and is famous for a rocky fastness into which Reynard tries to make his way when hard pressed by Mr. Robson's well-known trencher pack. It is a ravine in the rock along the bottom of which a little stream creeps down to join the more important water. It forms a resting-place from which one can easily take in the main features of the Northumbrian moor. Sundaysight is further up and commands a still wider view of Cheviot moorland, high ridges, deep ravines, great bare sheep-walks, with green plantations in the slacks down which streamlets percolate or dance according to the season. They dry up to nothing but a damp trickle in summer, but in winter can race down in torrents. The farm stands bare and alone, though the inmates will not confess that they ever feel dull. They have so much to do is the explanation. The neighbourhood is close to Otterburn and part of that country where Percy and Douglas had their famous hunt. Indeed, when one has turned again towards Bellingham and walked for some distance along the unfenced moorland road and reached once more a country of enclosed fields, there stands a milestone which tells that Otterburn is but six miles away.

CHAPTER XXIX

CAPHEATON, WALLINGTON AND BELSAY

An old Northumbrian family—Swinburne's poetry of Northumberland—" The chiefest house of the Fenwicks "—A Chaucerian jest—Sir John Fenwick and William of Orange—The builder of the modern house—William Bell Scott and his cartoons—Ruskin and other guests at Wallington—Cambo and Capability Brown—Early history of Belsay and its owners—A rebel and his fate—The best example of castellated architecture in Northumberland.

CAPHEATON'S main interest to-day lies in its association with the poet Algernon Charles Swinburne. Although Swinburne is the greatest poet the county has produced, he was not born there but in London. The family, however, is a very old one in the north. It existed previous to the thirteenth century, when it possessed Swinburne. The name seems to have been taken from Swin, or Swine Burn, as Dr. Furnivall used to recall in the days of the famous " flyting " between him and the poet. The Swinburne family produced many members distinguished as soldiers and sailors, but Mr. Gosse in his biography of the poet rather laments that it attained no literary distinction. Swinburne had no ancestor to whom his temperament can be traced. The house at Capheaton was built in 1688 by Robert Trollope, who was also the architect of Netherwitton Hall and the old Exchange at Newcastle. Much alteration has been done in the course of time, and although the back is still a piece of beautiful and practically untouched Tudor work, the front is modern and the roof of Westmorland slate. In Leland's time the family inhabited the ancient castle of Swinburne, which was moated and fortified, and had a great stone or Menhir in the park. The moss-troopers used to be as much of a danger to Capheaton as to Swinburne Castle, besides which the owners were implicated in the many political movements and rebellions which occurred in the seventeenth and eighteenth centuries. It is no wonder that in Capheaton there used to be many priest-holes and hiding-places, but these have all but one disappeared in the process of the many alterations made.

Algernon was born in Chester Street, Grosvenor Square, London, in 1837. Lady Jane Swinburne had been on her way to the seaside home of the family on the Isle of Wight. In spite of being born in London, Swinburne was thoroughly proud of being Northumbrian.

At one time I saw a good deal of him, and his talk ran very much on the ballads and superstitions of his county. He delighted in reading his own Northumbrian ballads, and the curious chanting sing-song was singularly appropriate. His memory was full of strange legends, many of which tempted him into verse. But a considerable number of the ballads he read to me have not been published. There is a great deal in his work to stir the imagination of Northumbrians. It may be divided into two classes, one in which the external characteristics of the region are dwelt upon, and the other which glows with the spirit of wild and romantic Northumberland. His pride and affection came out most conspicuously in the early drama called "The Sisters." In a letter to Mrs. Lynn Linton dated 1892 he said he "never wrote anything so autobiographical as Redgie's speech about Northumberland, done in the Eton midsummer holidays":

> The crowning county of England—yes, the best ! . .
> Have you and I, then, raced across its moors
> Till horse and boy were well-nigh mad with glee
> So often, summer and winter, home from school,
> And not found that out ? Take the streams away
> The country would be sweeter than the south
> Anywhere : give the south our streams, would it
> Be fit to match our borders ? Flower and crag,
> Burnside and boulder, heather and whin,—you don't
> Dream you can match them south of this ? And then
> If all the unwater'd country were as flat
> As the Eton playing-fields, give it back our burns,
> And set them singing through a sad south world
> And try to make them dismal as its fens,—
> They won't be.

It was a Northumbrian neighbour, Pauline Lady Trevelyan, wife of Sir Walter Trevelyan of Wallington, an old friend of his

father, who was the first to discover the genius of the
strange youth, then a puzzle to less appreciative minds.
The friendship was only ended by the lady's early death.
The letters Swinburne wrote to her show more than anything else
the terms of confidence on which they stood. In the description
of Wallington will be found some account of the brilliant company
Sir Walter and Lady Pauline used to get together. Young
Swinburne, in addition to the friendship he formed with Ruskin
and Rossetti, both of them intimates of Sir Walter Trevelyan,
had also included William Bell Scott in the number. In a few
lines written to the old Newcastle drawing master and litterateur
we have a most engaging picture of the poet, in the careless grace
of early youth, galloping from Capheaton to Wallington, his
mind seething with rhymes and ideas :

> Whenever in August holiday times
> I rode or swam through a rapture of rhymes,
> Over heather or crag, and by scaur and by stream,
> Clothed with delight by the might of a dream,
> With the sweet sharp wind blown hard through my hair,
> On eyes enkindled and head made bare ; . . .
> Or loosened a song to seal for me
> A kiss on the clamorous mouth of the sea.

But it was in the best of his ballads that he rendered the true
spirit of the county. Northumberland was indeed part of his
very life and blood. From childhood he had at Capheaton
listened to reminiscences connected with the stirring deeds of
Border strife. The raids of the Scots, the gatherings at Capheaton to organise defence and counter-attack, the legends of
the rebellions of the Fifteen and Forty-five, in which his family
had taken the side of the Stuarts, formed his common conversation. His knowledge of the Stuarts was not obtained entirely
from books, but was part of the lore instilled into him at
Capheaton. That was what enabled him to write "A Jacobite's
Exile." I quote pretty fully from the poem, because nothing
finer has ever been written about Northumberland, and because
of the exquisite and intimate pictures it gives of the braes and
burns :

> The weary day rins down and dies,
> The weary night wears through :
> And never an hour is fair wi' flower,
> And never a flower wi' dew.

O lordly flow the Loire and Se'ne
  And loud the dark Durance :
But bonnier shine the braes of Tyne
  Than a' the fiel ls of France ;
And the waves of Till that speak sae still
  Gleam goodlier where they glance.

O weel were they that fell fighting
  On dark Drumossie's day :
They keep their hame ayont the faem
  And we die far away.

.   .   .   .   .

On Aikenshaw the sun blinks braw,
  The burn rins blithe and fain :
There's nought wi' me I wadna gie
  To look thereon again.

On Keilder-side the wind blaws wide :
  There sounds nae hunting-horn
That rings sae sweet as the winds that beat
  Round banks where Tyne is born.

The Wansbeck sings with all her springs,
  The bents and braes give ear ;
But the wood that rings wi' the sang she sings
  I may not see nor hear ;
For far and far thae blithe burns are,
  And strange is a'thing near.

.   .   .   .   .

We'll see nae mair the sea-banks fair,
  And the sweet grey gleaming sky,
And the lordly strand of Northumberland,
  And the goodly towers thereby ;
And none shall know but the winds that blow
  The graves wherein we lie.

With this should be read the fine poem on Northumberland
which he contributed to the first number of that most interesting
but too short-lived magazine which Mr. Howard Pease started
years ago. Of this the following verses have the true Northumbrian spirit. These are the first, third, and fourth verses :

Between our eastward and our westward sea
  The narrowing strand
Clasps close the noblest shore fame holds in fee
Even here where English birth seals all men free—
  Northumberland.

The splendour and the strength of storm and fight
    Sustain the song
That filled our fathers' hearts with joy to smite
To live, to love, to lay down life that right
    Might tread down wrong.

They warred, they sang, they triumphed, and they passed,
    And left us glad
Here to be born their sons, whose hearts hold fast
The proud old love no change can overcast,
    No chance leave sad.

Wallington Hall is interesting *per se* and also because of some old and many modern associations. It was built by Sir William Blackett towards the middle of the eighteenth century on the site of a mansion described by Leland as " the chiefest house of the Fenwicks." Earlier still the family of De Strother had there an ancient peel house. Strother is a Northumbrian name of not infrequent occurrence, and no doubt many who bear it would like to trace their pedigree back to the ancestor who had been at college with Chaucer and whom the poet with characteristic humour made one of the leading characters in " The Reeve's Tale "—a story too broad for modern refinement but related with a terseness, skill, and point unexcelled in any of the other Canterbury stories. There were two brothers,

John highte that oon and Allyn highte that oother ;
Of o toon were they born that highte strother
Far in the North I kan nat telle where.

The " town " appears to have been near Kirknewton in Glendale, but no trace of it now remains, unless there be some truth in the surmise of Mr. Crawford Hodgson that some of the stones have been built into Kirknewton Church. But the name frequently crops up in the annals of the county.

Sir John Fenwick is the most historical of his family. He was out in the '15 and the part he played is described at great length in Macaulay's " History of England." After his execution his goods were forfeited to the State. William of Orange chose for his personal share a famous horse, named Sorrel, that according to tradition grazed the excellent pasture in front of the house. This was the animal he was riding through the park of Hampton Court when, urging his steed to a gallop, it accidentally put its foot in a molehill. It stumbled and threw the rider, whose collar-bone was broken by the fall. William's health had previously begun to fail, and he never recovered from the accident. As he had been far from generous to Sir John, there were some who saw a wild justice in the accident. In the songs of the day frequent reference is made to the Wallington cellars and wines, and the impression is produced that the Fenwicks belonged to the jovial, hearty, and hospitable type of Northumbrian squires, such as Sir Walter Scott has depicted in the Osbaldistones of Osbaldistone Hall.

The Blacketts belonged to a different category. Newcastle often from its whirl of business enterprise throws out remarkable men. For generations the Blacketts were leading men in the county—parliamentary representatives, high sheriffs, merchant princes—of whom the builder of Wallington was a notable example. He must have had a lively imagination to foresee that out of the bare and dreary solitude could arise a fine mansion surrounded by a noble park going down to the edge of the gleaming Wansbeck and set about with sylvan beauty. Well-wooded and fertile as the estate is now, there was not, at the time of building, a scrap even of the light timber needed for the fencings and the gates. Many travellers bear witness to the bareness of Northumberland in the eighteenth century. Sir Walter Blackett had indeed to start from the beginning. But his taste and resourcefulness proved equal to the demand on them, and the solid and handsome eighteenth-century mansion is the proof. The house was on the model of a French chateau, with a courtyard in the interior.

This courtyard became notable in the nineteenth century. By that time the house had fallen into possession of the Trevelyans through the marriage of Sir Walter Blackett's sister with Sir George Trevelyan, Sir Walter having died without issue. It occurred to Sir Walter Trevelyan and his friend John Ruskin that it would make an excellent picture gallery, an idea ultimately carried out by Dobson of Newcastle. Part of the decorations were effected by that gifted and singular half-member of the Pre-Raphaelite brotherhood, William Bell Scott. To many he is now but the shadow of a name, or only a gifted drawing master. Nevertheless, he was in his day a poet as well as a painter. One of his poems, the strange, fantastic, fanciful Witches' Ballad, holds a place in the anthologies, and deserves to do so were it only for that grotesque immortal daylight dance of witches in the market town.

> Arms and legs and flaming hair
> Like a whirlwind in the sea.

Scott is not seen at his best as a painter in the cartoons he did to adorn the panels on the ground floor. The typical Northumbrian scenes are too conventional for his brush. The building of the Roman Wall, Cuthbert being offered a bishopric, Danes landing, the Venerable Bede, the Charlton Spur, Bernard Gilpin, Grace Darling, and the iron and coal of the busy nineteenth century are all important landmarks in the history of Northumberland, but not necessarily the best subjects for wall decoration. Much more appropriate to the purpose are the illustrations of Chevy Chase on the angles and spandrels of the upper series of arches, where eighteen scenes from the ballad are depicted. Here imagination may work its will, because the ballad-maker wanders far from the region of fact. The painter therefore had the same free scope as Sir Noel Paton claimed for the series of pictures called the Dowie Dens of Yarrow.. Here Mr. Bell Scott achieved a pleasing effect even if he did not represent deer-hunting in the fourteenth century as described, for example, in " Gawaine and the Green Knight," the author of which was apparently a gentleman of the North of England. A more modern painter would have gone to the " Master of Game," a treatise of the same date, for realistic detail. But one does not tire of the lords and ladies gay, of the dogs and the deer and the bowmen, of the fighting, the slaughter, and the sad return.

John Ruskin was frequently a guest of Sir Walter Trevelyan, and he occupied part of his time in teaching the ladies how to paint on stone and in practising that beautiful form of architectural art. His handiwork and the handiwork of his pupils are seen in the rendering of tall flowers and plants such as rushes and sheaves of corn.

Lady Trevelyan, beautiful and kind and tactful, was an attractive centre round whom gathered many of the Victorian celebrities arrived or going to arrive. Young Algernon Swinburne, whose letters to her bear the stamp of a tried and intimate friendship, reflected the esteem in which she was held by Rossetti, Ruskin, and other frequent and brilliant guests.

No account of Wallington would be complete without a reference to the curious picture of Miss Sukey Trevelyan. As it stands it is a composite production. Originally it was painted at Bath by Gainsborough and, in the words of Sir George Trevelyan, " it subdued an over-bold expression and her strongly marked features by a large hat of the prevailing fashion." About 1767 Arthur Young made that pilgrimage through Northumberland which will be found recounted in his " Northern Tour." Young was a man of taste and a judge of pictures as well as an eminent agriculturist. He described the Gainsborough as " a portrait of a hat and ruffles." This very much disturbed the equanimity of the Blacketts and Trevelyans, for Arthur Young's dictum carried far in those days. So it happened that when Sir Joshua Reynolds was on a visit to Wallington some years later they persuaded him to paint out the hat. He did so with so much thoroughness that nothing was left untouched except the face, the white and gold gown, and the right arm, thus spoiling what, in spite of Arthur Young, must have been a very fine portrait.

It would take many pages to describe the contents of Wallington Hall. Sir Walter Trevelyan made many fine collections, of which the most important is that of old china. It includes many fine and even famous examples. The pictures too are notable. Sir Joshua Reynolds, Sir Peter Lely, Hoppner, Cornelius Jansen and Pietro della Francesca are among the artists represented. There is some interesting tapestry, too, and, as is well known, Lord Macaulay left his library to his nephew and biographer, Sir George Trevelyan, who in a supplement to the biography has reprinted many of the annotations on the Greek and Latin classics and also on the works of Shakespeare and other English writers.

The village of Cambo, which closely adjoins Wallington, has been to a large extent rebuilt, and no greater compliment could be paid it than to say it fits in beautifully with the gardens and grounds of Wallington. It was here that Capability Brown, as he came to be called, received his education. Little did the schoolmaster guess that his pupil would have the shaping and re-making of many of the most beautiful gardens in England.

Belsay Castle differs from Capheaton and Wallington in the vital particular that it is no longer inhabited. It was probably built in the reign of Edward III by an ancestor of Sir Arthur

Middleton, who owns it at the time of writing. Sir Arthur has
written an elaborate and learned account of the manner in which
for a time it passed out of the family. Sir Gilbert de Middleton
was the grandson of that Richard Middleton who was Chancellor
to Henry III. But in the subsequent reign Sir Gilbert de
Middleton was the instigator of a rebellion against the weak
rule of Edward II and was, after many exploits, captured at
Mitford, carried to London, executed, and his estates forfeited.
Sir Arthur gives a most interesting list of the other landowners
who lost their estates in the counties of Northumberland and
Durham for being adherents of Sir Gilbert. The estate came
back to the family in the time of Edward III by marriage.
Sir Arthur Middleton inherited Belsay through his grandfather,
Sir Charles Monk. This gentleman had been a sort of Ruskin
of his own time, and he thought that Grecian buildings alone
were worth imitation. It was this notion that brought into
existence the mansion in which the Middletons now live. The
taste of a later time would almost certainly have inclined Sir
Charles Monk to make the most of his castle which the Rev.
John Hodgson, the historian of Northumberland, thought was
the best example of castellated architecture in Northumberland.

The surroundings of the modern house are as interesting as
the house itself. Minor features are the fine hedges of yew and
Lawsoniana, but the most striking is the rock garden. It
happened that the building-stones were quarried close at hand,
and the quarry, which is sheltered, has been laid out and planted
as a rock garden with rare skill and taste. The majestic old
house stands empty, but the old outbuildings and walls have
been carefully preserved, so that the place looks as if it were
waiting for a tenant. The interior of the walls has often been
described owing to their having been ornamented with coloured
stencilled drawings. Fortunately everything worth preserving,
everything old, has been taken great care of, and Belsay as it
stands is a joy to the architect and antiquarian.

CHAPTER XXX

The Course of the Coquet—Guyzance and Brainshaugh—Felton—
Brinkburn Priory—From Pauperhaugh to Rothbury, the
capital of the Dale—Whitton—Rothbury—Tosson and Burgh
Hill Camp—Selby's Cove and a famous Inn.

NEAR the Roman station on Thirlmoor emerges the loveliest
of wandering, winding Northumbrian streams, the much-sung
Coquet, and forty miles further on it reaches the sea at Amble.
Going up-stream past Warkworth and Morwick Mill, its secluded,
sylvan beauty continues. At Guyzance on a green haugh are
the remains of a monastic cell. In the years when such things
were neglected it was used as a quarry for building-stone. The
walls have now been enclosed and the beautiful base of the
ancient columns revealed. On the north of the chancel is a
curious blocked doorway. The burial ground is still open
to the inhabitants of Guyzance and Brainshaugh. The windings
of Coquet are here very marked, with the wooded banks rising
above. A horseshoe fall, set amongst overhanging trees where
the river throws its whole length of tumbling water, is very
beautiful.

The construction of this dam in 1776 is said to be the cause
of the lack of salmon in the upper reaches, as it is impossible
for them to jump the weir. Two miles inland from the river
at Swarland is an obelisk erected in 1807, to the memory of Lord
Nelson, by a gentleman who placed an inscription on the pedestal
saying it was " not to commemorate the public virtue and heroic
achievements of Nelson, which is the duty of England, but to
the memory of private friendship." An extraordinary method
of calling attention to the friend of a great man.

Where the north road crosses the Coquet by a quaint fifteenth-century bridge stands Felton, in as beautiful scenery as can be found in the vale. Several events of historical importance occurred at Felton. On October 22nd, 1215, the barons of Northumberland did homage to Alexander, King of Scots, being not unreasonably dissatisfied with John Lackland, who in revenge reduced it to ashes the next year. In 1715 Tom Forster had his miserable following augmented here by seventy Border horsemen. In '45 the " butcher Cumberland " stayed at Felton on his way to dark Culloden. John Wesley remarks in his journal, after giving a stirring address in the village on a missionary tour in 1766, " that very few seemed to understand anything of the matter." Rural Northumberland was not given in those days to revival meetings, just as it had been the despair of early missionaries who found that their hardly-won adherents were ready to drift back to the old gods at the bidding of their lords.

On a crest of land above the Coquet on one side, with a ravine formed by the Back burn on the other, stands the church of St. Michael. The chancel and nave belong to the thirteenth century, but it was rebuilt with aisles in the fourteenth. In the north wall is the upper part of the effigy of a priest holding a chalice. There is a pre-Reformation bell with the inscription " Ave, Maria, Gracia, Plena " hung in the double turret, where is also one of the eighteenth century. It is an ancient and interesting building, and until sixty years ago the singing was accompanied by a clarinet, bass fiddle, etc., which gave so much more scope to village talent and musical development than does the solitary instrument of to-day.

From Felton, past Elyhaugh, to Weldon Bridge is a delightful walk of over four miles. Here is the Anglers Inn, where the mail coaches used to stop. It was and is a much frequented resort of anglers. Along either the river bank or by a carriage road is the approach to Brinkburn Priory, which some consider the highest architectural achievement of Northumbria. Descending a steep hill from which lovely glimpses of the Coquet are seen among the trees, the Priory is hidden until suddenly this most beautiful of Northumbrian abbeys appears on a green peninsula. It is almost enisled by Coquet,

> Whose winding streams sae sweetly glide
> By Brinkburn's bonny Ha'.

Many a solitary monkish fisherman must have lifted his voice in praise of Coquet, whilst the sandstone cliffs caught the echo of his happy melody.   Turner, the supreme, came here and laid the dreamlike beauty on canvas.

Brinkburn was already known by that name when Bertram de Mitford selected it for the site of a convent of Austin Canons. With the consent of his wife and sons he commissioned Osbert Colutarius, possibly a master-builder, to commence it for Sir Ralph the priest and his brethren.   The Bertrams made valuable grants of land, but the Chartulary shows that they were often very impoverished by Scottish raids.   Tradition says that once the Scots could not find it amongst the thick woodland, and the marauders had turned their horses north when the deep bell of the monastery ringing thanks for the inmates' deliverance guided them back, to leave behind fire and slaughter in the peaceful valley.   Either they or the monks threw the bells into a pool in the river still called the Bell Pool, where they may yet be discovered with other treasures.   The canons were always complaining of poverty, and it was evidently not without good reason, for the Commissioners reported in 1552 that they had only found at Brinkburn " one tene challes, ij owlde westmentes, one owlde coppe, ij small belles, one small hand bell, one holly water pot of bras."   It is a pathetic list. But though the Scots had an ill name, there must have been other influences of a disintegrating nature at work, for four years later the prior was found guilty of immoral conduct and the canons guilty of venerating a girdle of St. Peter.   For these diverse reasons, perhaps the second included the first, the convent was dissolved and the prior, William Hogeson, dismissed with an annual pension of £11.

Religious services were still maintained by chaplains, as a parochial district appertained to the convent.   The church and its lands have passed through many secular hands since then till they came to the present owner, who lives in the ad-joining mansion.

In the seventeenth century the roof of the abbey fell in at the south-west angle, but the greater part remained, a beautiful blending of the richest Norman work with purest Early English. Pointed and semicircular arches intermingle with the most graceful freedom, which with the rich varied ornaments make it one of the most interesting examples of the transition from the earlier to the later period. The shape of the church is cruciform, and it is 130 feet long and of noble height.

Brinkburn is earlier than Hexham Abbey, and it is possible that its lancet windows have been copied in many churches of south Northumberland. It may have been a genius of a master builder that Bertram of Mitford found.

> In the elder days of Art
> Builders wrought with greatest care
> Each minute and unseen part
> For the Gods see everywhere.

The building was restored and roofed in 1858 and has suffered little by the process. The only discovery of note was an unused grave-cover inscribed to Prior William, Suffragan Bishop, etc., a great dignitary evidently, but his greatness is covered now by the two narrow words " Hic Jacet." Still the river murmurs past ; the old millrace that he saw working still flows. No spot more exquisite or peaceful could be imagined, and the piety of man has enriched it with the serenity of perfect art.

From Pauperhaugh, about two miles further on, is a charming walk along the valley to Rothbury. The Forest Burn comes down from Simonside's eastern slopes through Rothbury Forest, which covers a great tract of country crossed by the railway from Morpeth. The burn is still wild and remote, running through woodland and flowery glades. Its banks are the haunts of badgers, foxes and otters. In early times anyone hunting in the Forest without leave had to pay a fine of ten pounds of silver to the King, and his dogs and horses were forfeited to the lord of the manor. Within half a mile of Rothbury is the Thrum, where the river races through a narrow chasm which is only about two yards wide and sixty yards long. It has been enlarged, as the easy leap which looked so tempting led to drowning accidents.

Rothbury is the capital of the Dale and the best centre for exploring the Coquet. It is almost enclosed by hills, with the densely-planted grounds of Cragside belonging to Lord Armstrong rising steeply up rocky heights covered with heather and bracken. Its first recorded name was Rodeberia, and as there are the remains of a tenth-century cross it is probable that it owes its name to the rood, meaning the burgh of the Cross.

The manor of Rothbury was granted by King John to Robert

Fitz Roger of Warkworth. He had large powers, and it seems a far cry from the equality of to-day to the privileges granted to Roger. He had the power to apprehend, try, and hang malefactors. Their goods became the property of the Crown, but all lost property and stray cattle became his. He had an assize of bread and ale, a ducking-stool and a pillory. On the way to Thropton is Gallowfield, where Roger executed justice. In regard to seignorial misuse of privileges he shut the free sokemen out of a portion of Rothbury Wood, where they grazed their stock, and diabolically bought off the parson's opposition by presenting him with six acres of the common pasture. This was one of the ways in which enclosure started. There must have been many acrimonious disputes between powerful baron and powerful priest. On one occasion recorded, the parson's servant was returning with a cask of wine in a wagon to Rothbury and, having enjoyed part of his cargo too recklessly, he fell under the wheel and was killed. Oxen, wagon, and wine, being the instrument of death as the law ran, were forfeited to the Church and had to be redeemed. The servant must have surely been a relative of the man drowned in the Tyne about the same time with the festive name of Adam Aydrunken.

The inhabitants suffered greatly from the incursions of the Scots, who were always driving off their four-footed wealth. In 1586, in a book giving losses due to the Scots, the value of the various animals is given—an ox 13s. 4d., a cow 10s., an old sheep, wether, or ewe 2s., a hogge or goat 1s. 4d. The people were of a wild and warlike disposition, as they had to be constantly ready to fight. About this time they are thus described : " If any two be displeased, they bang it out bravely, one and his kindred against the other and his ; such adepts were they in the art of thieving that they could twist a cow's horn, or mark a horse, so as its owners could not know it ; and so subtle that no vigilance could guard against them." According to this account, the wily Scot must have needed all his wits to best them. Nothing remains of the fortress called the " brave castle " of the Barons of Rothbury, and only a few houses survive in the town with seventeenth- or eighteenth-century dates on them. The raiders from Scotland did not often leave the roofs above the heads of the natives. Edward I signed one of the many truces with the Scots here, and John also stayed in the village for a time and signed the town's

charter, finding shelter in the valley from the cold blasts
that blow across the Borders. A delightful picture of Rothbury
is given by Thomas Doubleday, who published " Coquetdale
Fishing Songs " in 1852 : " Rothbury is cheerful at sunny
mid-day, but dimly sober towards evening, for then the hills
close in again, and in their gorge the town of Rothbury stands.
Its site has evidently been selected for shelter, being shut in
by hills, save towards the west. To the north, behind it, the
hills are steep and broken into crags, amidst which the goat—
numerous here—alone finds footing. To the south are the

The Coquet at Rothbury.

hills forming a portion of the great Simonside ridge. And to
the east the crags close in and cross each other, as if determined
to bar the Coquet from further passage. The town has all
the marks of hoar antiquity in its aspect. The stone bridge
of four arches which here spans the Coquet bears the mark of
age. The low tower of the church, which stands near the river,
is weather-worn and the whole structure the worse for time.
The houses have all the impress of time, and the very orchards,
with their moss-grown trees, seem to have smiled for years
gone by and for generations now buried. The old market
cross is half in ruins, the very stocks in the churchyard, like

a toothless mastiff, seem to have lost their terrors amidst the ravages of age."

Alas ! the medieval bridge since then has been almost ruined by the County Council. The old market cross which used to shelter the countryfolk with their farm produce (it must have been a covered market greatly like that at Hexham) when it got ruinous was pulled down instead of being restored. A very old man within recent times remembers watching the countrymen at the fair going unto the shelter of the cross to try on the leather breeches they were about to buy. The village stocks and pillory and the bull-ring all went about the same time. This piece of ground is now enclosed and has a cross to the memory of Lord and Lady Armstrong. Rothbury, being so favourably situated for such a fine trout stream as the Coquet, has always nourished many anglers in its bosom, and original characters abound in those who practise the solitary art. But things are not what they used to be even amongst the finny tribes, and a piquant observation on that point may be quoted from " Rambles in Northumberland," by Stephen Oliver. The old Coquet angler speaks in his own tongue : " Talk o' fishen there's na sic fishen in Coquet now as when I was a lad. It was nowse then but to fling in an' pull oot by tweeses and threeses, if ye had as many heuks on, but now a body may keep threshin' at the watter aa' day atween Hallysteun and Weldon an' hardly catch three dozen, an' mony a time not that. About fifty years syne I mind o' seein' troots that thick i' the Thrum below Rotbury, that if ye had stucken the end o' yor gad into the watter amang them it wad amaist hae studden upreet."

Such a speech, with the inimitable accent and emphasis of the Northumbrian, must be heard on its native soil to get its full flavour.

The interest of Rothbury Church lies almost entirely in its font. The basin is seventeenth-century, but it stands on the shaft of a pre-Conquest cross of red sandstone. On one side is a headless figure, with another on the right that seems to be holding back a curtain, and, underneath, numerous heads looking upward. It may represent Christ and suppliant sinners. Another side has intricate knotwork and a bronze spout intended to run off the water. The other sides are covered with dragons and nondescript animals. Other parts of the cross were found at the restoration of the church in 1850.

Holes have been drilled in it evidently for candles, which were lighted at the consecration of a Saxon churchyard.

Opposite Rothbury is Whitton Tower, the parsonage of Rothbury, and a prominent mark in the landscape, standing on a ridge of the Simonside hills. It was built towards the end of the fourteenth century and has been well preserved. It has modern portions built by successive rectors. The vaulted basement would be used to hide the frightened women and children during a Scottish raid, and in the courtyard the cattle would be secured.

> Nae bastles or peles
> Are safe frae thae deils.
> Gin the collies be oot or the laird's awae—
> The bit bairnies an' wives
> Gang i' dreid o' their lives,
> For they scumfish them oot wi' the smoutherin' strae.

The Scots had a habit of setting light to straw at the inner door if they could, and the inmates got suffocated in the thick smoke.

The first floor, now the rector's study, is also vaulted, and while alterations were being made in it a piscina was discovered in an alcove, pointing to a pre-Reformation oratory.

A mural shield on the west wall of the tower has a coat of arms either of the Umfravilles or of Alexander Cooke, the rector from 1435–74, who probably built the upper storey of the tower. The reigning rector is still lord of the manor although the lands and village of Whitton are his no longer. The villagers of " Wutton, Roberie " in the thirteenth century had to render an account of one mark for " frussure." They had ploughed pasture lands without leave—a reversal of the procedure during the Great War, when ploughing of pasture was compulsory.

From Whitton Dene an ancient trackway goes in the direction of Lordenshaws Camp on the Simonside hills, one of the most complete of the many British camps in the Coquet valley. It is encircled by three ramparts with a deep ditch between the two outer ramparts. The camp forms an irregular oval. The eastern entrance has grey lichen-covered gateposts which appear almost in their primitive condition. Earthworks extend from the inner to the outer ramparts. In the camp are some well-defined hut circles. One of them has walls two feet high and a paved floor, one flagstone carrying traces of fire. From the eastern gate a hollow way drops into the slack towards Garley Pike, where a spring and a small burn supplied the water for the camp. Several large stones in the vicinity have the mysterious markings to be found in many parts of Northumberland.

On the north-east side of the hill are a number of grave-mounds, and some have been excavated, and a line of stones may be traced from the camp towards two of the excavations. On the neighbouring Garley Pike are other hut circles, and there are ramparts and a ditch at Pike House. Many evidences of British occupation have been found, cists, axes, pottery, etc. A splendid view is obtained from Lordenshaws Camp, Upper Coquetdale to the west bounded by the dark heather-clad hills beyond Holystone and Harbottle. To the east the Coquet winds to the sea, and the broad expanse of Druridge bay, with the shining sea beyond, is visible. And all round can be seen the crests of hills crowned by prehistoric camps that have been very fully explored and written about by Canon Greenwell.

West from Rothbury, half a mile, the Lady's Bridge crosses the Coquet, where after passing along pleasant meadows are the noted Tosson Woollen Mills. They have been worked for a century by one family and their durable and handsome products have many admirers. Beyond the farm buildings which are all that is left now of the ancient village are the ruins of a pele tower which belonged to the Ogles. It was one of a line of towers extending from Harbottle to Warkworth as a defence against the reiving Scots. A complete system of watchmen was maintained whose names and duties are found in all the records of towers and villages along the Northumbrian border. " Every man do rise and follow the fray upon the Blowing the Horn, Shout or Outcry upon Pain of Death." The massive walls of the pele, about nine feet thick, still stand to the height of thirty or forty feet, although the large outer stones have long been removed for neighbouring buildings. The tenacity of the masonry is due to the method in which all Border peles were built, small boulders, taken here from the Coquet, being welded with hot lime. The lords of Hepple held their court in Tosson after the Scots had destroyed their own castle. Before Tosson's decay, the village inn stood opposite the pele, and the stump of the oaken beam from which the " Royal George " hung is yet to be seen in the house wall. When its doom as a hostelry was sealed, the village joiner " grat " as he mounted the ladder to cut it down. A green spur of the Simonside hills rises above the trees and grey walls of Tosson's tower. Burgh Hill Camp occupies over an acre of the summit, from which a wide and lovely view of Coquet rewards the climber. The high civilisation of the Britons can be well gauged by ornaments and weapons found near this camp. Two leaf-shaped bronze swords discovered had the pommels of the handles made of lead, which is regarded as unique. Bronze rings for fastening the swords to the warrior's belt were found beside them. Jet buttons and a well-designed food-vessel in a cist which had probably held a woman's body were dug up near, and also amber buttons or amulets and a bronze axe.

The Simonside Hills extend from Hepple to Pauperhaugh, near Brinkburn, along the south bank of the Coquet, and reach their highest point south-west of Rothbury. They are studded by great boulders, the largest of which have names. Between Tosson and Simonside a high perpendicular rock with a shallow cavern on the side of the hill is called Little Church. Simonside, 1,409 feet high, is a bold hill, the most noticeable on the Rothbury landscape. On the south of the hill is Selby's Cove ; an opening in the rock, where once a moss-trooper called Selby is said to have had his retreat. Croppie's Hole, not far off, was the lair of a well-known fox without a tail—a cropped fox. This original animal survived for many years by his superior cunning, but at last was run to death on Amble sands, having led the hounds and a single huntsman right down the valley of the Coquet. It is sad to think of plucky Reynard, reared in the dark recesses of Simonside, after so many years of superior wit, meeting a dazed end with the strange tumult of the sea in his ears. Another fox, after a long run, found shelter on Simonside, where a local character, old Will Scott, found him and told the Squire, who inquired if he was quite sure. " Sure," said the old fox-hunter, " hevvent aa his aan handwritin' for it," holding out his hand the fox had bitten. South of Selby's Cove over the moors is Fallowlees, a farmhouse, and two loughs on which the black-headed gull breeds. On Chartners Lough, about a mile north-west of Fallowlees, grows a variety of the lesser yellow water lily. Two dangerous morasses cover many acres, from which issue numerous watercourses. One of these, Coe burn, after rushing impetuously down, disappears in a chasm on the hill. By the banks of these runnels grow many flowers and ferns. It is a wild and lonely land, amidst heather moorlands which gaze down on rocks and woodland with the bright river wandering amidst meadows.

The Coquet at Warkworth.

CHAPTER XXXI

Bickerton and Hepple—How age was proved in the fourteenth
century—The Tower of Hepple—A curious epitaph—A
Coquetdale poet—The legend of the Five Kings—Paulinus
and his record baptism—Holystone and its famous Prioress—
Ned Allan, weaver and fisherman—Harbottle Castle and the
link between the kingdoms—A ghostly threat.

THE Coquet at Thropton, two miles west of Rothbury, receives
its largest tributary, the Wreighburn. Thropton is a pleasant
village possessing a pele tower, now a farmhouse. In the early
nineteenth century a cross stood at each end of the village. One
may have been placed there as a guide to the Hospitium of
St. Leonard, which stood on the opposite side of the Coquet.
It seems quite unnecessary to have removed medieval crosses.

A mile above Thropton, on the summit of a ridge, stands the
curiously-named village of Snitter, between the Wreigh or
Rithe burn and the Whittle burn. The original manor was
called Sencher. The picturesque fourteenth-century ruins of
Cartington Castle lie three miles north of Thropton, on the
slope of Cartington Hill, looking down on the Coquet, with
the Cheviot range to the north. In 1515 Lady Anne Radcliffe
was hostess, in the old tower, to Margaret, Queen of Scotland,
and her infant daughter, who had been born at Harbottle
Castle. During the Civil War Cartington stood for King
Charles, and Sir Edward Widdrington, who owned it,
suffered great loss. The castle was besieged and badly damaged,
and Lady Widdrington was fined £400 for giving intelligence

to the Royalists. It may have been the same lady who in 1682, being asked her advice " of a childe in sad condition," said that she could not understand its illness unless it were bewitched. A witch at Long Edlingham was accused of looking at the child with an evil eye.

Two miles up-stream, on the opposite side of Coquet, is Bickerton, now only a farmhouse, where were noted osier beds. From Thomas de Bickertone the monks of Newminster had a right of way to the osier beds to get supplies for basket-making. The willow still grows, and the yellow iris on the marshy ground by Bickerton burn. A family who once lived at Bickerton and lost it through extravagance were thus described by Will Scott, who made the witty comment on the fox that bit him : " Bickerton was beyked rig by rig i' the big yuven o' Bickerton a pie every day."

> The peewits are mustering on Bickerton haugh,
> And the swallows are racing round Hepple's dark tower.

The grey walls of Hepple's fourteenth-century pele still stand at the east end of the village. It was held by the de Hepples, the Tailbois, the Ogles, and several later owners. In the fourteenth century is a record of the proving of age of Walter Tailbois at Newcastle which did not rest on the word of any document, but on the evidence described in old law books as that which a man cannot deny before his neighbour :

Robert de Lonthre deposed that the said Walter was 21 years old on the Feast of the Purification last past ; that he was born at Hephal and baptised in the church at Routh-bury. He recollected the day because he was a godfather. John de Walington recollected the day because he had a son baptised there on the same day. John Lavson recollected the day because he had a son buried there the same day.

This heir, so quaintly and well attested, was taken prisoner in a raid by the Scots when he was commissoiner in defence of the Borders. He was exchanged for a Scottish prisoner called Peter of Crailing, evidently not a person of importance, as forty quarters of malt were also required by the bargaining Scots. The raids remind us of the weather conditions necessary for Zeppelins, for they always occurred on moonlit nights.

> For they'll be there by moonlight
> Though hell should bar the way

to adapt a line from " The Highwayman." September and October were favourite months for the pastime of getting rich at the Northumbrians' expense. When November came, as there was no winter feeding-stuff, nearly all the sheep and oxen still left were killed and salted. Much indifferently cured mutton lay in the vaults of the pele towers. Even as late as the eighteenth century, Hepple had a number of bastle houses, the fortified type of houses still to be seen on the Borders. The tower of Hepple was about fifty feet high, the usual height of these strongholds, surmounted by a battlement. The basement vault, chiefly used for storing provisions, was seventeen feet high, with slits for light, and the holes for the sliding bar of the door are still to be seen. The internal arrangements were simple, uncomfortable, and badly lighted. Roaring fires no doubt helped to cheer the inmates " when winter winds blew loud and shrill, o'er icy burn and sheeted hill." After the battle of Neville's Cross, the landowners were encouraged to build and fortify these towers. Previous to that a special licence was required from the King, who feared the barons' growing power. The ruinous state of Hepple Tower is said to be due to the Scottish moss-troopers.

About half a mile west of Hepple, on Kirkhill, an ancient chapel stood, the remains of which were removed in 1760 to build a farmhouse. The baptismal font and pedestal were still in good preservation and are now at the neighbouring farmhouse. At the removal, a tombstone was found with a nearly obliterated inscription : " Here lies . . . Countess of . . . who died . . . her age." Underneath were a number of verses said to have been composed by the lady herself, probably the wife of a lord of Hepple. The English does not seem older than the eighteenth century, and it may probably be a forgery handed down by an audacious local maker of ballads and accepted by later authorities. One verse is pretty :

> Then lay my head to Long Acres
> Where shearers sweetly sing
> And feet toward the Key heugh scares
> Which foxhounds cause to ring.

Scares, of course, is Scars.

The Keyheugh Scars are a mile over the moors in a wild

and beautiful district where the Grasslees, Darden, and Keenshaw burns run, hiding-places for badger, fox and otter. In
the sandstone cliffs or scars the raven and falcon are said
to nest. The inaccessibility of these ravines can be gathered
from the fact that in smuggling days an illicit still used to flourish
up the Keenshaw burn. The three burns unite and make the
Swindon burn, which runs past a small hamlet of that name,
where once lived a Coquetdale poet called Lewis Proudlock,
who died in 1826. An elegy he wrote on a tree that grew in
front of his cottage is still remembered. The sooty ones mentioned were the pitmen who then worked for coal on Hepple
moors :

> Lament ye, Swindon, sooty thrang
> Lament it sairly, loud and lang ;
> Alas ! a muckle, waefu' wrang
>   Ye noo maun dree !
> For handsomeness, it sure did bang
>   Maist every tree.
>
> It was by monie a sangster haunted,
> Oft linnets thro' its leaves hae chanted,
> Oft round its roots hae tinklers ranted
>   In merry key.
> It was the loveliest e'er was planted,
>   My favourite tree.

It is perhaps the usual poetic plaint for wanton destruction
of the " Woodman, spare that tree " variety. But the jolly
tinkers and sooty pitmen have passed away for ever from
Swindon. Where boisterous crowds once gathered to watch a
main of cocks or a badger-baiting there is now a population of
quiet rustics.

The Swindon burn runs round the south side of Harehaugh
Camp, one of the strongest in the district, which has the Coquet
on the east and the Harecleugh burn on the north. On the
west, where there are no natural defences, are three earthen
ramparts with ditches. On the high moor to the west, called
Woodhouses Beacon, 988 feet high, is an immense cairn of stones,
and on the slope were the standing stones known as " The Five
Kings " ; but only four remain, as one monolith has been removed
to make a gatepost. They are from five to eight feet high and
may once have formed part of a monolithic circle, or of an
avenue. Local tradition says they were to the memory of five

XXXI HOLYSTONE AND MARJORIE THE PRIORESS 321

kings, brothers, to whom this countryside belonged. Wood-house pele or bastle house, on the banks of the Coquet, is a picturesque ruin now used as a byre with the date 1602 over the doorhead. The road from Woodhouses to Harehaugh winds through a lovely dene.

From point to point here we move with gentle interest. Whitefield to the south-east, a prehistoric camp; Hetchester, probably a Roman camp; half a mile off, Wreighill—now a one-housed village, visited by the plague through a packet from London and devastated, and the birthplace of a mathematical celebrity. Wreighill Pike looks north on Plainfield Moor, to which Derwentwater summoned his timid mob in 1715.

Holystone, on the south bank of the river, is a tiny, diminishing village the claim of which to fame is the possession of the Lady's Well, where Paulinus made his record baptism. The well is a quadrangular basin and the spring bubbles up clear and sparkling in numerous jets. In the centre is a cross with an inscription, " In this place Paulinus the Bishop baptised three thousand Northumbrians Easter DCXXVII." A stone statue of an ecclesiastic brought from Alnwick Castle in 1780 stands at the west end of the sacred pool, which is surrounded by a grove of fir trees.

A Benedictine Priory founded by an Umfraville has left hardly any traces, a few stones near the church on the roadway, and a field called the Nuns' Close, and St. Mungo's Well on the Holystone burn. The sisterhood was very poor, owing to the constant depredations of the Scots, and in 1311 they were granted the churches of Harbottle, Corsenside, and Holystone for ever. In 1296 Marjorie, the Prioress, did homage to Edward I at Berwick and signed the Ragman's Roll. The seal is preserved still on a fragment of Homage. and represents a church with central tower, the crowned Virgin and Holy Child with a nun praying beneath, and the inscription " Tu virgenis fili succere Marie." It sounds more pathetic than usual when the position of the nuns subjected to the continual inroads and horrors of the Scots is considered. Holystone is now so remote amidst the hills, with the silver Coquet at its feet, that only the dark towers in the neighbourhood speak of the wild thud of horses' hoofs, the shouts under the suddenly lighted autumn sky from the fired cottages, and the succeeding desolation. In the beginning of the nineteenth century a great

Y

character and sportsman at Holystone was Ned Allan, the weaver, who was described in a fishing article in *Blackwood* in May, 1820. He was probably the most proficient of his day in handling the " five-taed leister." Mr. Dippie Dixon tells the following story of him in his book on Upper Coquetdale, to which the writer is very greatly indebted. Allan was one day asked by a farmer to help during the harvest, and he replied : " Ye should saw ne mair nor ye can shear. A'll help nane o' ye." One winter morning he arrived at the inn at Harbottle very early, much to the surprise of his friend the landlord, whom he called up. " What's fetched ye here se sune Ned ? " " Sune," says Ned, " a' the watter i' the Hallysteyn wunna myek a crowdie th' mornin'." It was oatmeal he was in search of. The village schoolmaster, Robert Hunter, wrote a very good epitaph for his grave, but no stone was ever erected to the wayward original.

> Here lies old Ned in his cold bed,
> For hunting otters famed,
> A faithful friend lies by his side,
> And " Tug 'em " he was named.
> Sport and rejoice ye finny tribes
> That glide in Coquet river,
> Your deadly foe no more you'll see
> For he is gone forever.
>
> The amphibious otter now secure,
> On Coquet's peaceful shore,
> May roam at large for Ned and Tug
> Will never harm him more.
> Up Swindon burn he may return,
> When salmon time comes on ;
> For poor old Ned in his cold bed
> Sleeps sound at Holystone.

The Coquet has no village on its banks more beautifully situated than Harbottle, surrounded by hills purple in August with heather and topped by the historic ruins of the castle.

The Conqueror gave the lordship of Redesdale to Robert de Umfraville to be held for the service of defending that part of the country from enemies and wolves. Of the Saxon owners and the village then existing little is known. " Har " is Anglo-Saxon " here," an army, and " bote," abode—the abode of an army or military station. There was probably a Saxon stronghold, and a mote hill, as there was at Wark, Elsdon, and Haltwhistle, on which the inhabitants met to settle disputes and dispense justice. The Umfravilles died out in 1436 with Sir Robert, a Vice-Admiral of England, and Harbottle then went to the lords of Hepple, changing owners often in the centuries.

The famous castle of Harbottle was built by Henry II to protect the borders, and it had a history not unworthy of comparison with Wark and Norham. A great waste lay around it stretching to the marches of Scotland, unprotected and open to attack. The castle was captured not long after its erection by William the Lion, but after his defeat at Alnwick the Scots had to evacuate it. It suffered constantly from their attacks in the succeeding centuries. An event of great human as well as historical importance occurred at Harbottle in 1517, when the Dowager Queen Margaret of Scotland under obscure circumstances here gave birth to a daughter. Little could anyone have foreseen that this would lead to the fulfilment of Henry VII's dream when he dispatched his little daughter on her nuptial pilgrimage to Scotland. It will be remembered how she was escorted by that Earl of Northumberland who was called the Magnificent, what a Receivyng she got at Lamberton, how she danced with James IV and was welcomed to Holyrood by Dunbar as the " princes most pleasing and preclare." But marriage to a Lothario like James has its drawbacks. Soon after he was killed at Flodden, Queen Margaret married Archibald Douglas, Earl of Angus.

Henry VIII had granted the temporary use of Harbottle to his sister and she occupied it at her confinement. But the ill-feeling left by Flodden had been fanned by many raids, and the Governor of the Castle, Lord Dacre, Warden of the Middle Marches, or his myrmidons, were not enthusiastic over their guest. Admission to any Scottish female attendant was refused and the birth took place under cruel circumstances. It is not to be surprised that her position at Harbottle was described as " uneaseful and costly, by the occasion of the far carriage of everything." So she was removed to Morpeth via Cartington Castle. A letter to Henry VIII gives an account of her journey. " She was so feeble that she could not bear horses in the litter, but Dacre caused his servants to carry it from Harbottle to Morpeth. I think her one of the lowest brought ladies with her great pain of sickness I have seen and scape. Nevertheless she has a wonderful love of apparel. She has caused the gown of cloth of gold and the gown of cloth of tynsen sent by Henry to be made against this time and likes the fashion so well, that she will send for them and have them held before her once or twice a day to look at." A true picture of a Tudor with unquenchable vitality and frivolity, though she has just escaped the agony of death.

The surveys of the sixteenth century disclose a terrible state of affairs in Redesdale, for the raids of the Scots were not more disastrous than those of the Northumbrians from Tynedale. A clanship system prevailed and justice was impossible. The men of Redesdale would pour into Coquetdale and burn and destroy, and the men of Coquetdale, who were even more active in such campaigning, carried retribution into Redesdale. In later days animosity was often expressed through the medium of doggerel verse, insulting the *amour propre* of the dalesmen more subtly than using sticks and stones to break their bones.

> Upper Redewitter for mosses and bogs,
> The main o' their leevin' is titties and hogs,
> An' if an aad ewe chance to die o' the rot
> There's nae loss at her, she's gud for the pot.

At Harbottle Fair grudges were often settled and free fights took place between the men of Rede and the men of Coquet. A story is told of some years ago, before the Fair was discontinued, of a Redewater man heard to exclaim as he paraded Harbottle Street, " Sic a fair ! here we are ! it's eleven o'clock i' the fornyun an' never a blow struck yet ! "

Within six miles of Harbottle there were sixteen Border peles, the traces of which are now gone, but they availed little against the fierce lawlessness of the times. " Villages, castles, and manor-houses were given to the flames ; border hate and border warfare recognized no distinction of age or sex, of things sacred or profane. Devastations were followed by famine and pestilence." Sad accounts were sent by the wardens of Harbottle Castle praying for further up-keep, as it was gradually becoming very ruinous. In 1543 it is called the key of Redesdale, though falling into decay. After the Union, it was allowed to go to ruin, like many another Border stronghold. The new peaceful social conditions demanded more comfortable dwellings than could be found within the stark walls of peles. James, indeed, with that fatuousness in his character which was always cropping up, absurdly proscribed the use of the name Borders, and substituted Middle shires, to extinguish the memory of past hostilities. He also ordered the iron gates of strongholds to be converted into ploughshares and the inhabitants of the country to betake themselves to agriculture and peaceful arts.

Time and the hands of stonebreakers have dismantled the walls of the Umfravilles' proud castle and the prison of many a Scot and Redesdale man who may well have wept in a barbarous age when he looked his last on the bright sky and Coquet water. A dungeon, however, must have survived the amenities of the Union if Mr. D. D. Dixon is correct in assigning to Harbottle Castle the honour of secreting Christie's Will's captive. The story is known to the readers of the Minstrelsy as the " Ballad of Christie's Will," and the prison is the Tower of Graham in Annandale. Will Armstrong, or Christie's Will, was in Jedburgh Jail in the reign of Charles I, when the Earl of Traquair happened to visit it. Inquiring why he was there, Will replied, " For stealing two tethers," but on being more closely interrogated he admitted there were two delicate colts at the end of them. The joke amused the earl, who succeeded in getting Will released. Some time after, the earl was engaged in a lawsuit in which he knew that the president, who had the casting vote, was against him. He reminded Will of his service to him and the dilemma he was in. So, when the judge was taking his airing on Leith sands, Will kidnapped him and conveyed him to Harbottle.

> He shot him down to the dungeon deep
> Which garr'd his auld banes gie mony a crack.

There the president was kept till the trial was over. The only voices he ever heard was the old servant calling on Maudge, the cat, and the herd shouting to his dog, called Batty. These he thought were spirits being invoked by the ghostly inmates of the castle, for he never saw anyone, and was conveyed away, as he came, in the dark. The fact of the dog being called a Northumbrian name like Batty favours Harbottle as the place of detention.

The Coquet, after winding nearly round the castle, makes a sharp loop known as the " Devil's Elbow." Hugh Miller notes it as the most interesting change of channel in Coquetdale. " This curious bend is a scoop in the bank almost at the very point at which the modern gorge leaves the ancient valley, and is doubtless caused by the softness of the deposits that occupy the latter." The buried channel is possibly underneath the village. On Harbottle Crag is the Drake Stone, a huge sandstone rock thirty feet high. A footpath leads past it to Harbottle Lough, a lonely tarn in the hollow of the hills, very pure and intensely cold, above which in summer the gulls wheel and scream, with gleam of erratic wing above the dark moor. Tradition says there was once a scheme to drain the water, but the workmen fled when a ghostly voice from among the rushes uttered the words :

> Let alone, let alone
> Or a'll droon Harbottle
> An' the Peels
> An' the bonny Hallystone.

From Harbottle to Otterburn there is a beautiful walk across the moors going past the Drake Stone.

A sketch on the Coquet.

CHAPTER XXXII

TO THE SOURCE OF THE COQUET

Alwinton—Northumbrian luxuries in the thirteenth century—
Gilbert de Umfraville and the Gallows—Drowning the goose
at Netherton—Biddlestone Hall—Upper Coquetdale and a
medieval lease in the nineteenth century—Setting the Watch
at Passpeth—The Wedder Loup—Spirits in the dales—Battle
of Fulhope Edge—The Land Debateable—Watling Street and
the Roman Ad Fines—The last homecoming of Douglas to
Scotland.

ALWINTON is perhaps even more exquisitely situated than
Harbottle, standing on the green haughs between the Coquet
and Alwin, which here unite. Its church of St. Michael
has some points of interest and contains a little work of the
twelfth and thirteenth centuries. In the eighteenth century
it had fallen into a wretched condition and had been badly
repaired. In 1851 it was completely restored. A curious
feature is the elevation of the chancel by ten steps above the
nave, with another three steps leading to the altar. This was
rendered necessary by the slope on which the church is built.

Beneath the north aisle rest many generations of the Clennel
family, to whom belong some eighteenth-century tombs. In the
south transept, called the Biddlestone porch, lie the Selbys
of Biddlestone. A fragment of light on the luxuries esteemed
in out-of-the-way Northumberland in the thirteenth century
is found in an agreement between the rector of Alwinton and
the Abbot of Newminster concerning tithes at Kidland, about
which there seemed very strong feeling. The seneschal of
Gilbert de Umfraville was one of the arbitrators, and it was
arranged that the monastery should give the parson half a

mark of silver, a pound of pepper, and a pound of incense annually at Michaelmas.

Gilbert de Umfraville had a gallows—that outstanding medieval necessity—at Alwinton, and the hill known as the Gallow Law stands above the village. The Norman barons kept order with a strong hand, though it is said William of Normandy had a great aversion to taking life by process of law. Gilbert, however, had evidently no scruples in that way. He took prisoner, for some offence, an unfortunate wretch called Thomas de Holms, who escaped from Harbottle and fled to Alwinton Church for sanctuary. He forswore his country and was going to leave it, but two of Gilbert's men followed him and cut off his head on Simonside, brought it back, and hung it on Harbottle gallows in ghastly revenge for the loss of a victim. Old animosities have a pleasanter outlet at the annual meeting of shepherds at Alwinton. A football match is still played between men of Redewater and men of Coquet, and the old slogans ring out—" Tarret Burn and Tarset Burn, Yet! Yet! Yet ! " and " Coquetside for Ever."

A house which stands on a green patch near the heather on the south bank of the Coquet has an interesting name— Angryhaugh. It is derived from *anger*, a meadow or pasture ground, and " haugh " is evidently a mere repetition when the origin of " Angry " was forgotten.

The green foothills of the Cheviots shelter Alwinton on the north, and issuing from a narrow glen the silver Coquet broadens out to take its gracious charm through the lovely valley it creates.

To the north-east of Alwinton, on a slope of the Cheviots, which rise 1,300 feet above it, is Biddlestone Hall, the ancient seat of the Selbys, which may be the Osbaldiston of " Rob Roy." It stands amid a grove of oaks beside a deep ravine. Biddlestone Hall, or Tower, appears in a ballad by the Ettrick Shepherd describing a raid of the Carrs of Cessford :

> Ride light, ride light, my kinsman true
> Till aince the daylight close her e'e,
> If we can pass the Biddlestone Tower
> A harried Warden there shall be.
>
> He reived the best of my brother's steeds,
> And slew his men on the Five stane Brae,
> I'd lay my head this night in pawn
> To drive his boasted beeves away.

The adjoining village of Netherton was once one of " the ten towns of Coquetdale." In later times it was known for its brisk social life, greyhound coursing, cockfights, merry nights, etc., and many stories are told of its characters and their habits. One of them is about the Netherton carrier, a century ago, who had been at Alnwick and had goose for dinner, evidently a very large helping. He tried to " droon her " before leaving Alnwick, made another attempt at the Bridge of Aln Inn, and also at Whittingham, but he declared he never " gat her drooned till he gat to Netherton " ! The old " Fighting Cocks," the scene of many a main, is gone now. After Waterloo a renowned battle took place here as elsewhere, when the feathered warriors were named after the French and English generals. They fought to the wild hoarse yells of the natives and the visiting team from Bickerton. That particular form of Northumbrian jollity has gone for ever. The old Star Inn is now a hotel and the " Fighting Cocks " is the schoolmaster's house.

Clennel Hall, where stood an ancient tower of the Clennels, is on the banks of the Alwin, secluded amid sycamore and ash trees at the base of the Cheviots. The old tower is incorporated in the modern mansion. Over a window on the first floor is a piece of frieze carved in bas-relief representing some scene like Chevy Chase, which Mr. Cadwallader Bates described as " the most interesting bit of ancient work he had ever seen in Northumberland."

Coquet, issuing from the hills, tempts the wanderer's feet. It is no longer the serene water whose murmuring voice fills the lower valley. Wilder and lonelier becomes the stream the further we follow it, and ever wilder and more untravelled is the country through which its slender, tumbling tributaries, descend. Here and there are the stones of peles, once indistinguishable doubtless from the lofty scaurs that edge the water. The raiders from Scotland and Redesdale often found the rough roads and raging torrents to their mind when the watchers, giving the alarm, lost their enemies in the thick mists or dodged them in vain up the boulder-strewn ravines. In later times old customs died hard in a solitude where only the sound of water and cries of birds fell on the ears, where sheep baa-ed indeed, but seldom horse's hoof fell on the miserable tracks. From Alwinton only necessity took travellers to shepherd's hut and lonely shieling. Linn Brigg, a short way up, is the last foot-

bridge, and over the moor above, beyond Selby's Lake, lies
Wilkwood Farm, and a scrap of history about it tells strangely
but truly of the remoteness of Upper Coquetdale in 1818. The
Princess Victoria was already destined for the throne and
England had changed from agriculture to humming industries
when a lease was drawn up for East Wilkwood Farm. The
lease between Daniel Wood, the farmer, and Walter Selby stated
" that he shall and will make use of one of the corn mills belonging to the said Walter Selby for the grinding of all such corn as
the said Daniel Wood, his servants and cottagers shall have
occasion for." Daniel had also " to walk a game cock, feed a
spaniel dog, and spin four pounds of lint yearly for the squire
of Biddlestone."

It would be hard to find the charm of running water more
beautifully exemplified than where Ridlees burn comes singing
down to Coquet. Its waterfalls, pools and rippling shallows are
delightful. Above Linsheels the Coquet narrows into the heart
of the hills. On the right bank are lofty cliffs from which a
dizzy path looks down on the dashing stream. On this height
one of the many hundred Border watches was kept against the
Scottish freebooters. The two peles mentioned lower down the
river are both described as having been attacked and " brunt "
by the Scots. But they watched too for the men of Redewater,
their own countrymen. The watch at this point, " Passpeth,"
is thus set in the " Border Laws " :

The Day Watch of Cookdaill beginning at Passpethe
Allenton (Alwinton) to watch to Passpethe with two men every
day : Setters and Searchers of this Watch, John Wylkinson, the
Laird of Donesgrene, John Wylkinson otherwise called Gordes
John.

The watchers were visited any time by a searcher and fined
if absent. The name of Linsheels came from the shiels that
the farmers lived in when they pastured their flocks in the
summer months among the valleys or on the high waste grounds.
This was called summering, or shieling, and is described in a
survey of 1542.

At Shillmoor the Coquet receives the Usway, a beautiful
tributary which rises at the base of big Cheviot, not far from
Scotsman's Knowe. It passes three shepherds' houses in its
course of eight miles, Uswayford, where is a fine waterfall,
Fairhaugh, and Battleshield. The latter name is a striking

instance of word corruption. It seems to speak loudly of border warfare and some lonely fight of desperate men disturbing Cheviot's sleep. But it was only a shiel, or summer farmstead of Henry de Bataile. A grazier in far-off times he must have been, as it is the Newminster Cartulary that reveals his name and calling. Below the waterfall, " Davidson's Linn," on the Usway, in a lonely glen called Harecleugh, are the remains of an illicit still which belonged to a noted distiller of mountain dew called Rory. Rory's still is said to be in a very good state of preservation. Past Shillmoor the Coquet falls over rocks, making a fine cascade with a deep pool for fishing. A spot well known to anglers, where a fence stops on the rock above the stream, is " The Rail End." Shillhope Cleugh, below Shillhope Law, rises precipitously above the bed of Coquet. Further on is a long, deep pool where the Coquet pushes its way through solid rock. It is called " The Wedder Loup," and is famous for big fish. Its name arises from a fatal accident to a Border thief who, being followed, tried to jump to the other bank with a fat sheep he had lifted. The weight of his booty made him miss his footing, and both he and his struggling victim were drowned. At Windyhaugh the Barra burn rushes into Coquet, and three shepherds' houses appear in sight. The monks of Newminster had a fulling mill at Windyhaugh. Their monkish finger is met everywhere in Coquetdale. It was granted to them by Gilbert de Umfraville " for the salvation of my soul and of the souls of my ancestors and heirs." He must have required the intercession of the Church acutely. The stones from the mill can still be seen in the old house at Windyhaugh, and the foundations of the mill were visible at low water a few years ago.

Above here is Rowhope burn mouth, where between steep hillsides the burn enters Coquet, having a little higher up been joined by the Trows burn. The anglers' song says:

> Oh, come, we'll gae up by the Trows
> Where the burnie rins wimplin' an' clear,
> Where the bracken and wild heather grows,
> An' the wild rose is sweet on the briar.

The Coquet and its tributaries have surely evoked more fishing songs than any other Northumbrian stream. Close to a huge rock at Rowhope burn mouth there stood an inn called

Slyme Foot, where the eighteenth-century farmers of the district spent much of their time gambling and drinking illicit whisky which came from numerous distilleries among the hills. In such an inaccessible district this cheerful traffic flourished amazingly. The older dalesmen can still remember the visits of smugglers carrying " grey hens " to the farmhouses. When there were no bridges the fords were very dangerous in rainy weather, and the gauger found it difficult to round up the hardy rogues. Indeed the exciseman was apt to develop a taste for the peat-flavoured spirit, and one of them stationed at Harbottle had a frequent entry in his official diary, " Stopped wi' witters."

Carshope and Carlcroft are the next two shepherds' cottages up the water, and at Carlcroft is a ford.   At Blindburn House the Blindburn joins Coquet, and a pool here is beloved by anglers. Up the Blindburn, Rory had another still so well hidden that on four different occasions the gaugers were within a short distance of it without it being discovered.   At Blindburn the Coquet, the infant stream, first reveals itself as a fisher's joy.

At Fulhope is a shepherd's house, and the tiny Coquet is augmented by the Fulhope burn, which is as large as the parent stream.   On the hill called Fulhope Edge a fierce battle was fought in 1399.   It was previous to that the Scots destroyed Wark Castle and carried fearful warfare into Northumberland, which was then also under the black hand of the plague.   Sir Robert de Umfraville, giving chase, fell on the Scots and routed them among those streams which tumble from the high hills. Past lonely Makendon cottage, below Thirlmoor's frowning rocks at the south of Chew Green, lies the source of the Coquet. Hill rises upon hill, dark and rugged where the fairy stream has birth, and Watling Street crosses the moors into Scotland by Brownhart Law, which forms the boundary.   From its crest the view reaches far as Eildon's triple heights, and on the west are the hills of Dumfriesshire.   On the east side is Great Cheviot, Cushat Law, and the conical green tops of the Cheviot range.

Makendon estate runs up to " the Scotch edge " and marches with the property of the Duke of Roxburghe.   On the debatable land the boundary line has always been a source of contention, and even recently the Ordnance Survey was the occasion for a revival of opposing claims.   A part of Watling Street south of Chew Green, during Border wars, was an appointed place for borderers to settle disputes by combat. It was here that Robert Snowdon of Hepple, in his sixteenth year, slew in a combat with small swords a celebrated Scottish champion, John Grieve. Here also in this wild debatable land the Earl of Northumberland and Earl Douglas met in 1401 in a futile attempt to bring their respective countries the blessings of peace.

Two blocks of stone in the vicinity are known as Outer Golden Pot and Middle Golden Pot. They were long supposed to be of Roman origin, but are now known to be ancient boundary stones between the parish of Elsdon and the chapelry of Holystone as guides to the traveller in this unpeopled country. Chew Green, a very large camp, also called Makendon, is the Ad Fines of the Romans lying far behind the Wall. Watling Street traversed these desolate moorlands and may possibly have been founded on a British trackway. For centuries it has been the common highway between England and Scotland. After the Battle of Otterburn the Scottish army halted one night at Chew Green. They carried with them the bodies of the Earl of Douglas and two squires who fell near him, which lay on slender biers " of byrch and haysell graye." A mournful procession, with the gallant dead leading the way, they marched across the Border and reached Melrose next day. Our hearts are still moved by the spectacle of that antique woe as we watch in fancy the silent and unbeaten host crossing the hills—the dark true men of the North.

CHAPTER XXXIII

THE VALE OF WHITTINGHAM

Alnham—How the Wardens encouraged the raids—The False Alarm in 1804 and some shirkers—George Collingwood and his sad fate—A Border otter hunter and his dogs—Callaly Castle and a lady's stratagem—Newcastle's Whitecoats and how they were dyed scarlet—Hob Thrush's Mills—Whittingham, an Anglo-Saxon village—Its church, ruined by Victorian restoration —Whittingham Fair and its song—Peg Macfarlane and a proverbial saying—The buzzum-maker and the sodgers—Northumbrian folk rhymes—Glanton.

THE vale of Coquet can be left at Netherton by a road which goes to Screnwood, where once was a border tower, the home of the ancient Northumberland family of Horsley. The hamlet stands on the pleasant banks of the Rithe. Into the valley of the Aln the road descends where Alnham, locally called Yeldom, lies at the base of the outlying slopes of the Cheviots. Being only six miles from the Border it suffered severely from raids. In 1532 the Earl of Northumberland writes from Alnwick to Henry VIII that the Scots have " brunte a towne of myne called Alenam with all the corne, hay and householde stuf in the said towne and also a woman." The last inconsiderable item comes in with the suggestion of an afterthought, just to weigh down the scale of the Scots' enormities. The next month he writes another " forray did run down ye watter of Bremysch and another com to the watter of Aylle."[1] But in his indignation he has forgotten that in a raid organised on the English side previously he wrote that he will " lett slippe secretlie them of Tindaill and Riddisdaill for the annoyance of Scotland. God send them all good spede." The conscienceless connivance of

[1] Alnmouth is still locally called Alemouth.

the Wardens on both sides of the Border in these raids is amusing. They seem to hold back the fierce borderers in a leash when it suits them, then with a great whoop start them galloping with the historic cries of "A Percy, a Percy"; "A Fennyke, a Fennyke"; "A Douglas, a Douglas."

The foundations of a large tower are still visible on a green mound in Alnham opposite to the church, and in the vicarage is incorporated another tower. The beautiful little church is of the Transitional period. After being allowed to go nearly to ruin it was rather poorly restored in 1870. It has some quaint sepulchral stones. On the Castle Hill, where there is a British camp, a magnificent view is obtained by looking south to the Simonside Hills with the Cheviots on the north. West of this hill the Rithe rushes down on its journey to the Coquet past Hazelton Rig woods.

The False Alarm in 1804, when the fear of "Boney" was strong in rural Northumberland, has left in this district some happy anecdotes, of which the most amusing were collected by Mr. Dippie Dixon and printed in his book, "The Vale of Whittingham." The beacon was lit on Ros Castle in Chillingham Park, easily seen from the Castle Hill. Its conflagration signalled to the beacon hill watchers in Coquetdale and Alndale. The excuses given by those who did not yearn to go to the muster were hardly to be expected from the descendants of the bloodthirsty rieving Borderers. Tom Bolam "had a pain in his breest" and needed three glasses of whisky to cure it. Willie Middlemas was seized with violent pain, and Jack Dixon's horse wanted shoeing. Curiously enough, when the alarm was proved false, they all had joined the troop and were ready for the dinner at Collingwood House. The Netherton miller was drying oats in the high kiln when the bugle sounded. He shouted to his wife: "Come here, Mary, an' kill thur yetts, an' grind them an' if the French dis land at the mill, we'll let them see she's no toom." With which spirited if confused reasoning Tommy mounted his nag and hastened to Caisley Moor.

On the north of the Aln, two miles from Whittingham, is Eslington Hall, a seat of Lord Ravensworth built on the site of an old Border tower. It was held originally by a family called Eslington, and afterwards by Hesilriggs, Herons and Collingwoods. The estate of George Collingwood was confiscated and he was executed for his share in the '15.

Tradition says that like Lord Derwentwater he was urged
by his wife to join the Jacobites. On an eminence at Thrunton
Crag End, as he rode to the rendezvous, he pulled up his horse
and gazed back wistfully over the fair lands of Eslington with
a foreboding that never again would he see the ancient home of
the Collingwoods.

> And fare thee well, George Collingwood,
> Since fate has put us down
> If thou and I have lost our lives
> Our king has lost his crown.

So his unfortunate leader, Lord Derwentwater, laments.
George Collingwood was described as a Papist, of a valuable
estate and very quiet and unoffensive. His execution at
Liverpool, he being unable to reach London through an attack
of gout, was generally deplored. Sir Henry Liddell, the ancestor
of Lord Ravensworth, bought the confiscated estate and built
the present mansion in 1720.

There are many members of the ancient family in the locality
still. A rhyme about their crest, a stag at full gaze under an
oak tree, is neat, though it possibly signifies nothing, indeed it
seems only a variant on the Buccleugh rhyme.

> The Collingwoods have borne the name
> Since in the bush the buck was ta'en,
> But when the bush shall hold the buck
> Then farewell faith, and farewell luck.

The rich, well-stocked pastures of Eslington were a great
attraction to the Scots, and the Collingwoods were often besieged
in their tower. In 1587 it was taken by the Duke of Buccleugh,
and a glimpse of the uncertainty of life in those days, even
within the security of a fortified dwelling, is given in a letter
from Sir Thomas Fairfax.

" My brother Bellasis has met with a misfortune which is a
sorrow to us here. He was garrisoned at Eslington and had a
hundred soldiers dispersed through four towns. The Scots
ran a foray and before his people were assembled he was taken
prisoner by the Lord of Buccleugh. His brother James has not
been heard of since, and James Godson and his ensign, one
Harte, and fifteen soldiers slain." Weeping and dolour must
have often followed these sudden raids, wounded men left

reddening the moss with their blood and captives carried struggling and dazed over the border. The English ambassador wrote in 1586 to the Scottish ambassador : " The complaints that we have against you are so many that seek redress from what time ye will, all the thieves in Scotland are not able to satisfy the losses of England. But what need I to babble or prate with you of this matter. You shall hear enough of them at your coming to London ; how many of our men have been murdered and slain, how many maimed and hurt, how many spoiled and burnt ; besides the goods and insight they have carried away." An indictment not lacking sarcasm ! No wonder that the children in Northumberland still play " Scotch and English " with such gusto to this day. The feuds had left deep imprint on the racial memory. What sort of Borderer was left after feud and foray were over is delightfully shown in one or two salient anecdotes preserved by Mr. Dixon, who thoroughly understands the poor sports and ne'er-do-weels whose occupation was gone when thieving was no longer in fashion. The best are about Will Allan, who in the eighteenth century used to go to Eslington from Hepple with his dogs Charley, Phoebe and Peachem. They killed the otters for Lord Ravensworth which were too plentiful for the prosperity of the fish in the Aln. Will used to say : "When my Peachem gies mouth, I durst always sell the otter's skin." Lord Ravensworth wanted to buy Charley, and told the agent to say that Will would get any price he liked for the dog, but his reply was : " His hale estate canna buy Charley."

This is the account Will, who was used to wrap himself in a plaid and sleep on settle or by hedgeside, gave of the comfortable bed at Eslington :

" When night cam on they put me amang some things they ca' sheets ; I slid, and I slid, and I slid aboot, and rolled first on ane side and then on the other, just iv all the warld as tho' I had been thrawn in to sleep amang salmon. At last I kicked out the things they ca' sheets, and fell in amang the blankets, where I got foothad and slept till the mornin'." Ignorance of what many regard as ordinary civilised usages lingered long in out-of-the-way districts. We remember well the astonishment of a village carter when he saw the new curate shaking hands with a parishioner in the street : "Go set," he exclaimed, " he worked Johnny's airm up and down like a pump handle."

z

Will died playing on the Northumbrian pipes his favourite tune, " Dorrington Lads Yet."

> An' sweetly wild were Allan's strains,
> An' mony a Jig an' Reel he blew,
> Wi' merry lilts he charmed the swains ;
> Wi' barbed spear the otter slew.
> Nae mair he'll scan wi' anxious eye
> The sandy shores of winding Reed,
> Nae mair he'll tempt the finny fry
> The king o' tinklers—Allan's deid.

The Lady's Bridge at Eslington is the subject of one of Bewick's woodcuts.

A mile south of Eslington is Callaly, where the remains of an ancient tower are incorporated in the seventeenth-century mansion. This was the home of the Claverings for centuries. It stands at the base of the characteristic hill called Callaly Castle Hill, on which are the remains of extensive foundations, probably British, followed by a Roman camp. They occupy two acres, and the ditch in places is deeply cut in the sandstone rock. In parts, the stones are squared and bedded with lime. The remains of building gave rise to a curious legend. Once a lord of Callaly started his castle here, but his lady objected to the position and bribed a servant to dress in a bearskin and pull it down nightly. This continual undoing of the day's work by the next morning became terrifying to the superstitious lord, as the lady insisted that higher powers were on her side. A watch was kept and the bear was seen pulling down the walls and crying :

> Callaly Castle built on the height
> Up in the day and down in the night,
> Builded down in the Shepherd's Shaw
> It shall stand for aye and never fa'.

This settled the matter ; the wily lady had her way, and the tower rose on the lower ground. The Claverings were Cavaliers during the Civil War. In 1644 Sir John was taken prisoner by the Roundheads, and " after being barbarously used in many prisons and common gaols dyed a prisoner in London in 1647."

Even now the fate of the Northumbrian lords who gave up all then and later for "those who knew not to resign or reign " seems piteous.

Sir Robert, his son, raised a regiment of troops for the King's service who formed part of the Duke of Newcastle's forces and were known as Newcastle's Whitecoats, from the colour of their doublets. He had no scarlet cloth, but they swore to dye the white with the enemy's blood. A brave boast, but fulfilled in another manner. At Marston Moor the Northumbrians, the men from the valleys and hills, stood like a wall when victory was no longer possible, and when the day was done and the armies melting away a long white line, streaked at close view with a darker colour, showed where they lay. Their doublets were dyed with true blood. Out of a troop of 1,000 only 30 survived.

The Claverings lost part of their estate and had to pay heavy fines. In 1715 they again came out, and the chief of the house, a nobleman of seventy, was taken a prisoner to London, where the mob terribly insulted the captured Jacobites who, on horseback, with tied arms, were led through the streets. Strange it seems that the fierce foes on either side of the Border should have the same tragic loyalty to the Stuarts. South of Northumberland the deposed house was regarded with indifference, except among a few Catholic families of high estate.

From Callaly Crags is seen one of the most beautiful and diversified scenes in Northumberland, over Whittingham Vale and the Cheviots. The crags form part of a ridge which, after bounding the valleys of Till and Breamish, rise above Doddington, form Ros Castle at Chillingham, and sweep round by Beanley and Alnwick Moor to Thrunton. In one of the huge fantastic rocks among the heather is Macartney's Cave, a little oratory hewn out of the sandstone by a former chaplain of Callaly Castle. Some curious boundary stones carved with a Maltese cross are near the summit of the crag. A precipitous watercourse goes down the crags where the pot hollows are known as Hob Thrush's Mills, the haunt of a sprite or brownie. The " mills " are set going in a spate which brings down stones that rattle in the pot holes, like the grinding of a mill. He is generally coupled with Robin Goodfellow in folk-lore. He had a haunt in Hob Thrush Island at Holy Island, but St. Cuthbert frightened him away. He is an ancient brownie of the north. Near Oakenshaw Burn and Caplestone Edge there is a Hob's Flow.

A majestic avenue of beeches leads along the Callaly estate

towards Whittingham. Emerging from it can be seen the church and red roofs of the old village through which runs the Aln.

Whittingham gives its name to the vale, not the river, and for centuries has been its principal town. It was an Anglo-Saxon village, as the church bears witness to this day, and it was part of the possessions of the see of Lindisfarne given to the monks by Ceolwulf. There is no notice of Whittingham till 1161, when Ughtred de Witingeham was lord of the manor. Whittingham had two towers, one that the parson lived in, and another which belonged to the Herons and Collingwoods, restored in 1845, and now used as an almshouse. It stands on the brow of a steep green knoll on the south bank of the Aln. The basement of the tower has walls eight feet thick, and an arched doorway is part of the original fourteenth-century work. In 1542 both the towers were " in measurable good repar'ons." The imagination is most stirred in Whittingham by the church which for a thousand years has seen the devout homage of the Vale. It was probably built in the eighth century, but a most disastrous renovation in 1840 marred its antique features. The tower, the west end of the aisles, and an arch on the north side were early Saxon. The corners of the tower and the exterior angles of the aisle walls had that quoining which consisted of a long stone set at the corner and a short one lying on it, which is a characteristic of Saxon work. A very plain arch and a square pier remained of the old nave. This was all removed and the upper part of the tower pulled down and re-erected in sham Gothic. The window next the pulpit in the north transept has a fragment of early English architecture. An early English piscina is in the south transept, which had been a chantry dedicated to St. Peter, probably founded in the thirteenth century by the Eslingtons. Over the gable at the entrance, also early English, is a sundial, near one of the stiles which give access to the public footway. In the churchyard is an ancient cross, and hosts of the grim memorials which the rude forefathers of the hamlet found so pleasing to the eye and instructive to the mind. Skulls, crossbones, hour-glasses met the villager as he proceeded leisurely over the sward on Sabbath mornings. In youth, even at its most unreflecting stage, these, with the stiff consciousness of unfamiliar boots and clothes, were apt to cast a passing gloom over the spirit, which fell still further as the damp, musty air, thick with emanations from the bones of county families, met it at the church porch. The inscriptions at Whittingham are so dismal as to be humorous to the modern mind. The following is not particularly dismal, but is curious:

" In Memory of Ralph Rutledge who died at Barton Sept. 1st 1765 aged 60 years, also his son William Rutledge who died December 20th 1782 aged 45 years, also his wife Margret Rutledge who died October 1st 1790 aged 35 years. Also 9 small children."

Poor Margret ! And her relationship remains obscure as her nameless children, as, dying at the age of 35 in 1790, she could not have been the relict of the Ralph who died in 1765. Perhaps she was the son's wife.

Whittingham Fair was a great event long ago, when the countryside was more populated and fairs were the times of replenishing the household and all sorts of merchandise was on sale. To read of the games and merry-making at Whittingham Fair makes us believe that the happy, light-hearted age has gone for ever. The day of cinemas will never again permit the bailiff, leading a long cavalcade of the manor's tenantry to the music of fiddlers, to enter the fair with the ancient cry," Oyez ! Oyez ! Oyez ! " After a long recital of the laws that governed the fair, the most necessary injunction in " Northumberlonde hasty and hot " followed : " If any person or persons shall use any violence, by drawing any weepon, or shedding any blood shall forfeit to the Lord of the Manor 100 shillings."

The ballad of Whittingham Fair is a localised version of an older one :

> Are you going to Whittingham Fair,
> Parsley, sage, rosemary and thyme,
> Remember me to one who lives there
> For once she was a true love of mine.
>
> Tell her to make me a cambric shirt,
> Parsley, sage, rosemary and thyme
> Without any seam or needlework
> For once she was a true love of mine.

From Thrunton Crags, where the cliffs rise to a height of one hundred and two hundred feet, is a magnificent view. A dense plantation of firs clothes the hill. There is a cave called "Wedderburn's Hole," the hiding-place of a noted moss-trooper on the crag. Wonderful, wild scenery is found on this range of crags and moors, and in the recesses of the rocks are the retreats of badgers and foxes, and owls, hawks, peregrine falcons, and goatsuckers nest there. Blackberry bushes cover the ground. In a plantation called Blackcock, on the wild moor, grows the black crowberry, an acid fruit eaten by the moor fowl. The plant is unknown in the south of England. Blackcock Plantation is notorious for the number and size of its adders.

At the beginning of the nineteenth century, in a hovel on Thrunton Moor, lived a besom-maker called Jamie Macfarlane, whose daughter called Peg travelled the countryside selling his wares. One afternoon she was asked where she was " bound for that night," and her answer originated the popular proverb addressed to those who " swither," " ye'r like Meg Macfarlane who had a twenty hundred minds whether to go for the night to Whittingham or to Fishes-stead "—places about twelve miles apart. It is curious that in Glendale there is a Fishes-Stead, about which a similar story is told.

Mr. Dixon has a very good story about Jamie Macfarlane. On the day following the False Alarm, when the whole district was seething with excitement, three Coquetdale Rangers, returning home in the February afternoon across Rimside Moor, saw Jamie, and thought it would be fine to make him believe they were French and take him prisoner. Putting spurs to their horses they galloped with drawn swords towards their victim. But the besom-maker was a match for any martial jesters. As they approached him he suddenly turned his back to the foe, stooped down and, with acrobatic skill, looked out between his legs and ran backwards towards them, shouting wildly. The horses, unaccustomed to such a spectacle, reared and plunged and would on no account face the onset of Jamie Macfarlane. The cavalry had therefore to retreat, with Jamie shouting triumphantly after them : " Hey, three bonny sodgers canna tyek a buzzum-maker ! "

The children of Whittingham used to shout after an old trooper of the Coquetdale Rangers—a troop of volunteer cavalry raised during the Napoleonic War :

> Reed back'd brummeller,
> Cock-tailed tummeller,
> Fire-side soldier,
> Darna gan te war.

It was very expressive, and north country children sing many funny old rhymes.

The people returning from a Northumbrian fair such as Whittingham or St. Ninians, locally called Trunnion, would be greeted with :

> Fair folk ! fair folks ! gies wor fair
> Yor pockets is ripe an' wors is bare.

The miller going round the village with the flour he had ground for the hinds, who were paid in kind with corn and had to send it to the miller, would often hear :

> Millery ! millery ! moonty poke !
> Put in your hand an' steal a loke.

The moonty is from the old custom, the mouter or multure, the miller's wages, also taken in kind, and he was often credited with helping himself well. A " poke " is a bag (hence the miller's common name of Poker) and " loke " a small quantity.

On the road leaving the village for Glanton is an old house, with a flight of outside stone stairs, which used to be an inn called " The Hole in the Wall." Two miles further on, Glanton stands on a ridge that divides the valleys of the Breamish and Aln and looks over the vale. Glanton Pyke rises above and used to be the beacon hill, but now a mansion stands on its summit. It is a pretty village and has many visitors.

CHAPTER XXXIV

THE HOME OF THE PERCIES

The Barony and its first owners—Building of the Norman castle by
Ivo de Vesci—The coming of the Percies and the state in which
they found the county—Border life after Bannockburn—
Alnwick fortified against Scotland—England turns the tables—
Hotspur and Prince Henry—The Hector of the North—
Subsequent Percies—Advent of Sir Hugh Smithson, the first
Duke—Decay and restoration of the Castle, Alnwick Abbey—
Hulne Park and its birds—Northumbrian Carmelites—Bishop
Percy at Alnwick.

Some say it was Alnwick, says Mallory of Lancelot's famous
Castle, Joyous Gard, which speaks at least for its early renown.
But he must have been thinking of a fortress earlier than that
rebuilt by the first of the Northumbrian Percies. No such
records exist as those that relate to the more romantic Bamburgh.
A great many lands had been massed together to form the barony
of Alnwick before the Conquest. Tradition avers that after the
battle of Hastings William bestowed it on his standard-bearer,
Gilbert Tyson, but on the other hand the chronicle of Alnwick
Abbey gives Bisbright Tisonne as the owner before that event.

The Norman Castle was in the first place built by Ivo de Vesci,
who was Lord of Alnwick at his death in 1135. Thirty-eight
years later, when it was besieged by the Scots under William the
Lion, it was commanded by William de Vesci, "the brave natural
son of the lord of the Castle." It remained in possession of the
De Vesci's until 1297. Often in early Northumbrian history a
de Vesci plays a leading part, but the interest of the Castle
begins in earnest with its purchase by Henry Percy in 1309.
It was a critical period. During the twelfth century Northumberland had enjoyed unexampled prosperity. " Right down to

the Pyrenees there was no country so well provided with the
necessaries of life or inhabited by a race more universally
respected." The stress of war had made itself felt during the

Alnwick Castle.

long successful reign of Edward I who had been dead for two
years and had as successor the weak Edward II. Percy must
have thoroughly understood the state of the country, but he

belonged to a race not easily discouraged by difficulties. The first Percy to settle in England had not come over with Duke William, but immediately after. It would appear that the name was originally that of a Norman village, probably connected with *percée*, a glade in a wood. The founder of the English family had a friend at court in the person of Hugh d'Avanche, a cousin of the Conqueror, and this may explain how he came to receive a grant of land in Yorkshire, where the Percies originally settled. An heiress of the family married Jocelyn, younger son of Godfrey, Count of Louvain, who had risen to be Duke of Brabant. Their son adopted the maiden name of his mother and thus became Henry Percy I. So many Henrys came into the succession that they had to be distinguished by numerals like a race of Kings. It was a Percy III of Louvain who became Percy I of Alnwick.

The purchase was a transaction that casts a brilliant light on the men and manners of the time. At his death William de Vesci had left his property in Alnwick in trust to Bishop Bec for his natural son, William of Kildare. Bec was a great ecclesiastic, and, like many of his day, was notorious for characteristics little akin to those of Christianity. He was able, but grasping and dishonest. Making his pretext certain " warm words " of his charge, he sold the castle and estate to Percy and pocketed the money. Fortunately for William Kildare the purchaser became his friend and protector, undoing the wrong to some extent.

It was the son of Henry Percy III who, when he came into possession, did most of the building. Well he might, for in Edward II's reign things had gone from bad to worse and the condition of the Borders became terrible. It was no wonder that the Scots were roused to a fury of revenge. Gray's famous lines were as applicable to Edward in Scotland as to Edward in Wales :

> Ruin seize thee ruthless King .
> Confusion on thy banners wait
> Tho' fann'd by conquest's crimson wing
> They mock the air with idle state.

Aged and worn as he was with campaigning and grief, Edward's fury knew no bounds when in 1306 Robert Bruce stabbed the Red Comyn, the Lord of Badenoch, in the church of the Grayfriars in Dumfries. Although nearing that fatal illness which seized him on the Solway Sands, he dealt out stern punishment to the Scottish nobles. Green says in his " Short History " :

Bruce was already flying for his life to the Highlands. " Henceforth," he said to his wife at their coronation, " thou art queen of Scotland and I king." " I fear," replied Mary Bruce, " we are only playing at royalty, like children in their games." The play was soon turned into bitter earnest. A small English force under Aymer de Valence sufficed to rout the disorderly levies which gathered round the new monarch, and the flight of Bruce left his followers at Edward's mercy. Noble after noble was hurried to the block. The Earl of Athol pleaded kindred with royalty ; " His only privilege," burst forth the King, " shall be that of being hanged on a higher gallows than the rest." Knights and priests were strung up side by side by the English justiciaries ; while the wife and daughters of Robert himself were flung into Edward's prisons. Bruce himself had offered to capitulate to Prince Edward, but the offer only roused the old king to fury. " Who is so bold," he cried, " as to treat with our traitors without our knowledge ? " and rising from his sick-bed he led his army northwards to complete the conquest. But the hand of death was upon him, and in the very sight of Scotland the old man breathed his last at Burgh-upon-Sands.

Edward II was ill suited to stand in his father's shoes, and when he lost the field of Bannockburn in 1314 the tables were completely turned against the English. Northumberland felt the full brunt of the Scottish ire. " For fifteen years after 1316," says the historian, " the whole county remained waste, no one daring to live in it except under the shadow of a castle or walled town." Those who wish for details of the devastation and plundering should read the excerpts made by Raine from the accounts sent from the Lindisfarne Chapelries to Durham. No crops, no cattle, no household goods and no life was safe.

Standing on the battlements of Alnwick Castle and looking north over the little river Aln gliding under the bridge, and glancing down between its green banks, it is easy to see how the animosity to Scotland must have been at its height when the second Percy was adding new towers and fortifications to the ancient stronghold. Every tower looks towards Scotland like a soldier waiting for his foe, every stone lion *couchant* or *gardant* has his head turned in the same direction, while the images of fighting men surmounting the old towers signify battle and nothing else. The Percies were well aware that the Castle standing on the edge of the wild, hilly moorland in the level country between the Cheviots and the sea was a bastion against which waves of soldiery must beat if they would win their way to the south. They were aware, too, that the Scots, most tenacious and stubborn of nations, would not be easily stopped. Ballad and chronicle alike bear witness to the pride and self-confidence that characterised them after the battle of Bannockburn. It took many a hard fight on the part of the English to redress the balance. But between two nations equally brave the stronger is bound to come out top in the end. It took the whole of the fourteenth century to do so and it was a glorious but troubled century in the annals of Northumberland. The tables were first turned at Halidon Hill, where the Scottish army lost in a great measure through the arrogance and over-confidence of their leaders. Another disastrous day for Scotland was that in which the battle of Neville's Cross was fought. Otterburn was not a national trial of strength, but the glorious end of a Border fray from which victor and vanquished emerged with equal honour. Homildon Hill, 1402, was the decisive English victory in this contest. Flodden came later and was fought on new issues.

Of all the figures in this drama the one which left the most abiding name in Northumberland, and even on the whole of England, was " Harry Percy, that Hotspur of the North," whom Shakespeare with a regal disregard of time and date makes the protagonist of his darling prince. Prince Henry was born in 1387 and the battle of Shrewsbury was fought in 1403, so that he was then sixteen years of age. The chroniclers say nothing of any rivalry between them or of the Prince killing Percy, whom he knew well, as Hotspur had been his military adviser when he was learning the art of war in Wales at the early age of thirteen. Hotspur, under Henry IV, in addition to being Warden of the East Marches, was Justiciary of North Wales and Constable of the Castles of Chester, Flint, Carnarvon and Conway—a fact which explains a passage about Homildon in Bates. " Unfortunately for northern pride, the retinue lists and muster rolls of the period show that these archers, instead of being raised from Bamburghshire, Islandshire, and Norhamshire, must have been mainly Welshmen." The celebrated description of Hotspur put into the mouth of Prince Hal is chiefly interesting as showing how all England knew of Hotspur's fame: " He that kills me six or seven dozen Scots, washes his hands and says to his

wife, ' Fie upon this quiet life ! I want work.' ' O my sweet
Harry,' says she, ' how many hast thou killed to-day ? ' ' Give
my roan horse a drench,' says he and answers ' some fourteen,'
an hour after—' a trifle, a trifle.' " This is not a boy's merriment,
but the boisterous laughter of him who created Falstaff. Hotspur
is a more popular hero than Lancelot because he is more real
than any of King Arthur's legendary knights. Gallant, hasty
and hot, he and no other would answer to the Trojan Hector if
the epic of the county were to be written ; and if an Andromache
were needed she would surely be found in the lady to whom Dr.
Bruce referred when he said of the chief entrance to Alnwick,
with its two flanking towers : " Oft times from the windows of
these towers will the spouse of Harry Hotspur have waved a
parting adieu to her heroic husband as he valiantly rode forth on
some warlike expedition." The play of Henry V is a tribute to
the bravest and well nigh the best of English Kings ; and Shakespeare, bending everything to the end he had in view, uses the
greatest warrior of the day to show his hero greater still.
The latter was greater in organising power and generalship,
but he could not have been braver.

Hotspur's father was the third Percy of Alnwick and the first
Earl of Northumberland. Few of the name died in bed, and he,
after a stormy life, was killed at Bramham Moor.

The second Earl was slain in the battle of St. Albans, 1455,
and four of his sons fell in the Wars of the Roses, and the third
Earl was killed at Towton in 1461. The fourth Earl was murdered by a mob at Thirsk. He had been trying to enforce a
war tax of Henry VII. He was described as

> Of knightly prowess the sword, pomel and hilt
> The myghty lion doutted by se and land.

It was he who had the lion rampant carved and placed over the
outer gate of the Castle. The original has been removed and
another substituted, but the cornice and the ledge are still
preserved in Alnwick Castle with the motto " Esperance ma
comfort."

His successor was he who escorted the Princess Margaret, as
described in a previous chapter. They nicknamed him The
Magnificent, and he was the first to die in his bed. The sixth
Earl is famous as the lover of Anne Boleyn. He was a good
soldier, but, from his prodigal way of life, called The Unthrifty.

The seventh Earl was executed at York for taking part in the Northern rebellion against Queen Elizabeth, and his successor was found in bed killed by a pistol shot, fired by himself it is thought. He had lost influence in the North by long absence in the south. The ninth Earl was mixed up in the Gunpowder Plot, sent to the Tower and ultimately released on the conditions that he should pay a fine of £20,000, then an enormous sum, and stay away from the North. For a time the Percies were over-shadowed by the Radcliffes, who at this time added Alston, with its lead mines, and the barony of Langley to Dilston and their other properties. But the eclipse of the Percies was only temporary.

The daughter and heiress of Josceline had married Algernon Seymour, the seventh Duke of Somerset, and the only survivor of their union was a daughter, who insisted on marrying Sir Hugh Smithson, a Yorkshire baronet of good family. The Duke did not like the match, and left the great Percy Estates in Yorkshire, Cumberland and Sussex to his nephew, Sir Charles Wyndham, so that only the Northumbrian estates remained to his daughter and son-in-law. Sir Hugh Smithson changed his name to Percy and became Earl, and subsequently the first Duke of Northumberland. He proved to be a very successful and able administrator, who vastly increased the value of the estates and was responsible for what the architect of to-day properly regards as a disastrous restoration of Alnwick Castle, which, amid the changing times and fortunes, of which this is only a bird's-eye view, had fallen into decay. A more enlightened modern effort on the part of Algernon, fourth Duke, was begun in 1854.

Alnwick Castle fell into ruins when the wars with Scotland were drawing to a close. In early days the walls appear to have enclosed the same area as they do to-day, five acres. The walls were probably built by Eustace Fitzjohn, who after his marriage to the heiress adopted the name of de Vesci, and Clarkson, who wrote his survey in 1558, gives the names of the following towers on the walls : Armourer's Tower, Falconer's Tower, Abbot's Tower, Barbican, Garrett, Round Tower, Auditor Tower, Record Tower, Ravine Tower, Constable's Tower, Postern and Sally Port. The garrets—a word akin to the French *guerité*—were huge stone sentry boxes. The Barbican was probably erected by the first Percy. It was the aim of the first Duke to restore the Castle so as to make it habitable, and it was his misfortune that Gothic was fashionable at the time, and he was led into doing his restoration in the wrong way. Duke Algernon converted the stately building into an equally stately pleasure house—notable for its magnificent rooms and great staircase, its museum and collections and noble library. It is a place to make you dream as Coleridge dreamt,

> At Xanadu did Kubla Khan
> A stately pleasure dome decree,

till some grim heritage from the savage wars, like the deep and

Street in Alnwick.

horrible dungeon, spoils the vision by intruding less agreeable fancies. Alnwick sleeps under the castle walls ; a quiet old-fashioned town of curious streets, chares and ancient buildings of which one of the most interesting is that called Hotspur Tower.

You cannot imagine either town or castle without trying to picture the Abbey, too. This has been rendered easier by the

work done by St. John Hope in 1884. Till then only the gatehouse of the Abbey was visible, but the great antiquary had the
turf cleared away so that the bases of the walls are seen, and
thus he who would form a mental picture of the ancient church
has at least a ground plan on which to work.

Hulne Priory is about three and a half miles north of Alnwick,
and in Hulne Park. No one could wish for a more beautiful
and interesting walk, for the famous park stretches right away
from the outlying spurs of Cheviot to the gates of Alnwick.
The late Henry H. Paynter, a well-known ornithologist, who for
many years was honorary secretary to the Farne Isles Association, and who when consulted in any year and in any moment
of the year used to give one the latest information of the comings
and goings, the nesting and increase or decrease of the tribes of
bird folk, contributed to the Journal of the Berwickshire
Naturalists' Club a brief note of a page and a half, into which was
compressed an excellent summary of the ornithology of the
park.

Between 1866, when he went to Alnwick, and 1917, the year
before he died, he found no fewer than sixty-seven species nesting
in the park. This is a striking tribute to its manifold attractions.
The reason as he gave it is that on the one hand the Park reaches
the uplands that roll away north and westward, and with the
other hand touches the belt of fat, rich land which borders the
sea. Heather on the west, and on the east fair meadows, on the
river bank great trees and luxuriant vegetation offer a varied
bill of fare to the birds, and they have the protection of private
ground. Of the rarer birds noticed he enumerates a Black
Kite trapped in 1866, the only one taken in Great Britain.
Among others he observed Ospreys, the rough-legged Buzzard,
a honey Buzzard, three Ruffs, a Roller and a Wryneck. Before
Lord William Percy began breeding waterfowl, and ringing them
to trace their migration or other movements, Wild Duck,
Pochards, Widgeon, Pintail and Scaup Duck visited the park.
On the heather and crag are Grouse, Blackgame, Curlews,
Woodcock, Nightjar and occasional Merlin, Golden Plover and
Teal. Kingfisher and Dipper, Pied and Gray Wagtail, Summer
Snipe, Mallard and Moorhen breed. So, too, does an occasional
Sedge Warbler.

Among the birds nesting in the woodland are Sparrow Hawk
and Kestrel, Rook, Magpie, Woodcock, Woodpigeon, Carrion

Crow, Tawny and Long-eared Owl, and occasionally are also to
be found nests of the Heron, Great Spotted Woodpecker and
Jay. This is a 'ist which shows that an idle day in Hulne Park
may be filled with the interest of watching birds as well as
enjoying the charms of Nature. Hulne Priory is said to have
been founded under romantic circumstances. The story is
repeated by Grose from ancient writers. It is briefly that the
Lord of Alnwick and Richard Gray, two Christian warriors,
when in the East visited Mount Carmel and found there a saintly
monk named Fresborn, who had been a Crusader. On returning
home they begged the Superior of the Carmelites to let him
accompany them, which leave he reluctantly granted. The
particular hill was chosen for the site on account of a real or
fancied resemblance to Mount Carmel. According to Mr.
Reavell, of Alnwick, the oldest documentary evidence is an
undated charter by John de Vesci, which must have been granted
between 1265 and 1288 A.D. It recites that John's father,
William de Vesci, had previously granted a site for the friars.
Like all the first buildings of this preaching brotherhood, the
church originally built was an aisleless parallelogram. The
ruins are very interesting even though tampered with by the
first Duke, and they have been technically and admirably
described by St. John Hope.

Bishop Percy, the author of the famous " Reliques of Ancient
Poetry," though not an Alnwick Percy, was, on account of his
name and position, invited to Alnwick in the latter half of the
eighteenth century, and in a letter has left a fine description of
the surroundings as they were in 1765. After telling about the
start and his first view of the Cheviots, which astonished and
delighted him, he goes on, in a passage as interesting to-day as
it was a hundred years ago, to say : " After winding round the
edge of a most astonishing precipice, the first object the eye looks
down upon at the foot of the mountain is the River Alne,
winding in the most beautiful and whimsical irregularities.
This is to be received into a large lake on the right, which will
cover 200 acres of ground. On a little hill on its margin, are
seen, as in a picture held far below the eye, the fine remains of
Hulne Abbey : more to the left are little swellings, the hollows
of which are fringed with a chain of small, rough thickets.
Beyond these rises a vast extent of wild, naked plains, with here
and there a single farm or plantation scattered like solitary

islands in a wide, unbounded ocean. Over these the eye gradually rises to where the vast mountains of Cheviot erect their huge conic heads ; between the openings of which, the sight gains a glimpse of the still more distant blue Hills of Tiviotdale in Scotland. The top of Cheviot is distant more than twenty

The Aln in the Park.

miles : the Hills in Tiviotdale near forty or fifty." He finds the British Carmel clothed with young plantations of evergreens and forest trees, and looking to the west finds a more extensive view of that amazing wild prospect towards Cheviot ; to the sea, fine green valleys " in the midst of which the town of Alnwick,

overlooked by the Castle, has a most picturesque appearance."
Below it the river Alne is seen beautifully winding towards the
sea. The prospect terminates with the Farne Islands to the
north and a fine, moving picture made by the shipping. On the
seashore he sees the ruins of Dunstanburgh Castle and the little
Port of Alnmouth. To the south-west is a wild, rude moor,
part of the ancient forest of Haydon.

Between Wooler and Alnwick.

Oldgate Street, Morpeth.

CHAPTER XXXV

MORPETH, MITFORD, AND KIDLAND

The castle of the de Merlays—Morpeth an easy prey of the Scots—The homeliest of Northumbrian towns—" Canny man gie's a ha'penny "—Newminster and its history—A beautiful valley—The visit of Miss Mitford—Newminster and " the great waste ground called Kydlandes "—Perilous shepherding in the old time—The chaplain who lost a day at Memmerkirk—The shepherd's dog and stick—Birds of the moorland.

ON a peninsula of the Wansbeck, in a fertile valley, lies the ancient and attractive town of Morpeth, thought by some to be the most beautiful town in Northumberland. It is not associated with any events of historical importance, though the ruins of the large castle of the de Merlays, standing on a wooded eminence above the town, show the might of the Norman barons who reigned there. Later it came into the possession of Belted Will through marriage, and his descendant the Earl of Carlisle is the present lord of the Manor. Morpeth had its share of the raids and burnings of the troubled centuries. One time John, in his infuriated march north to be revenged on the barons, burnt it. The terrified Northumbrians had already devastated the country in the vain hope of retarding his advance. In Elizabeth's time Morpeth was in a woeful state. It is said that the Scots rode to it for plunder as they might ride to a market. On their way home, driving the cattle before them, they looked like farmers returning from a fair. Horses were restored only at a blackmail price. The walls of the Castle, which had been built by the de Merlays when they received the barony of Morpeth from William at the Conquest, were shattered during the Civil War. They were never repaired, and nothing of the Castle itself exists but the gatehouse, supposed to have been built in the fourteenth century.

West of the Castle is the parish church of St. Mary, built at different periods of the fourteenth century. The chancel contains some beautiful Curvilinear work, sedilia, priest's door, and the low side window through which afflicted persons received the communion, and squints or slits on each side of the chancel arch. On the north side is an aumbrey with a hinged door and the original old ironwork. In the west wall of the vestry is a curious recess with a small circular window looking into the north aisle. It is supposed to have been an anchorite's cell, and the aperture (as there was no external door) his means of communicating with the world.

Coming down the avenue of trees from Morpeth station the visitor is greatly impressed by a stately building looming up before him. It was the county prison, the present cells being now in Newcastle. In the nineteenth century Morpeth Gaol was a terror to the horsecopers, muggers, and other gangrels who were credited with the thefts and burnings which constituted the more ordinary forms of crime in North Northumberland. The clock tower surmounted by quaint figures, once the town jail, at least the stocks were there, the town hall built from designs by Sir John Vanburgh, a very picturesque building, and a number of old hostelries, give Morpeth a charming, old-fashioned air. The Old Grey Nag Inn has an Elizabethan front. Either at the Nag's Head or Queen's Head Sir John Eldon and his bride slept on the way back from their runaway marriage from the old timbered house in Newcastle. Collingwood House was occupied by the great admiral, who spent his scanty leisure in planting trees.

Morpeth is thought by many to possess a greater natural beauty than any other town in Northumberland. To me it is always the homeliest, in many ways the most typical of day-to-day life. The stranger who on a summer day leans over the walls of the footbridge which replaced the medieval bridge in 1831, spanning the Wansbeck as it ripples through the town smiling and friendly, will gather what I mean from the boys and girls plodding among the stones. They assail the stranger in words used by hundreds of generations before them: " Canny man, canny man, gie's a ha'penny." Should the traveller good-naturedly respond by tossing a copper or two into the water he will be rewarded by the sight of a ducking and diving and scrambling inspired far more by the spirit of frolic than desire for money. It speaks of days when the poor were much poorer than they are now, and also affords evidence of the fact that nowhere in the North of England are the old tongue and the old customs more cherished than in Morpeth. Nearly all that survives in the folklore of Northumberland may be found in this little town. The history of the place is that of an open village, which makes its annals very different from those of Berwick and Alnwick and other fortified places. At the end of the bridge, on the north side of the Wansbeck, stood the Chapel of All Saints, where services were held and the dues collected. Unfortunately it is now transformed into a business property.

About a mile and a half from Morpeth is Newminster Abbey. Crossing the river by the west bridge the High Stanners are passed. This unenclosed ground gets its name from the small stones and gravel on the margin of the river. The Low Stanners, formerly the place of execution, is on the eastern outskirts of the town. The walk by the riverside is called the Lady's Walk, as it was the way to Newminster dedicated to the Virgin Mother. The avenue called the Lovers' Walk ends in the sheltered haugh over which is spread the ruined buildings with steep wooded scaurs rising above. Only a fragment of the Abbey remains, the solitary arch of the northern doorway, though excavations are recovering much of the original building, which is almost identical with that of Fountains in Yorkshire. It was founded for the Cistercian monks by Ranulph de Merlay in

1137, who was buried there with Juliana his wife. It became the burial-place of many noted families. One knight lying there was the great Robert de Umfraville, known as Robin-Mend-the-Market. The possessions of the Abbey were extensive. Lands on the Wansbeck, all up Coquetdale, fisheries on the Tyne, salt works at the mouth of the Blyth and Coquet, helped to form a great ecclesiastical property. Its value in modern money

Newminster Abbey.

would be £20,000 per annum. But they were doomed, though on the visitation in 1536 no charge of laxity could be brought against Newminster, Alnwick or Blanchland. The relic the monks then still venerated was the girdle of St. Robert, the first abbot. Eight wax candles burned before his tomb. The name of the last abbot is unknown, and the roof fell, smashing the tombs, when the monastery was rifled at the Dissolution. Many of the English sovereigns had visited Newminster, and it had

escaped every visitation of the Scots except the burning of
David I, when it was rebuilt.

The Wansbeck valley, extending about two miles between
Morpeth and Mitford, has often been extolled for its
loveliness. The best description is that of Miss Mitford,
who when she was eighteen years of age was taken by her
father to see their grand relatives in the North. Her
account of the journey is a reminder of the travelling methods
in the first decade of the nineteenth century, which, though they
would not have been found suitable by those in a hurry, did not
lack attraction to a romantic girl just entering the borders of
womanhood. The party travelled to London by stage coach,
but afterwards had the advantage of Mr. Ogle's private carriage,
the said Mr. Nathaniel Ogle being a cousin of Dr. Mitford and a
Northumbrian landowner. They changed horses at Royston
and Wade's Mill, and, after several days, reached Little Harle
Tower in Northumberland. Miss Mitford writes enthusiastically
of the ruined Castle and of " the wild and daring Wansbeck almost
girdling it as a moat." Lord Redesdale, in his " Reminiscences,"
published in 1915, explained the claim of the family to be of
Saxon descent. At the Conquest the Castle and Barony were
held by Robert de Mitford, whose only child and heiress was a
daughter named Sibella. William bestowed her in marriage
on Sir Robert Bertram, who seems, from a contemporary document, to have been deformed, *estoit tort*. In the reign of Henry III
the estates were forfeited to the Crown and then seemed to have
passed into possession of the Pembroke family. They belonged
to that Aymer de Valance, Earl of Pembroke, who was slain in
a tournament held in honour of his wedding. It was said of
this family that for several generations no father ever saw his
son. Charles II restored Mitford to the Mitfords, and with one
or two vicissitudes it has been held by them ever since. The
history will explain the local couplet pointing to the great antiquity of Mitford :

> Midford was Midford ere Morpeth was ane
> And still shall be Midford when Morpeth is gane.

The old Castle had been beautifully situated, with the Wansbeck
flowing close to the Mound on which it was built and plantations
framing it. The Wansbeck, which receives its tributary the
Font a little above the village, breaks into a dance over its bed

of sandstone as it passes the Castle. The place has many literary associations. Reference has just been made to Lord Redesdale, a man of singularly varied accomplishment—a novelist, a really great gardener, a wit and diplomatist,

Mitford Church.

antiquary and collector. Captain Meadowes Taylor, who wrote the " Confessions of a Thug," was the son of a Mitford.

Overlooking the village stood St. Leonard's Hospital, founded by Sir William Bertram in the reign of Henry I. The village, once more important than Morpeth, is now only a few cottages dominated by the ruins of the ancient and mighty castle. It was built by William Bertram, who founded Brinkburn Priory. It was captured by the Scots in 1318, and after being dismantled passed into the hands of the Mitfords, who left it at the beginning of the nineteenth century to live in a manor-house in the valley which is now also ruined. A portion of the later tower remains west of the church with the Mitford arms above the doorway and the date 1637. A part of it in which is the great kitchen is converted into a cottage, and the dog spit wheel is preserved.

The church of St. Mary Magdalene, after being long dilapidated, has been restored. There is a fine thirteenth-century chancel with sedilia and aumbrey and a crude effigy with a tender inscription to Bertram Reveley, who died in 1622: " Bertram to us so dutiful a son, if more were fit it should for thee be done." There is another monument on the wall above to him commemorating his virtues. He was descended from

> " . . . a race of worshipful antiquitie
> Loved he was in his life space of high eke of low degree
>   Rest Bartram in this House of Clay
>   Revely until the latter day."

Belonging to the monks of Newminster in the Middle Ages there is a wild mountain country reaching to the Borders. It is known as Kidland, where a few shepherds tend thousands of sheep. Part of it was granted to the monastery in 1181 by Odinel de Umfraville, who stipulated that " the dogs of the monks were to lack one foot that the lord's wild animals might have peace." The lordship of Kidland belonged to Newminster until the dissolution of the monasteries. In 1541 the Survey described the " greate waste ground called Kydlandes of iiij myles or more of breade and vj myles or more of lenthe. All the said Kydlande is full of lytle hylles or mountaynes and between the saide hilles be dyvers valyes in which descende litle Ryvelles or brokes of water spryngynge out of the said hilles and all fallinge into a lytle Rever or broke called Kydlande water which falleth into the rever of Cokette nere to the town of Alyntoun, within a myll of the Castell of Harbottell." This naïve account needs no alteration to-day ; though more than three and a half centuries have elapsed, the natural features remain untouched by man's activities.

Kidland was much exposed to the attacks of the Scots and Redesdale men, and the monks found it more profitable to let the grazing to the men of Coquetdale; but shepherding in Kidland was never considered an easy way of making a living, " being so farre also fro' the strength of the plenyshed ground of England." The monks, when they found tenants scarce, stocked the farms and sent lay brethren to tend the flocks. Along the banks of the streams are many foundations of buildings once accepted as British dwellings, but now supposed to have been the shielings of the monks or the Coquetdale men. At the junction of the Yoke burn and Sting burn, near Cushat Law, the Monarch of Kidland, are the remains of a chapel called Memmerkirk, built for the devotions of the monks and their servants when " summering " in Kidland.

There is a story of the chaplain in those early days when it was just as lonely as it is now. To keep record of the days of the week he made a bee skep each day. But a week came when he mislaid one, and the lay brethren assembling for Sunday Mass from their duties on the hills were scandalised to find him busily engaged on his daily task. The monks gave up attempting to carry on the farms, as the border thieves lifted so much of their stock and murdered its guardians. The men of Coquet, when they held these wild upland pastures, were not at all reluctant to make reprisals on the foe by removing some of his cattle, and the monastery found it safer to let them remain as tenants. The gentle men of God were no match for their turbulent neighbours.

There was rough law administered, and justice meetings were held at regular times, when both sides of the Border were represented. Prisoners were exchanged and claims laid for damages. At one of these meetings on Windy Gyle, a usual place for a rendezvous, Sir John Forster, the English warden, had with him many Northumbrians and also Lord Francis Russell. Sir John sent to the Scottish warden the customary assurance of peace, when the Scots made a sudden attack and the unfortunate nobleman was slain in what seemed a most unjustifiable fray. This was in July, 1585, and a cairn still marks the place, called Russell's cairn. Gamels path, a part of Watling Street, on the western slope of Thirlmoor, was another recognised place of meeting. The other one was Hexpeth gatehead, on Windy Gyle.

The other noted Kidland hills are Bloody Bush Edge, which must have seen some terrible, forgotten fight. Cushat Law is 2,020 feet high, and from its summit a view to the east looks over woods and valleys and winding rivers to the North Sea, and away to the west are the Cumbrian hills. Enormous flocks of sheep wander on the Kidland hills, and the shepherds who live in the widely separated cottages are a race of intelligent, interesting men. In winter their life is very hard, and many have been lost in the great snowstorms. In summer, mists descend very rapidly, to the confusion of the traveller, but the shepherd's wife is very hospitable and pleasant to the lost wayfarer. Where the distances are long and the flocks immense, much depends upon the dogs, which are wise and well-trained.

> At Milkhope, Dryhope, Kidland Lea
> Their value is well known.

The shepherd is entitled to a number of sheep as a part of his wages. There is a joke that the shepherd's own sheep never die from the afflictions that beset his master's animals.

Besides his dogs, of which each shepherd has several, he needs also a good supply of sticks.

> In the long nights of winter
> When the girls are weaving baskets
> And the boys are making bows

the shepherd dresses his hazel sapling and ornaments it with his pocket-knife.

A story is told, by Mr. Dippie Dixon, of an old herd who had a new stick sent him by a brother herd who was a famous stick-dresser. He inspected it and then tried walking with it, muttering " Heavy ! heavy ! heavy ! " ; then, flinging the stick from him in disgust, exclaimed, " A'll nivvor wear it ! "

In the lovely secluded ravines the " burns tumble as they run," often making gleaming waterfalls with ferns and flowers along the banks, and in the boggy places are many varieties of moss. Wild fruits are plentiful in August and September, for the blackberry, cranberry, red whortleberry, and blaeberry are found. On Cheviot particularly, and also on Cushat Law, Bloody Bush Edge, Windy Gyle, and Thirlmoor, is the delicious cloudberry, known to the natives as " noop." Ospreys and golden eagles are occasionally seen, and a raven still nests in Ravens

Crag, near Milkhope, but seldom brings off its young. An eagle has occasionally been seen on Windy Gyle. A noted ornithologist gives this picture of the birds on the hills : "During the heat of the day all the bird life of the district appears to collect near the burns. Wild duck and teal rise from the quiet pools ; the blackgame startle us as they spring from the bracken on the brae. One hot day in July we noted no less than seventeen species in a distance of three miles up the Eelrig—a lonely burn leading into the Coquet above Blindburn ; these were the heron, lapwing, wheatear, whinchat, grey wagtail, dipper, common sandpiper, kestrel, merlin, sparrow hawk, curlew, mountain linnet, ring ousel, meadow pipit, wren, sandmartin, and carrion crow."

The Briton has left traces of his habitations in Kidland. The Roman came and passed, but his camps and the road of his genius remain. Raiding Scot and plundering rogues from Redesdale have had their day, and the frightened monk has watched his flocks and raised his shrine in the waste. But no change has come over the face of Nature in the centuries, no village smoke ever rose to the deep sky. The shielings that clung to the sheltering edge of the burns have gone, and the succeeding herds' huts also. Mostly on the heights now, grey and fearless, the shepherds' cottages gaze over valleys and hills that seem numberless. But wandering in the heather, or where the burn chatters in the deep ravine, it seems like a land "where no man ever comes or has come since the making of the world."

CHAPTER XXXVI

OLD CUSTOMS AND SUPERSTITIONS

A bloodcurdling tale, the devil in a hurry—"Thrice the torchie, thrice the saltie"—Birds of ill omen—An old woman and her ballads—Bee superstitions—Poor Wat and the traveller—First footing and Hogmanay—The wise woman—The ghost and the gamekeeper.

THE world has changed so much during the last half-century that it may be interesting to recall what one remembers of old Northumberland. But I must premise that it is purely a matter of personal recollection, not of reading and collocation, so that no one need expect an account that pretends to be exhaustive. It is more an attempt to indicate an atmosphere than to make any elaborate study.

Before the hustling and busy times began there were many idle ne'er-do-wells in the typical village, objectionable from one point of view, but good-natured and amusing in their lazy paganism. There was one such at Belford, who was known far and wide because he was an itinerant barber who visited the farmhouses, shaved the good man before fairs and markets, and cut the hair of the boys by clapping a basin on their heads and clipping round it. At the time, there was a clique of godless young farmers who in the current phrase feared neither god nor devil, and performed pranks that congealed the blood of the righteous. About one of these, awful whispers went round. In a drunken ploy they had done a deed of blasphemy and sacrilege so wicked that pious lips would not describe it. Only very recently the secret was told me by one of their contemporaries, then approaching his own end. It was a bloodcurdling tale of a mock sacrament and an old horse that need not now be more fully described. One of the perpetrators took so ill that a fatal end was inevitable. Watty, in accordance with an old custom, was sent to shave the dying man, and what happened was given in his own words. He had performed the first part of the operation, and was about to lather for the second when a dreadful voice from the other side of the bed exclaimed : "That'll do, Watty, I'll just take him as he is." Whereupon the sick man turned to the wall and passed away, and the affrighted barber, without waiting to collect his instruments, fled in terror.

In the rites pertaining to the dead, solemnity and mirth were grotesquely mingled. I think that curious and beautiful legacy from Elizabethan times, the Lykewake Dirge, which seems to have been in use from Yorkshire right up to the Lowlands of Scotland, is a homely rendering of medieval beliefs about death. Its haunting burden reminds one of an owl's melancholy to–hoo on a winter night.

> This ae night, this ae night
> Everie night and alle
> Fire and slet and candle light
> And Christ receive thy sawle.

An eminent authority on dialect words holds that " slet " means the hearth or the home, but that it is a rendering of "salt " is far more probable. Among the things waved over the corpse, " thrice the torchie, thrice the saltie " came first, and in Northumberland, as in South Scotland, a plate of salt was placed on the breast of the body. Only in a district of moor and fell could such a journey of the departed soul be conceived. It is as elemental and primitive as the picture of lost souls being carried to hell in the ancient painted glass windows :

> When thou from hence away art past
> Everie night and alle
> To Whinny-muir thou com'st at last
> And Christ receive thy sawle.

That the funeral guests had to travel over such wild country probably accounts for the custom that they were to be provided with plenty of good meat and good drink. Cards and other games were also played, but here I write of the tradition of the elders. These customs had been greatly modified in my young days.

Forebodings of death were innumerable. One of my earliest recollections is that of hearing one grizzled rustic say to another : " I told the wife his end was near when I saw the corbies (carrion crow) settle on the roof." Crows, ravens and magpies, especially the last, were reckoned birds of ill omen. So was the bat, which was a bird, in the rustic mind, as sure as a whale was a fish. There was a beetle which they called a coffin-breaker, whose very appearance caused old men and women to shudder. Anyone killing it was sure to be the next victim. Once I committed that crime and thereby threw into gloom the old woman in whose charge I was at the time. Poor body, she could be easily forgiven her superstition, for she could neither read nor write, had never been inside a church or a school door, and her only learning came from the Scottish ballads she had picked up. I seem to hear her now crooning, or, as she would have said, " raiming over "

> Bonnie Mary to the ewe-bucht has gone
>   To milk her daddie's yows
> And aye she sang her bonny voice rang
>   Right over the tops of the knowes, knowes,
>   Right over the tops of the knowes.

Or the most melancholy of them, " Lord Ronald," with its piteous refrain :

> Mother make my bed soon for I'm weary wi' huntin
> And fain would lie doon.

Bees were intimately associated with the fortunes of their owners, as in other parts of rural England. They used to be kept in straw skeps before the invention of the modern box hive, and two honey harvests were obtained, one from the lowland flowers, of which wild white clover yielded the best, and another from the heather. To obtain the latter the hives were carted to the hills, an operation that had to be performed by night so that the little creatures could be fastened up after finishing the day. Also it was cooler. The bees were treated as little family friends. Ill luck was sure to follow if they were not informed of any death or birth. When they swarmed, a kind of savage music was made with the tongs and the frying-pan or girdle to charm them into settling close at hand.

Among wild animals the hare was considered the best augur. If you were going a journey, and met poor Wat come lopping along the dusty road, you had to observe whether on seeing you he took to the right or the left. If the latter, the traveller would turn home and eat a meal before adventuring forth again. Otherwise he would be challenging misfortune.

Of days, the first of the year was most pregnant with fate. It was and still is important that the first foot, that is the first person crossing the threshold, should not come empty-handed. Many made Hogmanay the jolliest as it was the last day of the year, by setting out when the clock struck twelve with a piece of cake and a flask of whisky to ensure good luck to their friends by arriving before any chance, unwary caller brought calamity on the household. The Northumbrian peasant is as a rule simple and abstemious in his habits, but he used to let himself go in the dark days of Yule.

The utmost faith was felt in "the wise woman," a kind of white witch, who could unravel a present mystery or unfold the future. I remember the case of a poor man who lived by carting coals and lime, having his stable burnt down and with it his three horses, which were his means of livelihood, travelling twenty miles on foot to ask a wise woman who was the culprit. She indicated that a trade rival, who was a horse-coper and widely known by his nickname of " Was," had done the deed, and he was ultimately convicted and punished ; but whether she was aided by supernatural power, or only made a shrewd guess, " let the learned decide when they convene " ! The yokel had no doubts. He was no fanatic about church doctrine, but his faith in ghosts and witches was implicit ! It was considered impious not to believe in the old Lady Delaval, who " walked " at Ford Castle for half a century after her death. He would in proof tell the story of a reckless gamekeeper who volunteered to sleep in the haunted chamber with nothing at his bedside save his hobnailed boots. Presently the ghost appears and glides towards him. " I ken your tricks," he exclaimed bravely, though one suspects there might have been a quaver in his voice, and as she continued her silent advance, " Take that, then," he cries, heaving a heavy boot at her. " But believe me or believe me not," concluded the narrator of this tale, " the shoe went clean through her and he up and ran for it. His hair stood on end and neither oil nor watter could gar it gan doon again."

There used to be few country ways which had not a spot to be avoided after dark. At such-and-such a cut through a plantation there was a risk of meeting the spirit of someone revisiting the scene where, by his own hand or that of another, he had been forced to quit this mortal frame.

National schools, cheap reading, and cheap travel have not altogether rooted out these old superstitions. They lurk still in the more remote villages and farms. I do not know that they were more absurd than some of the notions by which they have been succeeded. I know a village blacksmith who ekes out his earnings by taking and selling spirit photographs.

Bunkered in Northumbria.

INDEX

INDEX

E

D

F